Heart by Heart: Mothers and Daughters Listening to Each Other

❖

An Anthology of Love Stories by and about Mothers and Daughters with Commentary

Marianne Preger-Simon, Ed.D.

iUniverse, Inc.

New York Lincoln Shanghai

Heart by Heart: Mothers and Daughters Listening to Each Other
An Anthology of Love Stories by and about Mothers and Daughters with
Commentary

iUniverse, Inc.

For information address:
iUniverse, Inc.
2021 Pine Lake Road, Suite 100
Lincoln, NE 68512
www.iuniverse.com

ISBN: 0-595-30592-X

Printed in the United States of America

Contents

Acknowlegements

I want to express my gratitude to many people:

to my mother and my children, from whom I learned what it means to be a mother.

to my husband, for his interest and confidence in me, for making sure that I say what I mean, and for his intolerance for jargon.

to Lynn Hoffman, for encouraging me to write outside the culture of wounds and pain, for nurturing my creativity in composing headings and titles, and for helping winnow out stories and poems which did not belong in this book.

to all the talented and generous authors for their contributions to my book....both those whose work was included and those whose work was not.

and above all, to the mothers of the world, who are doing the best they can with the resources, information and energy available, to raise daughters safely in a world which is challenging, unpredictable, beautiful and often dangerous. God bless you all.

Introduction

"I have something I need to say!" exploded Ellen.

Ellen's demand, and the following revealing conversation, occurred at Esalen Institute in California. I was leading a workshop for mothers and daughters to explore the delights and difficulties in their relationships. Participants in this interaction were Ellen, a mother in her mid-forties, her college-student daughter, Jane, nineteen, and myself as facilitator. Ellen and Jane had been very sweet to, and appreciative of each other for the first three sessions. During a momentary lull in the fourth session, Ellen burst out:

"I have something to say, but I don't want to hurt Jane's feelings…she's very sensitive."

I reassured her, Jane had plenty of support here in the group.

Ellen began, in a tone somewhere between belligerence and petulance:

"I'm not satisfied with our relationship as it is. I want to *mother* Jane more. She treats me mostly as a friend. It's only when she's feeling bad that she wants me to mother her. I want to mother her and take care of her, and I want her to let me."

Jane protested, "I like the way our relationship is. I like having Mom for a friend. And she's a big help when I have problems. But that's all the mothering I want."

Ellen elaborated on her complaint and her longing, with more urgency. Jane began to cry, and couldn't say anything.

"I want to hold Jane and cuddle her and mother her. I'm ready to be a mother now, in a way that I never was. And I don't want her to feel abandoned and neglected the way I did when…."

Suddenly, Ellen collapsed in heavy sobs. After a few minutes, she wailed:

"This is all about me and *my* mother, and I'm laying it on Jane. That's not right. I have to deal with my own feelings of abandonment. Jane is just fine."

Jane looked very relieved.

The next day, Jane announced softly, "I'm realizing I'd like more mothering".

Ellen learned something very important in this conversation. She discovered, by talking out loud, having attentive listeners around her, and listening to herself, that she was trying to get rid of her own feelings of neglect and abandonment by pushing herself on Jane. She said she was wanting to use Jane as a surrogate for herself, to slather on Jane all the affection that Ellen had longed for all through her childhood.

The problem was not in wanting to be an affectionate mother; it was in treating her daughter as if she were herself, Ellen, which Jane most definitely was not. Jane, like all daughters, needed to be seen and heard and understood for the unique and separate person she was. Jane had no responsibility for her mother's old painful feelings. It was certainly not her job to heal them, even if that were possible (which it wasn't, and never is). Once Ellen was able to perceive the distinction between her own needs and feelings, and her daughter's, and to acknowledge that she was responsible for taking care of her own pain, then Jane felt free of the burden of making her mother feel good. Therefore, Jane was able to take a step closer to her mother.

The preceding story illustrates some of the complex factors impacting on the mother/daughter relationship...a remarkable and intricate relationship that this book was written to honor. The stories that follow demonstrate a variety of different ways in which mothers and daughters have been creative and effective in building their connections with each other, in thinking about each other, and in assisting and empowering each other. No one style or method is right for everyone, but perhaps the reader may find in these many tales and poems some inspiration to help blow away some of the fog in the matrilineal line, or to affirm the clarity that already exists there.

Our immediate impulse, perhaps, is to picture our mother/daughter relationship as involving just mother and daughter, but, as the story above demonstrates, the mother/daughter relationship never exists in a vacuum. Many external forces help to shape it:

The relationships within the immediate and extended family: Does Father demand a lot of Mother's attention, so that daughter Nora feels left out? Does big brother Al get into trouble often, so that sister Elaine is particularly praised and appreciated? Does Grandma take loving care of Grace while Mother is working so that Grace feels closer to Grandma than to Mother? Is daughter Beth the only intimate connection that Mother has?

Legacies from past generations: Is the alcoholism of Grandma and Mother creating a culture of addiction in the home that Joan is either capitulating to or fiercely resisting? Are three generations of women doctors putting pressure on the next generation to follow suit, despite Ella's desire to be a Kindergarten teacher...or would Ella really be more fulfilled handling the challenges of the medical profession?

The cultural customs and expectations of the group, region or neighborhood of which the family is a part: Does Gina and her family belong to an ethnic or religious group that prizes large, close-knit families where the girls model themselves after their mother's role as homemaker and care-giver? Does Maria live in an area where girls are encouraged to go off to college, pursue careers and live independent lives, with marriage as only one of many options?

The political, economic and physical environment in which the family exists: Did Dora grow up in a cotton-farming family, where, as an infant in a basket, she was placed at the end of a row of cotton, and had attention from her mother only when her mother picked her way to that end of the row? Did Janet grow up in a wealthy family where the children had their own rooms at one end of the house, with their parents in a wing of their own at some distance? Or was Lucille a member of a minority group that was discriminated against, so that her mother taught her to be silent and as invisible as possible, or to be proud, strong and outspoken? Perhaps Jennifer's mother belonged to a generation that believed men deserve to enjoy a privileged status in society; did Jennifer feel the need to liberate her mother from that belief system?

All the foregoing situations suggest some of the more obvious influences on this precious and primal mother/daughter relationship...a relationship which exists like a small, sturdy boat in a sea of pressures.

Inter-personal factors also impact on mothers and daughters: if mother and daughter resemble each other physically, have character traits in common, or share the same rhythm in their daily actions...such similarity can bring ease and delight, or it can cause stress (perhaps you have noticed that the trait you like least in yourself is the one you have most difficulty with in others!). On the other hand, when mother and daughter are very different, or if the daughter reminds the mother of someone she adores or can't stand...that also can be either pleasurable or difficult.

There are many reasons, therefore, why your mother-daughter relationship has its particular shape; furthermore, despite all that history, the relationship can change. Many of the stories and poems in this book demonstrate the actuality of change...all are stories of appreciation and/or transformation, not of unresolved problems.

When planning this book, I asked women to submit true stories about interactions between a mother and daughter, interactions that produced desirable change in the mother, the daughter, both, or their relationship. As the replies show, some of the interactions created new perspectives, others increased security and closeness, still others provided assistance, and some offered a sense of being understood and accepted. All the stories and poems are from the point of view of the mother or daughter who was involved, and are autobiographical. Most of the stories and poems were submitted as finished pieces, and are credited (brief biographies of the authors appear in the back). I transcribed and arranged a handful of the stories from interviews over the phone or in person…in some cases, names were changed, and no credit is given.

The authors included are women who, at some time in their lives, experienced, reflected on and integrated the transformative impact of a particular moment in their relationship with their mother or daughter.

The stories are arranged in ten categories, nine of which describe certain kinds of interactions; within each chapter, the stories are arranged as much as possible in order of age…stories about the youngest first. Many of the stories overlap categories…I've placed them where they seem best to illustrate that particular kind of interaction. As mothers and daughters, none of us can operate effectively all the time in all the categories…but we can all operate effectively some of the time in some, or even most of them.

I offered contributors ten questions to help focus memories and thoughts. They were as follows:

1. What are some of the times you've spent with your mother/daughter that you've felt have had a positive impact on you, on her, and/or on your relationship?

2. What has been a very effective way you've found to communicate with your mother/daughter, or that she has found to communicate with you, that allows, or has allowed, something useful to happen? Can you think of a specific example?

3. Was there ever a particular *exchange* that you had with your mother/daughter that made a significant positive shift in your relationship, or in the way you thought about yourself or her, or in the way she thought about herself or you?

4. Is there any *activity* that you've done with your mother/daughter that has had a positive effect on your relationship, or on either of you?

5. Have you ever had a fight with your mother/daughter that has had a positive effect on your relationship, or on either of you?

6. Have you ever invited another person into your relationship with your mother/daughter in a way that created a positive effect?

7. Have you discovered an effective way of communicating with your mother/ daughter that is not verbal, or that doesn't use words, or uses words in some unexpected way?

8. Are there particular places or situations in which you discovered you can have an effective interaction with your mother/daughter?

9. Has a crisis ever been precipitated outside of your presence that forced you into a new relationship with your mother/daughter, or caused you to think about her in a more positive way, or caused her to think about you in a more positive way?

10. What do you feel you have learned from your mother/daughter that has had a significant positive effect on your life or your perspective? Under what circumstances did you learn it?

Perhaps these questions will remind you, the reader, of some forgotten, special moment in your life. And, hopefully, the stories and poems in this book will stimulate some fresh and innovative ways of thinking about, or interacting with, your own mother or daughter.

1

Love Without Strings

One day, my two-year-old granddaughter was heard talking to herself about herself. Touching each of her arms, she said:

"This arm is named Love and that arm is named Scrumptious."

Where did such sentiments come from? They came from her sense of being just right the way she was, of being loved in every inch of her being. That is the feeling that comes from being loved unconditionally…the fertile soil in which children grow strong and sturdy, and in which adults also thrive.

Unconditional love doesn't mean a lack of standards or values, nor does it mean, "Anything goes".

It simply means, "No matter what, I love you. You don't need a different face or body or personality or higher grades or to become a doctor or a concert pianist, in order for me to love you. I love who you are (not who I wish you were) and I'm on your side. I will do all I can to help you become everything you can be, and want to be."

This chapter contains stories and poems in which mothers and daughters experience the giving and receiving of love without strings

Uncontaminated Bond

Maureen Flannery

My plum colored newborn,
perfect as your moment of emergence,
rare as the round blue moon that marked the month,
you squirm on my chest for a foothold,
waiting for the vine that wove you to me
to be still and force your first breath.
Tiny hands,
like sea anemone in constant motion,
recall their recent element.
All between us now is fresh,
not soiled even slightly yet
by harsh or cryptic words,
critical affronts, looks of
disappointment, disapproval, disavowal.

I wish your blue topaz eyes could find
in me such purity as I see now.
Though you perhaps hold more than I
of the history we will try to right,
for now we need not shun the depth
of one another's stare, so flawless
in this newness is our love.
You and I have not one time,
this life, provoked each other's tears.
No pain has clung like lint
to the hem of negligence
or well-meant hovering.
There's been as yet no blame between us,
no guilt evoking, and no shame,
not even an unconscious slight
to taint the clarity of our intentions.
This calls me tread so softly on the future,
I hesitate to let them cut the cord.

This story, and the two poems that follow, exemplify the mutual flow of love between mother and daughter.

Excerpts From a Journal

Annette Peizer

7/23/96

I showed Shoshi the moon tonight. She was tired and acting fussy in my hot upper unit that holds in summer heat like a greenhouse. She normally would be sleeping, so every little toy that dropped or any other disturbance caused her great distress since her resistance was down. Her temporary, ultra-sensitive mood reminds me of people who didn't get enough love as children so their resistance always seems down and every little disturbance throws them off.

To cool her off a little, I lifted Shoshana out of her baby swing by the window and walked with her onto the balcony. She has been there many times during the day and more than several times we watched the soft, baby-head pink, then Flamenco-red sunset together in the early evening. But it occurred to me tonight, by her somewhat startled response, that I was taking her into a strange environment, all dark with bright white, sparkling lights in the blackness above.

We looked at the moon together and I realized that this was probably the first time she had looked at the moon. As I held her in my arms facing away from me toward the magnificent new scene, she held onto my fingers tightly with her left hand and reached out toward the moon with her right hand. She remained in this pose without moving as minute after minute dissolved into the cool night air.

Aren't we all in Shoshana's pose? Aren't we a mix of instincts and vision, with one hand on comfort and security and the other hand reaching out in awesome wonder, toward the unknown?

After a long gaze, she moved her attention to the familiar treetop she has often studied during the day, as a type of grounding, I suppose.

She looked up at my face for reassurance, then again at the moon, her left hand curled tightly around my index finger, her right arm reaching up and out.

10/3/96

Babies touch our faces like blind people
like the tenderest of lovers
like petals blown from a cherry tree
like God whispering
melt into love melt
into love
melt.

Down My Mother's Hall

Patti Tana

Darkness down my mother's hall beckons
heart awake...I follow
stumbling against the walls
urged by the thrill of comfort.

At last I rest engulfed:
moist fur perfumes my body
large shapes yield to my touch
bad dreams drain from my night.

The next story reveals the mother's unconditional love making a safe space in which her daughter has the freedom to express powerful feelings without any loss of love.

Old Cow

Phyllis Woolf

One time Jekki became furious with me, why, I do not remember. With all the energy of her six-year old outrage, she shouted:

"You're an old cow!"

It was the fiercest thing she could think of saying. Then she became terrified of what she had done, and waited, holding her breath, to see what calamity would befall me or her. To her astonishment and relief, nothing happened. She looked so frightened that I could only look at her with kindness. I didn't melt into a puddle of water, like the bad witch in *The Wizard of Oz*, she didn't get punished, and the house stayed in one piece.

She had arrived at the realization that words could have power, that she could exercise it, and that I'd be okay and continue to love her.

Here, the daughter's unconditional love...of mother and life...dissolves her mother's anger.

Morning After

Karen Ethelsdattar

I woke before the clock struck, child crowed
knowing I ought to examine my mind,
its cover stretched taut like a drum's head
over yesterday's fury.

My child's voice called
   Conscience pulled me up
      I marched drum-headed to her room.

Raising the blind I turned to see her face, sunned-on,
arms reached to gather the day;
all wrath went slack as I hastened to her.

This letter expresses in great detail the lifelong, unconditional love of a mother for her daughter.

On Mother's Day...To My Daughter...

Elayne Clift

This is a day which traditionally dictates that you lavish attention on me. But it's also a chance for me to take stock, from the other side of the relationship, of our seventeen years together. As I think about it, I feel pretty lavish myself.

I'll never forget the day you were born. I'd had a lovely pregnancy: you were easily conceived, carried with grace (or did I just imagine I was Madonna?), and delivered naturally in very short order. You emerged, turned your pink face upward for a good look, and announced heartily that you were here to stay. From the very beginning you fit nicely into my life. You were a good nurser, an excellent traveler, and a charming guest. In time, you outgrew the first of these virtues; the other two remain to your credit.

I knew early that you were going to be bright and precocious. But it took a while longer to realize your determination, which emerged during your "first adolescence"...the Terrible Twos. What a shock! Toddlerhood is overwhelming to a mother, because suddenly we face the awesome responsibility of having another personality dependent on us, and frightening because with stark reality we confront our own inadequacy and needs. No one really prepares us. We only know, unconsciously, that as good mothers we must subordinate our own desires to those of our child. We don't really know how to handle our anger, frustration, and guilt...so often born of fatigue. The only thing we are sure of is our unequivocal and bottomless love; that tugging at the heart that goes all the way to our toes when a pair of trusting eyes twinkle, "I love you, Mom."

So there you were, viewing the world from its center, which you took to be your rightful place. And there I was, floundering to meet the demands of this very distinct personality...yet, in so many ways, the mirror of my own. There were times, and still are, when I see myself so clearly in your actions, your expressions, your judgments. I watch you struggle to cope with disappointment and it is me. I see your quick wit, and I recognize my own girlhood. I witness your compassion, and I feel my own pain. You thrust a hip, grin, gesticulate, and uncannily, you are me.

Is it in this mirror image that our conflicts lie? Are we so alike that we reflect not only the best, but also the worst, of each other? And if that's true, is it really so bad? Oh yes, we can be driven to profound rage; hurt to the essence of our souls; guilty beyond reason. That passion is played out precisely because we are safe with each other: because we know that the bonds of love, trust, and loyalty between us can never be broken, we can do our growing together. We can flourish, fail, be afraid, take pride, because no matter what, we know that we are grounded in each other's likeness and love. At the end of every day, regardless of what it has brought to each of us, there is security in our still-present bedtime ritual. When I tuck you in and kiss your cheeks, you know what is real in the world. And when you sing out "Love you, Mom," I know too.

There is less tension now, as you grow towards womanhood, and we come together on more equal ground. We are becoming friends, and I'm glad. I like you. When we talk things over...intimate, funny, sad, confusing things...I feel deeply satisfied. I'm proud of your emerging intellect, touched by your growing world view, delighted by your sense of humor. There is deep and abiding joy for me as I watch your potential develop, your sensitivity heighten, your spirit become strong. I know, with a mother's conviction, that you can achieve whatever you put your heart and your mind to, and that your future is bright with promise. Not because I'm your mother, and not even because you're my daughter, but because you are uniquely you. And it is that which makes this Mother's Day especially mine, and why I have chosen this moment to tell you that truly, and oh so deeply, "I Love You."

Mom

In the following story, a mother's unconditional love trumps ambivalence and conflict, and assists her daughter to accept her own ambivalence.

Motherlife

Maril Crabtree

My daughter Virginia, 34, sits in the rocking chair with her first child, an eight-week old miracle named Penelope, and sips hot tea as we talk. She takes her tea now with soy milk. For the baby, she explains. Her world right now is baby-baby-baby. Life is simple on the surface, filled with simple tasks: feed, hold, change, soothe. What lies hidden are all the emotions of new motherhood, all the insecurities, the uncertainties, even the disappointments.

Virginia surrounds herself with dozens of books on babyhood and magazines with names like *Parents, Child, Hip Mama*. Still, there is no certainty, no sure way to succeed. What is success for a mother? When does the hidden treasure of motherhood emerge? Or does it rise and fall, like a ship on a far horizon, throughout one's motherlife?

My own life as a mother weaves back and forth through tumultuous memories of failure and inadequacy, pride in watching my children accomplish new tasks, exhaustion in juggling law school and a new law career with making sure home-work was done, clothes clean, sleepovers with school friends arranged, guilt in never having time to make homemade chocolate muffins for school parties.

Most painfully, I saw my mother's conditional love repeat itself too often in the way I treated my children. I vowed never to yell at my kids, and I yelled; I vowed never to spank them, and in exasperation paddled my son with a shoe; I vowed always to be available to them, and saw myself marching away in anger, slamming the door, just like the rebellious adolescent teenagers who glared back at me from the breakfast table.

Fortunately, forgiveness is part of my memories, too. I have both sought and received forgiveness from my children…and most importantly from myself…for my shortcomings as a mother.

Still, I was totally unprepared for the telephone call that came from Virginia one day, 1,500 miles away, telling me of her pregnancy and asking me to be her birth partner. I was enthusiastic about the former, but cautious about the latter.

"What does a birth partner do?" I asked.

"Whatever I tell you to do," she said. "I'll give you instructions about how I want to have my baby, and it'll be your job, and Kevin's, to help make it happen."

I could picture my daughter in the throes of childbirth barking orders like a military sergeant. She has, unfortunately, inherited my own tendency to try to control the world around her at whatever cost, something that has, in the past, caused us more than once to rush at each other like oncoming trains determined to collide.

"It's been a long time since I had a baby. Don't people have to be, well, trained to be a birth partner?"

"I'm sending you a book to read," she said breezily. "Besides, I figure your most important job will be to protect me from the medical folks if they want to interfere with my natural childbirth wishes."

Mustering as much enthusiasm as I could, I agreed and said I'd look forward to reading the book. In the ensuing months we talked frequently, and I found myself mostly in a listening role, supporting her through familiar ills of morning sickness, swelling, and higher than normal blood pressure.

As the birth grew nearer, she grew more specific in her requests.

"Bring some of your New Age CD's," she said. "I figure they might come in handy to calm me down if things get too frantic."

"Great!" I said. "I even have one for reducing pain."

"There won't be any pain," she snapped. "I've cast a spell for a perfect, peaceful childbirth."

"Of course," I said, chastened. "I'll just bring my Enya tapes and…"

"Not Enya," she moaned. "She's too mournful. But don't bring anything too jiggly either."

"Do you have any favorite New Age artists?" I asked hopefully.

"Nope, just bring a variety so I can choose."

Finally the day arrived when I flew to Seattle and came face to face with my very pregnant daughter, a week away from due date. Grim-faced, she told me the doctor was threatening to induce because of her blood pressure. By now I knew better than to throw in my lot with any traditional medical opinions. I listened, nodded, murmured sympathetically.

We talk about plans. She's still determined to have the baby without drugs. She still wants me to be there with her. Solemnly, I give her permission to kick me out if she gets too nervous with me there. She laughs.

"I'll remember that if I can. But you'll probably be too busy keeping Kevin calm."

Three days later we are in the hospital. Virginia's labor was "naturally induced" with a substance inserted into her cervix; twelve hours later, when that didn't result in substantial progress, a second insertion was made and her water broke. Now, many hours later, she roams the birthing room, trying to hold out against the waves of pain that periodically engulf her.

Kevin and I take turns gently rubbing her back, holding her hand.

She has emphatically said, "Don't tell me to breathe!" "Don't touch me unless I want you to!"

My role as birth partner is reduced to fluffing the pillows and making sure the water in the tub is warm when she wants to get in. Her clenched fists tell me the pain is getting serious.

"Mom," she suddenly says, "is it OK with you if I ask for pain medication?"

I have been coached to ask her if she can hold out another hour. Instead, I immediately say,

"Of course, honey, whatever you want."

Kevin follows instructions and suggests she wait a few minutes, but when the nurse comes in Virginia says,

"Can you get the doctor in here? And is there something you can give me for the pain?"

Failure as a birth coach, success as a mother: my daughter and I see eye to eye at last, and I marvel at her strength and assertiveness as she shifts from the original birth plan to this one, which I would tentatively call "Let's Get This Over With." Her doctor turns out to be a marvelously sensitive woman who defines "natural childbirth" as "if you're a woman in labor and you give birth to a child ultimately, that's natural." She calls the anesthesiologist to give an epidural and starts a pitocin drip, procedures I'm familiar with because they were also needed at Virginia's own birth.

With pain no longer an ever-present specter, Virginia can relax and enjoy the process. Two hours later, the doctor announces the baby is ready to come through the birth canal and Virginia needs to push.

"How will I do that?" she says anxiously. "I can't feel anything from the waist down. I can't even lift my legs."

"Your birth partners will do that," the doctor replies. "All you need to do is push with all your might when I tell you."

The next several minutes go quickly. I am enthralled with the baby's dramatic entrance as she slides into her new life. But it is my daughter that I am wide-eyed with appreciation for. She has achieved what was once a distant dream. Her body has served her well, and has given her a beautiful baby girl, healthy and whole.

And not once have we yelled at each other or acted at cross purposes. Somehow, having this baby has given us both something grand enough to entrust ourselves and our hearts to, in a new and unguarded way.

I return to my role as birth partner: pay attention to the mother, make sure she's comfortable while holding the baby, step out of the way as Father cuts the cord, telephone others so that Virginia and Kevin can continue their joyful family reverie uninterrupted.

After a few hours I go home for the night, exhausted but pleased. Birth partner duties are over; now there's only the cooking, cleaning, and laundry to do, tasks which are, after all, second-nature to a mother/grandmother.

Three weeks later, I am back home. I receive a telephone message from my daughter:

"I always knew you loved me without ambivalence, unequivocally," she said. "But I also knew you felt ambivalent from time to time about your role as a mother, and about motherhood in general. I finally understand. I love Penelope to pieces, I could kiss every tiny finger and toe; but I feel completely ambivalent right now about motherhood. Just wanted you to know."

Yes, my darling daughter-mother, the ambivalence continues…but so, thank heaven, does the love, the fierce love that knows no uncertainty, that always knows its heart-path even when motherhood hesitates with indecision.

After thirty-four years of being a mother, I am sure of it.

In this story the mother's love overcomes her confusion and shock.

The Conversation

Fran Moreland Johns

"And another thing, Mom," my daughter said over the phone one balmy spring afternoon. "I'm gay."

"Oh my," I said. I felt suddenly upside down.

The phone call from Atlanta to San Francisco, linking us in comfortable familiarity, had begun with small talk and moved gently into the news that she and her husband of nine somewhat tumultuous years were getting a divorce.

"Oh my," I think I had said after the first shoe dropped. The questions had fallen on top of each other after the divorce announcement: "Are you okay? Are you sure? What will you do? Should I come?"

She was fine. The two of them had worked out everything, drawn their own papers, agreed to continue raising their 7-year-old daughter with two strong and loving parents, even though one parent (her dad) would move to another small house not far away. My daughter had explained this calmly and it seemed to make sense, and she did indeed sound better than she had in a very long time. But the other shoe was quite a drop

"I think I've always been gay," she said. My mind raced backwards into her childhood, through the intense high school relationship with a best girlfriend that I wrote off as part of the normal coming-of-age struggle, through her marriage to a closed-in but strong, handsome and decidedly macho young man she had known most of her life. "I know this is right."

It is the conversation every mother would like not to have. We talk about how the news is being received: She has told friends, and parents of her daughter's friends, and found most of them warmly accepting. Her older sister has exploded in disbelief for a moment or two before settling into her traditional role of helper/ advisor. Her father-in-law has driven over to hug her and tell her she would always be his daughter. Her mother-in-law will not speak to her again. Her (formerly) borderline homophobe older brother has been a rock of support. Her father offers to call in his lawyers, his shrink, his counselors. (She declines.)

"I just want you to be happy," I say. She knows that. "And I know there are going to be some really rough times ahead." Of course she knows that too, in her head; but I feel it in the pit of my stomach. "I love you," I say, and we hang up.

For a few minutes I sit on the side of the bed and consider my left toe. For years I have talked about "my daughter the free spirit," "my daughter the bonzai grower, the orchid expert." "My daughter the Deadhead," "my daughter the rock climber." Pride in her ferocious determination to dance to her own music has been part and parcel of my unabashed adoration of this youngest child. "My daughter the lesbian?"

She is unquestionably stronger, happier, better than she's ever been. I do not think of her as my daughter the lesbian. Only as my daughter the greatly loved.

I call some very close friends who are gay.

"You understand, people will say their marriage was a lie," says Jim, whose partnership with Richard, now past the quarter-century mark, followed a doomed attempt at traditional marriage and family. "That's not so."

"When you're gay," he continues gently, "it's the last thing you want to believe about yourself. So you do everything you can think of to prove it's not so. Including finding someone you really love and entering into a heterosexual marriage." Makes sense.

Another friend asks if I know why I'm distressed.

"Loss," I say. "I feel like the daughter I've known and loved for 34 years has suddenly disappeared forever."

"Think that through for a while," he suggests. So I sit down, finally, and make a list, my conditioned response to distress. On one side I put all the qualities that define my daughter: bright, funny, loving, pretty, outgoing, stubborn, curious, good with children…On the other side I intend to list everything that is changed by her being gay. It is blank.

In this poem, we hear the love directed both to the woman's child and to her mother.

Sweet Burden

Patti Tana

Carrying my child to bed tonight
I thought of all the times my mother
tucked me in to sleep with a blessing.
Sweet is the burden of cradling
an infant's head...how will we bear the old?

Mother, when you are old
let me keep your hair brushed smooth,
anoint your skin, surround you
with natural tones: brown green blue.
And if I have to carry you
and clean and feed and bring you
roses on a tray, this burden would rest
like baby's breath upon my mother's breast.

2

Looking and Listening

Newborn infants and their mothers look at each other a great deal of the time, and listen to each other's voices. It's how they get to know each other. The infant soon recognizes her mother's face and voice, and the mother soon begins to decipher the meaning of the baby's different cries. These are all very instinctive responses, and help to create the bond between mother and child.

One of the things that is so irresistible about babies and young children is the wide-open way they have of looking at whomever comes into view. They have vast amounts of attention to focus on everyone and everything...that's how they learn so much, so quickly.

However, because we have more and more things pulling at our attention as we grow older, many of us have a harder time listening in a focused way than our young children do. So we need to be consciously intentional about our looking and listening, and reflective about what we are learning.

In the following stories, mothers and daughters write of what they have learned from each other, sometimes through experience and sometimes through words; sometimes in passing and sometimes through effort; but in every case, the learning comes from looking, listening, and paying attention.

In the following story, the little girl has heard, over time, her mother's simple answers to people's curious questions…now the little girl gives a stunningly simpler response, because of her confidence and ease in herself.

That's The Way We Are

Annette Peizer

My daughter and I were at one of the neighborhood parks swinging together on the swing set. Summer was almost over, and even though Shoshana, who was still in her three's, was too young to pump and keep herself going, I just had to get on a swing as well. As a single mom, I wanted to have fun and feel like a little girl again for a minute or two. I gave Shoshi one more big push and quickly plopped myself down on a swing next to her and shoved off. Delighted that I was swinging alongside her, Shoshi called out and laughed with me.

I reminded myself of a bit of advice I read in some parenting article on how children really just want to see their parents enjoying themselves, and so continued to swing, guilt free.

A young girl of seven or eight watched us swinging and laughing together. "Is she your daughter?" she asked.

"Yes," I replied lightly. I was used to the question asked mostly by children who naturally say what they think.

The adults whose curiosity overtakes their tact, ask "Is she yours or did you adopt her?"

My daughter is biracial, African American and Caucasian. I've come to realize that most white people who don't know me see my daughter as light skinned African American. But most blacks and people in general who've had more exposure to mixed couples and biracial people recognize right away that she is of mixed race.

I made the decision early on to lightly respond that she is my biological child and either walk away or change the subject. What I really think is how this very personal question is absolutely none of their business! The people who usually ask me this question are strangers, people I may have just started chatting with for a few minutes if at all. Would these same people think for a moment to ask a white woman they had just met with a white child if her child were adopted or really hers? And even if I had adopted her, she would still be mine. I can see how if I had adopted her this question would be even more irritating.

But I've chosen not to have my daughter grow up with an angry mother every time the tiring question is posed. I've even grown to empathize with the nosy questioners. After all, they are just curious and don't really mean any harm. I might have asked the same question at another stage in my life if I were not feeling entirely centered or aware at that moment. Much worse things could be said. And they have, but that's another story.

The girl kept watching Shoshi and me swinging together.

"Then why does she look different from you?" she asked.

Completely unprepared for this immediate follow up, I hesitated.

Shoshi and I kept swinging toward the Pine and Maple treetops and the fluffy cotton candy clouds.

"That's the way we are," Shoshana answered for me in a confident clear voice with a patient little laugh.

The girl's expression softened in instant acceptance of my daughter's explanation.

I got off the swing to give the girl her fair turn. Of course I ended up pushing both of them, alternating arms, as they laughed together into the golden summer afternoon.

Observing her mother's adventuresome behavior challenges a more cautious daughter, and holds out new possibilities for her to explore.

Adventuring

Nomi Kluger-Nash

Mama always picked me up from school…and I was always so delighted to see her.

This was a brand new kindergarden for me, the third in an actively moving year, which movements made me even more delighted to see the reliable appearance of my beautiful Mama. I was therefore disconcerted this day when she arrived, cheerily announcing,

"Let's walk home a new way!"

"No. You'll only get lost."

(I was already well aware of her bad sense of direction, a genuine "non-sense" which was a family joke.)

"Maybe…but we already know the streets we've taken this past week, so let's try others."

"No."

"OK. You go the old way, I'll try another way."

And so we did.

I walked with stubborn resolution to our new home the way I knew. Sure enough, when I arrived no one was home, and so I waited proudly on our porch for my recalcitrant mother. She arrived sauntering gaily. I said to her (with pleasure in an "I-told-you-so" tone),

"You got lost didn't you!"

"Yes! But I had an adventure…and you didn't"

That struck me like a bolt of lightening. I considered it carefully, saw the truth of her ways, and since that time long years ago, I've taken many an adventure down many a wonderous lane.

Here, a daughter's courage inspires her mother to act more courageously.

A Moment With Jane

Kathleen Anne Smith

Jane looks at the birthday card that Allison made for her. It is a teenage work of art. Sassy magazine clippings, colorful words cut out one by one, arranged with skill and wit. It brings Jane to the point of tears.

"She lied to me," she says. "I hate it."

We are in Jane's room, hanging up clothes from a bottomless pile. I want to stop and hold her, but I don't want to short-circuit her talking. I know I can't fix the problem. Neither can Jane.

"It's a disease, honey," I say. "She can't help it."

"But, Mom, I'm her best friend. She shouldn't lie. Not about what she eats. Not to me."

"I know. But the lying goes along with the disease. Like being thirsty goes with diabetes."

"I don't care. I 'm so angry!"

She slams the card onto the dresser.

"Of course. I would be too."

"Will you just stop being so fuh…so…freaken understanding and just *listen*," she says.

She rubs angrily at a tear. I reach to touch her shoulder.

"Stop it!" She draws away.

I make myself still. It doesn't come naturally.

"How come she has it and I don't?" she says. "We were both on the same diet. Only I felt like I was starving. My thighs are so much fatter than hers."

She slaps the offending anatomy.

How easy now to say that mother-thing: Women's bodies need some fat, and besides, 112 pounds is not fat, you're perfect. I bite my tongue.

"She never eats in school. She says she only eats at home."

For the past few weeks Jane is saying she wished Allison didn't sit at her lunch table. Did they have a fight? No, it's just…Oh, never mind.

"When she goes home she tells her mother she ate at school, and I know she didn't."

Another slap on the desk. More tears.

"What does her mother say?" For God's sake, we're talking about a fourteen-year-old girl.

"Nothing."

"Nothing?"

"Her mother likes her thin. She likes things the way they are."

The way they are. Last weekend they invited Jane skiing with them. They planned to ski from 9:30 AM to 11 AM, home by 11:40. Cost: $38. I would have to pick Jane up at their house at 11:40. Right in the middle of my time at church.

"Can they drop you off at home?" I asked. "Or can I pick you up when church is over?"

No way. They had to be at her grandmother's by noon sharp. There was no time. I sigh.

"Look, Mom. She's the smartest kid in the whole school, the best piano player, the best athlete. Always the best."

"Where is she getting the energy?" I look down at my ample thighs and try to imagine myself a long-distance runner.

"I don't know, but I wish I had it."

Uh-oh, a Mother attack. "But not at that price," I say. "Anorexia."

I can't bear to tell her that up to ten percent of anorexics die. Then I realize she probably knows.

"…Well, anorexia is serious."

"She told me her mother put away all the scales, but she snuck one out and hid it in her room. That bothers me."

All the scales? How many scales does a family need?

"Oh, now I get it," I say. "Was that around the time you decided to put our scale in the closet?"

Jane smiles. "Yeah. You said it was a good idea."

"Yeah. Well, I got a confession to make," I say. "I sneak it out of the closet every once in a while to see how I'm doing."

"You cheat!" she hoots. "You said the only scale that matters to you is the one at Weight Watchers!"

"I lied about that too!" I laugh. "The one that really matters is the one in your head!"

"Well, I'm still weighing myself too. Sometimes it feels…well, sick, so I stopped."

Is there something I missed? She's down from a size nine to a size two. But she's in training for crew, and when she eats pizza there's no doubt she loves food...

"I hate it," My calm is vanishing. "I hate how you hate your thighs. I know every girl hates some part of her body. I hate that it's normal to be so...so obsessed."

"Mom, relax. I 'm not anorexic, all right?" She touches my arm. "It would be so easy to be. But even if I was, I wouldn't lie."

"It's a disease!"

"I know, I *know*." Her eyes are wet again. "She told me she would never go below a hundred pounds, but she is."

I sigh again. "I wish I could be wise for you. You've been a good friend to her."

"Yeah. Well..." She gazes off and grows silent. "That may be over after today."

I wait, clipping a skirt I've never seen before onto a hanger. "What happened?"

She bites her lip. "Me and Melissa decided we were really scared for her. So we went to the guidance counselor yesterday to get Allison some help."

"That's...That's amazing". I hold my tongue. "So what happened?"

"He made us go to the nurse."

"The nurse?"

"Yeah, the guidance counselor said the nurse had to weigh her, see if she's really lost weight, before they could do anything."

"I don't understand." It was hard enough for them to go to one authority, let alone two. "Why wouldn't the guidance counselor contact the nurse himself?"

"Mom, it's all right. It's anonymous. Once we decided to do something, well, it was easier to keep going."

I can't resist a hand on her shoulder. "Do you know how extraordinary you are?"

I feel her shoulders soften. I go back to hanging up a shirt. A very, small, shirt.

"They called Allison out of music class. When I saw her at lunch she said, 'OK, Jane, you're going to be next.' All year, whenever anyone tried to talk to her about not eating, she'd say, 'Jane's too fat. Jane's losing too much weight. Jane's not eating.' Anything she did, she'd say I did."

"I'm amazed you've stayed friends."

Soul mates, they had called themselves.

"Well, sometimes she brings in a bag of pretzels or carrots and I see her eat them. It's easier to talk to her then, and I think she's getting better. But then, well, she starts again."

She stuffs a green sweater into the bottom dresser drawer. Allison would have folded it very, very neatly. Suddenly I love Jane's imperfections.

"So what's going to happen now?"

"Probably nothing." She slams the drawer shut. A green sleeve peeks out. "She told the nurse she already sees a counselor about it. That part's the truth."

"Well, it's not doing her a whole lot of good. But I'm glad the school knows."

"Yeah, right. And what's the school going to do? Feed her lunch?"

"Your school has counselors! They must know something!"

"Yeah, right. All they know is how many great colleges she can get into!" We are close to shouting at each other.

"OK, but they might send her to a better counselor, someone who knows more about eating disord…"

"Why would they? The school thinks she's doing just fine! 'Excuse me, I have a 99 average over here, I need help!' Like, they're going to care."

I think about the scales, the skiing, Allison's family. I remember what it was like to be in my 30s and driven, like Allison's mother seems to be. There was so much I had to block out then…even parenthood itself…and I felt I had no choice but to forge ahead on the fast track, no matter what it cost. But from the perspective of my 50s now, I know there's another way. Part of it is just talking to someone who cares. Although I hardly know these people…Am I less brave than my daughter? I take a deep breath.

"I think, maybe I should talk to her mother."

No answer from Jane. Is that a yes?

If it's a "No," I would hear it.

I pick up the phone.

She doesn't stop me.

In the following story, mother and daughter learn from each other to be more open and to adjust to change.

Talking Things Out

Kimara Glaser Kirschenbaum

All during my childhood, my mother and I talked about everything that came up between us. This proved very useful when I entered college and our relationship inevitably started changing, producing all kinds of stresses and strains.

It started right away, when I came home for my first vacation during Freshman year. I had been on my own, making my own decisions and doing what I wanted to do when I wanted to do it. During the vacation, my Mom had lots of friends over to the house. I hung out with them, and felt like, in doing so, I was spending plenty of time with my Mom. In fact, I felt I was spending time with her, rather than doing what I wanted to do. She, on the other hand, felt like I wasn't spending time with *her*. I checked with a friend that I had brought home with me:

"Am I justified or not?"

She replied, "You're justified in your feelings, but I don't know what's going on with your mother, so maybe you ought to talk to her and find out."

This made sense to me, so I went to my Mom and said,

"We can fight about this or talk about it."

Because of our history, we talked about it. I realized what she was wanting, and she realized what I was wanting. The stress eased. We also realized that we needed to talk about our expectations in advance of any time together, in order to avoid problems and misunderstandings.

Midway in my Freshman year, Mom told me she had breast cancer and would be undergoing treatment. She didn't tell me much more, yet I really wanted and needed to know everything. But I was afraid to make demands on her or fight with her. It was a bad dynamic. Simultaneously, we came together to talk to each other.

I said, "I want to know your treatment, your options, your future."

She said, "You won't make me sicker if you tell me what you want, and fight with me...I'm still your Mom, and that's the most important thing to me."

That was a huge relief. She shared her story with me, and we re-connected.

When I came home in the summer, we had worked so much out that she was able to treat me more as an adult. She was just finishing her treatment, she was doing less, relaxing more, and realizing that she wasn't in control of everything in her life. I was trying to be more independent and she was respecting that. Instead of living at home, I lived next door, above her office. I spent time with her without running away, because I felt more independent. Also, I realized that she was neither immortal nor invulnerable, so I took more care of her.

Now when I come home, we block off a couple of days just for us together, as well as making time to do our own thing. It works well.

In the following story, the mother is opened to new experiences through her daughter's persistence in pursuing what she loves to do.

Sanmaria Gorge

June Calender

Greece was just what I expected; but it wasn't at all what Rachel expected...although she couldn't say exactly what she expected except that when she flew over it going home from a trip to Egypt with her father, she had seen mountains and they looked wonderful. But we hadn't seen any mountains. We had wandered the Acropolis where, when I began to tell her about its history, she put her elbows on a wall turning her back to the Parthenon, staring over the ugly rooftops of modern Athens. She was bored. At a lovely lunch on a flower filled balcony restaurant overlooking the Plaka, Rachel, who was then in the full throes of what would be a short lived vegetarian phase, frowned at my moussaka, and complained about her salad.

The Flying Dolphin, a hydrofoil, magically skimmed over the water taking us to the island of Poros but Rachel was not enchanted, she went to stand on the little back deck to avoid the smell of gasoline. On Poros I watched, secretly jealous of her daring, as she parasailed, but when she was back on the ground she was disappointed. She had been a competitive gymnast, and found the harness so restrictive she had little sense of freedom while flying through the air. She cheered up a bit at a splendid sunset and enjoyed a little festival in the town.

The bus ride to Delphi was a little boring, so I told her about the Pythia. Delphi itself was splendid. At the amphitheater I told her to imagine the dramas played there but she was interested in modern drama. When we got back to Athens we had coffee at Syntagma Square. I tore my attention away from other tourists and locals; it was time to decide what we could do the last few days that we would both enjoy.

A mother and daughter traveling together bring their old patterns of behavior. Rachel reverted to pouting when she was disappointed. As Mother-the-Educator, I lectured about history, mythology and the stories of the great dramas. I was thrilled to be in the ancient world. Rachel had just spent her first year after high school as an overworked apprentice at an Off-Broadway theatre, acting in a couple of plays and modeling to earn a little money. At this point she wanted a vacation, not an education.

I suggested Crete and started to tell her about the Minoan civilization. Rachel twisted her very expressive face into a mask of tragedy that portended tantrums when she was in the terrible twos and still did bad things to my blood pressure. I got out the guide book, wasn't Crete mountainous? Yes! A paragraph described Sanmaria Gorge as "one of the most spectacular mountain areas in all of Europe." An eighteen kilometer trail started at the top of a mountain and descended to the sea. Rachel cheered up. We found we could take an overnight ship from Piraeus to Chania.

The gods were with us, our timing was perfect. We arrived very early in the morning. A hotel had a room and would let us leave our suitcases. The bus station was only a couple of blocks away, a bus would leave in forty-five minutes for the head of the Sanmaria Gorge trail. That gave us time for coffee, rolls and a bag of delicious cherries for breakfast.

We headed up into wonderful, roughed mountains. Olive orchards clung to steep hillsides, curly horned sheep and nimble goats roamed among the rocks. We passed towns where men in dark berets had coffee and smoked pipes outside little shops. The ride took nearly an hour and left us beside a little snack bar at the trail head. We were totally unprepared for serious hiking, we didn't even have a water bottle and I was wearing thong sandals. At least Rachel was in sneakers. Neither of us knew eighteen kilometers was eleven miles. It was 10:30 in the morning, we had all day, we bought some candy at the snack bar and set out. The guidebook said there was another snack bar about half way along the trail at a now-deserted village, we could get lunch there.

Rachel was quietly happy as we followed the clearly marked trail. The early June day was perfect, the sun was bright and hot but we were under trees. By early afternoon we reached the deserted village but it was too early in the season, the restaurant wasn't open. No pouting or complaining, we ate our candy bars and drank at the water fountain.

A few other people were on the trail, mostly going down, although we met a few going up, which seemed to us a ridiculously difficult decision on their part. Mostly Rachel and I were quiet, being on a mountain trail inspired no tales of heroes of the Trojan war or philosophers who lived in barrels.

My sandals were threatening to tear but the walk was so lovely I would have gone barefoot if necessary. The actual gorge was as spectacular as the guidebook promised. The walls of the gorge stretched above us thirty or forty feet, the passage between them narrowed to less than the width of our outstretched arms. We had to wade in the shallow, cool stream.

The gorge opened out, the stream widened and the path began to level off, then we were among azaleas in magnificent pink, red and white bloom. As in fairy tales, we had traversed the wild forest and great rocky crevasse and were now in an enchanted land of flowers. Our feet were sore, shadows were lengthening. And then there was the sea! Rachel pulled off her sneakers and waded in; at a restaurant I got a cold beer. This little town at the foot of the gorge trail had only one road out...back up the trail! But a boat that would take us to a nearby town was due in twenty minutes.

The late sun glittered on the water as the little boat ferried us along the shore. We were so tired we nearly fell asleep lulled by the chug of the motor. Not far from the boat dock a bus waited for this boatload of tourists to get their tickets for Chania. As the road switch-backed up the mountain ridge and down the other side the afternoon light changed from dazzling to deep dusk. A proud ram posed atop a rocky cliff, magnificent horns silhouetted against a deep blue sky. Night had fallen when we reached Chania, we found a seaside restaurant. Fresh fish was allowed on Rachel's diet. The smell of frying food made us weak from hunger. While waiting for dinner, I asked,

"Do you like Greece now?"

"I'm glad we came to Sanmaria Gorge....It was a beautiful day," she added generously.

"Tomorrow when we go to Iraklion, we'll see the ancient city of Knosos and the labyrinth where the Minotaur was kept," I said. "Theseus and Ariadne..."

Rachel interrupted, "The guidebook says there's a nice beach, I'll go there while you see the ruins."

I shrugged. What's a mother to do?

Perhaps it's not strange that the enchantment of that day's walk stayed with me more vividly than the historical sites. Sanmaria Gorge was the first of what, in the next several years, would be increasingly exciting mountain hikes on three continents that would culminate in a trek to the foot of Mt. Everest. Little did I know that trying to please my daughter I had opened myself to experiences that would enrich my life beyond anything I could guess.

In this story, the mother's example of courage to pursue adventure ignites a new courage in her daughter.

Water Echoes

Gina Bacon

Water drips like mercury off my paddle, each shiny bead hitting the cold surface of the water below with a silver splash, sending water echoes dancing to the four flat corners of the earth.

Clouds form in the distance and bump up against the blue-gray mountains that frame the edge of the sea. A light breeze, warm in front, cold as it passes, pushes our sea kayaks gently, like secrets, toward the open water of the Puget Sound.

I hope for nothing but a safe, dry first kayak experience. It is enough to sit atop the water like a gull, drifting soft as smoke across the expanse. It is enough to enjoy the bigness of it all without anything big happening.

Adrienne, my adventure-seeker, 50-something mother pushes ahead with strong, swift strokes. My mother's brightness makes me want to turn back. I am more fearful than her. She is fuchsia. I am eggplant.

Adrienne is always zipping here and there, bolting, smiling, never gloomy, never pondering. She darts in her car, in her house, in shopping malls, on top of the sea. She is as fearless and as happy as any creature that does not know it should worry. She is always ready to enter any dark cave looking for light.

The wind picks up my mother's short curls and scatters them across her fore-head like shore grasses. She turns to me, a smile spread deeply across her tiny, square face. Her cheeks are flushed from the brisk sea air.

"The only thing I want to see in the whole world before I die is a whale up close in my sea kayak!" she yells, passionately.

I return the death wish with a half-smile and no comment. I shudder and pull on the old sweatshirt tucked between the boat and my right leg. My knees are cold and cramped, aching from pressing upward on the resin kayak. I follow Adrienne like a baby duckling in tow, but without the confidence that most ducklings have. I always take inventory of danger lurking around me. In my car, in shopping malls, on top of water.

Reach, dip, push, glide. Reach, dip, push, glide. The constant rhythm of the paddle, at least, is calming.

At one time in this very body of water, this Puget Sound in the upper, watery reaches of Washington state, I was fearless. I loaded up dinghys with my grandfather's fishing gear and went bottom fishing, sometimes with a friend or a cousin, but mostly alone. I caught nice fat sole, those awkward sideways fish with bulging eyes, and hauled them to shore in buckets. Once my cousin and I caught a couple of nice fish, but our fathers weren't around to help us kill them. We lugged our bucket to the beach cottage where our great-grandmother watched us whack them with various kitchen utensils in a futile attempt to do them in. She cried. She sat in her chair and cried and what was once just part of fishing became sickening and cruel.

Later, in college, I nearly drowned during a kayaking class. Actually, I never made it to the kayak lesson. The mere act of treading water during the pool swim test prior to being admitted to the class ended the experience early. Four laps fully clothed, then 15 minutes treading. I sank like a boulder and flapped atop the water before dog-paddling, sputtering, to the edge of the pool. Like drinking too much vodka one night forever ruining the pleasure of the liquor, the near-drowning tainted my perception and halted any desire to ever go near a kayak.

On this day my mother wants desperately to see a whale. Up close and personal. I used to yearn for excitement, but something happened along the way. A couple of car accidents, the near-drowning in front of my college peers, and reading far too many news accounts of tortuous, untimely deaths, has made me fearful of that big bad thing that will get me someday.

But I am drawn out here with her, made brave by her belief that if a big bad thing decides to get her, it is her time to be gotten. And because, despite the fact that I am no longer a child, I want my mother to be proud of me.

In the distance, a small cluster of fishing boats circles, like sea birds moving in over a school of fish.

"Look at the water," I say, lifting the flat edge of my paddle up, allowing the water to sheet over the edge. "It's full of plankton." The water is thick and dark and soupy with plankton.

Adrienne grins, knowing what I'm getting at, that the grey whales migrating here on their way back to Alaska for the summer, thrive on plankton that they filter through giant screens at the front of their mouths.

Ahead, where the boats are gathered, we recognize the excitement of something happening…perhaps a whale sighting. Adrienne takes off and I follow, fighting the urge to turn back. We are passing a small fishing village on the shore when the boats break up and begin to turn toward us. Then, 50 feet away, a fountain of shimmering rainbow spray breaks the surface. The spray is alive with the whooooffshh of air that comes from the whale's lungs.

My mother becomes quiet. I can hear her breathing. We paddle in place, as the whale, one of the great grey whales on it's migration from Baja to Alaska, slips through the water. The animal's giant ridged back heaves out of the water just 20 feet away from us. Then the tail, as smooth and black as a shiny polished beach rock, flips up and breaks the surface. I breathe in deeply, my hands shaking. Intuitively, I know grey whales do not toy with boats or bother people, that this creature is simply headed somewhere as our paths cross. But while Adrienne soaks up every glorious second in that wonderful space of time and allows herself to be lifted into the universe of another creature, I use my time to imagine the beast turning on us and batting at us with that enormous tail.

Then, the tail is gone, the whale gone. The water swirls in its place, the world begins to fold back into place.

"Come on!" Adrienne yells, giddy.

I begin to feel her excitement and try to forget the fear, let it leach out of me through my paddle, let the water take it up and carry it away.

"Let's follow him, come on!"

We paddle in the direction we think the whale is headed, through the gleaming water. We are going against the wind this time, but with the current, heading out, away from shore. We hope we are gaining on the beast, but have no way to know when or where it will reappear, when it spouts again. This time we can feel the spray on our arms and our faces. The whale's back bulges upward, piercing the swelling water. I sit bobbing in my boat, in awe of the creature, it's blackness peppered with white barnacles. The bone-roughed surface of the animal's back parts the water and I feel alive in my own skin somehow more complete.

What would it be like, I think, to topple in now and glide through the water on the back of the whale, or slip beneath it, staring into that intelligent eye as I go. I wonder if we are anything more than shadows to the creature. Does it feel my fear, seeping into the water like blood? Does it hear our excitement through the adrenaline surging through my pounding heart and into its sky? I hope not. A shadow is all I want to be, a curious shadow skimming the water like an insect.

The whale heads out toward the open sound, where only freighters pass at dawn and dusk, and whirlpools swirl dangerously and freak storms spin about on the water.

"Let's keep going," I yell, my fear chased away by the excitement.

The fishing boats have tired of watching. We are alone in our pursuit. We skip through the water, paddling ahead, throwing water with our paddles, as plumes from the whale's spouting part the water every few minutes. We know we can never catch up, but we cannot stop. Sweat is pouring down our faces. My knees are raw.

Without warning, a cold wind jumps off the mountains and blasts into us. Dark clouds spring out of nowhere, circling and setting in, determined to storm. The water turns cold and dark. We head back to shore and I glance over my shoulder several times as we go, but our whale has returned to the depths.

Back at the beach house, we dry off and make coffee and tell our whale tale to anyone who will listen. The water looks different now, more alive, as I sip at my steaming mug and look out at the white-capped waves frothing in the wind.

I find a beach chair on the porch of the family's waterfront trailer when my six-year-old son, Taylor, comes running through the sliding glass door onto the porch, binoculars dangling around his neck.

"A whale spout," he screams. "A whale spout! I saw a whale spout!"

I stand up and look out at the surging surf, but I see nothing.

"It was right there, by the ferry dock," he yells.

"The dock?" I ask him, unbelieving. "They don't come in that close."

"I saw it," he says. "I did."

A few minutes later, right by one of the pilings supporting the ferry dock, that now-familiar white spray blasts upward. It is followed by the rising back and the elegant tail flip.

Taylor is hopping up and down on the porch, emotionally charged.

"Wow" he screams. "Did you see that?"

"You were right," I tell him, giving his shoulder a squeeze and tousling his hair.

He hugs my right leg and squeals. Adrienne is now out on the beach in the rain, watching. I can just make out a satisfied smile. It is the look of someone content to live in the moment.

I wonder if I will ever lead Taylor somewhere, down some dark path, kicking and screaming.

We are quiet as the whale surfaces, spouts and breaches one last time before it is gone for good.

The daughter in this story observed, internalized, and passed on to her own daughter her mother's quiet persistence and belief in herself.

My Mother/Myself

Jeanne Quinn

I cannot say if my mother learned anything from me and since she's dead, I can only guess. But I can tell you my story and what I learned from her.

Oh, it's not the usual stuff like how to cook a turkey or how to mend a seam or even how to knit a sweater, although in truth, these things she did teach me. No, she taught me much more, like how to be a friend within the complexity of a mother/daughter relationship; how to change roles when the elder becomes old; how to love the written word and the smell of violets in springtime; and how to carry this knowledge down to the next generation and recreate it's goodness.

My mother was born an only child in a hospital in Lynn, Massachusetts, when most babies were born at home. She grew up in a transient family life; wherever her father could find work they went and that was long before airplanes and super fast trains.

My grandfather was a self taught electrician so for awhile they lived in Trail, N.Y. then Vancouver, British Columbia and Charleston, South Carolina. My grandmother told the story that the night she and her two year old daughter (my mother, Ruth) arrived at the train station in British Columbia after days on a train across Canada, an old miner was sitting smoking his pipe when someone mentioned the cute little blond-haired girl. The old miner said, "I'd rather have a dog." My grandmother never got over the affront.

When the first World War ended, they finally came to settle in New Jersey, where my mother virtually grew up and stayed for the rest of her life. She attended New York University's School of Journalism in hopes of one day writing the Great American Novel. She often said she was one of only three girls in that class.

My mother adored New York and as children, she often took my brother and me for trips to museums or to roam the mews in Greenwich Village where she'd been a member of a sorority, but more importantly where her idol, the poet Edna St. Vincent Millay, had lived. My mother dreamed of one day emulating her.

For many years Mom worked for a small town newspaper until WWII came along. With the men off fighting the war, the women filled their jobs. Mom gave up the newspaper job for a better paying one at a pharmaceutical company. But she never stopped writing.

On sunny winter afternoons, the sound of her typing on the old Remington typewriter on the dining room table kept her spark of writing alive and for me it was the sound of "Mom's home, all's right with our world."

After the war she went back to newspaper work and soon became the editor of the sister newspaper in the next town. She stayed at that job until she retired at the age of 71. When she retired she came to live with me but I was hard at work trying to pay the mortgage and get five kids off to college. (My husband had died some years before). I was physically exhausted and she was sicker than either of us realized. It frightened me to see someone I'd relied on all my life suddenly need me to parent her.

When at last I became seriously ill and she too was hospitalized for an infection that wouldn't go away, the ultimate pain came when she had to go into a nursing home. Neither of us wanted it that way, but I was fighting for my own life at the time and there seemed to be no alternative.

She was there only a brief six months when she unexpectedly died. But just before she died, she instructed my daughter Tara to find an old brown paper bag on the porch of my house and to give it to me.

"Don't go through it," she admonished Tara, "Just give it to your mother. She'll know what to do with it."

She died that night and caught up in the grief of her unexpected death, it was sometime after the funeral before I opened the bag. I spilled its contents onto my lap. There was so much some fell to the floor. There in crumpled bits of paper, some wadded into balls, old sheets of yellow tablet paper, were her writings, pencil markings faded now; words crossed out, corrected and written over.

The memories of her life captured on the bits and pieces of paper; the theme was the pain of loneliness after the death of a loved one, the anger of a lost love, walks with a boy (my father?) in a tattered coat in Washington Square. I started to read but tears blurred my vision and poured down my cheeks falling on the poems. More than 100 pages of poems from a woman I realized then I did not know.

To me my mother was so cloaked in the mantle of motherhood I had no idea such feelings raged within her. What life had she longed for, dreamed of, never talked about yet captured so succinctly on paper.

Recently an aged aunt remarked, "You have inherited your mother's love of the printed word."

Yes, I guess I have. But more than that Mom gave me a gift so magnanimous, her inmost thoughts, a legacy so intimate she never would have done that if we had not been friends, the best of friends. For here was a look into her soul through her poetry. While she could not speak to me of her dreams when she lived, in the end she entrusted them to me, perhaps in the hope that I would see to their being published. And I did.

But I think the deepest lesson I learned from my mother was perseverance. When she had to work outside her profession during the War she never stopped writing. It didn't matter if anyone every read any of her poems, she believed in them and in the end, she believed in me. And not so oddly, I see this same determination against all odds echoing again in my daughter.

(To honor her, my brother and I had her poems printed in book form for a small distribution within the family).

3

The Stamp of Legitimacy

Katya is three weeks old. She is lying in her mother's arms, her eyes glued to her mother's loving (though tired, of course!) face. Mama smiles at her, coos:

"Hi, my little one. I love you sooo much. You're just perfect in every way. You're the daughter I always dreamed of. You have such beautiful eyes, and such a sweet little nose, and your gurgles fill me with delight."

It is natural and easy for most people to notice, delight in and admire their infants. As children grow and develop, it takes more thought and perceptiveness to grasp the significance of each of their forward steps, and to acknowledge those steps with some fanfare…but fanfare that is precise, not general:

Rebecca, six, has been sitting on the trapeze bar, using it like a swing, for several months. Today, while sitting on it, she cautiously slides her hands down the ropes, letting her body drop backwards, til she is holding the bar with her hands and her knees, her head and body pointing down. She shrieks with pleasure. Her mother watches her and cheers:

"That's wonderful, honey! You're so brave and well co-ordinated! Congratulations! You're terrific!"

Mothers also need to take time to notice and acknowledge the particular qualities that make a child the unique person she is. Here is Elizabeth, age 11, cuddling with her mother, who says to her:

"I love being with you. I love talking with you. You're so smart and interesting, and you make me think about all kinds of different things that I ordinarily don't think about."

The appreciation, the validation, that Elizabeth's mother is giving her is not flattery…it's not generalized nor is it an empty cliché…it respects who Elizabeth is, and is about supporting her where she needs and deserves support.

All our lives we want to know that we are recognized as a special, remarkable, delightful person; that our existence matters; that we are worth being thought about and responded to; that we have a valid passport to being alive. When, as children, our elders reflect those realities to us, we gain strength and confidence. We can eventually carry those realities inside ourselves, even in the face of setbacks. And still, as adults, there are many times when we need to be reminded of our value and uniqueness, particularly in times of stress.

In order to validate another person, to give her that necessary stamp of legitimacy and approval, we have to pay attention to her, so that we can reflect back to her what we see and hear: her gifts, her passions, her unique qualities. This process begins from the first moments of life, and continues forever, as the anecdotes above exemplify.

The following stories and poems illustrate ways that mothers have validated the expression, the capacities, the interests and concerns of their daughters.

In this poem, the mother validates her young daughter's ability to be an effective teacher by becoming her student.

C-C-O Playmate,
Come out and play with me...
—*Traditional song*

Kathryn Dunn

My daughter teaches me clap-games
to songs I've known since childhood.
Our four hands slide and roll
like waterfalls in mid-air.

Slap, clap, back hands,
front hands: we meet as if
we have been doing this
a thousand years already.

Like Cat's Cradle,
it's one of those things
that can only be known
without thinking. It's how I felt

when the Beatles sang, "Blackbird,"
how I understood deep June green,
how I knew when I met her father,
that we could make a thousand years

work out. "Now," she says,
as she smiles and pushes her hair
away from her face. "Now..."
she sets my hands in midair

to begin again: "Now,"
she says, "close your eyes."

This mother understands and validates her daughter's need for pleasure.

Silver Dollars

Patti Tana

We were poor, but never broke. Hidden beneath a pile of old shoes on the floor of my mother's closet was a black pocketbook full of silver dollars. She had saved them from the tips she earned as a waitress.

When she came home from work, she emptied the coins from the big pockets of her apron onto the kitchen table, and I'd help her sort the pennies, nickels, dimes, and quarters. We'd count them as we stacked them into piles, then stuff them into paper wrappers of red, blue, green, and orange that we'd exchange for dollars at the bank. Usually there were a few half dollars, and these we put aside to spend or, if they were beautiful, save with the dollars. The most beautiful was Liberty striding across the earth in her long loose gown, seven stars above her outstretched arm, the sun blazing at her feet.

At least once a month Mom would bring home a silver dollar. I would get out the black bag and examine the date and picture of the new addition before I added it to the collection. The eagle stretches out its wings on some, holding them up or down, grasping arrows and a branch in its talons. On my favorite one the wings are folded and the eagle looks away into the distance behind it so I can only see its back. *Peace* is written on the mound where it perches. On the other side of the coin is the head of Liberty crowned with rays, her hair flowing back from her face. I'd touch her smooth cheek on one side and the fine rows of eagle feathers on the other, the raised numbers of the date and the letters of the words.

The coins were round and solid and heavy. They were made of real silver and they seemed to be worth much more than the green paper that creased and soiled and tore. The most I ever counted at one time was a hundred and fifty. When they ran low, down around fifty, I became nervous. Usually the black bag contained about one hundred dollars, and that was enough to give me a sense of security. I knew that when we had to we could dip into the stash and buy a quart of milk, a dozen eggs, and a large loaf of seeded rye bread...all for one silver dollar.

One time when I had my heart set on going to the movies, I was very disappointed that my mother didn't have enough money for me to go. The admission was twenty cents, the same as a quart of milk.

She thought for a minute, smiled, and went upstairs to her room. When she came down she placed a silver dollar in my hand.

"No," I protested, trying to give it back to her. "They're only in case of emergency...for necessities..."

"This is a necessity," she assured me. "The soul needs sweets."

I knew what she meant. She had often told me the story about her father, whom we called Papa. It was the Depression. She was raising her first child alone, with whatever help her father could give her. They were shopping together in a crowded grocery store when a young woman placed her selections on the counter, among them a small carrot cake. Quietly she asked the clerk if she could pay the bill at the end of the week.

"No cake for beggars!" he boomed, taking the cake off the counter and putting it back on the shelf. Everyone was stunned into silence.

And then Papa said, "Give her cake. The soul needs sweets."

I took the silver dollar and went to the movies. I even bought myself a chocolate bar with nuts to eat during the show.

This mother loves her daughter's talent, and is understanding and patient, awaiting her daughter's readiness to accept and live with her gift.

To A Young Poet

Barbara M. Simon

My daughter doesn't believe
she is a poet.
I watch her struggle
to fit herself
into an identity she doesn't understand.
The words she writes
frighten her. She can't accept
them. Her voice
is unique. I'd know her poems
the way I knew her cry.
They make me ache.

I watch her pull back
from what she must become,
force herself into the myth
of popularity, answer the septic lure
of action. She wants
to know what it feels like
to be ordinary, a part
of a group. I want to tell her
that already she is extraordinary,
the only gift
I'll ever give the world.

Here, mother and daughter learn from each other; in addition, the mother learns to respond helpfully based on what she longed for from her own mother.

Training Bras

Susan Crane

In the evening, she comes to me, sleepy and warm with questions and possibilities. My daughter is eleven years old and fresh with future. Usually, she's clutching the book I bought her, *The Body Book for Girls*. She studies this book as if she's preparing for final exams, and perhaps she is. She'll ask me a question, and then point to the section in the book where it didn't quite make sense. I'm so thrilled she comes to me that I often forget the question. My mind empties and I stare, beaming, into her soft face. Patiently, she asks again.

Tonight, this was the question: "Do you think I might need a training bra?"

It's a miracle, really, this recreating your own adolescence into what you wished it had been. As a young girl, I possessed all the tender curiosity my daughter does, but in my family, bodies and all subjects related to bodies, were strictly taboo. My mother and I never once had a discussion about bodies, breasts, periods or (Heaven forbid) sex.

In fifth grade, the girls in my classroom were solemnly led away one afternoon to a windowless room to watch the film *From Girl to Woman*. There was no discussion afterward, just giggles and whispers while each one of us received a small pink pamphlet containing the same information we had seen in the film. When I got home from school that day, my mother took me aside, dropped her voice to a whisper, and told me to hide my pink pamphlet where no one would find it. I shoved it to the bottom of my underwear drawer and only took it out late at night...reading it under my sheets by flashlight.

At eleven, I tentatively asked my mother for a bra. I didn't really need one anymore than my young daughter does, but I wanted one so badly. It felt like a ticket to a secret club that everyone else was joining. My mother flatly refused...she seemed angry somehow. While I know now that I must have eventually gotten a bra, I don't remember it. I remember only the refusal.

I ended up cutting the bottoms off my white undershirts and wadding them up to fit into my book bag, then changing into them inside one of the stalls in the girls' bathroom at school. I hoped that underneath my blouses, they'd look like bras. I even devised a way to undress in the locker room to hide my secret.

It makes me want to weep now to realize that it didn't have to be a secret. I was just a young girl, anxious to be a young woman.

I often wonder if as an adult, my mother and I would have been able to openly discuss the things my daughter and I take for granted. Sadly, I'll never know the answer to that question. My mother died of ovarian cancer at the age of forty-five, in part because she had been too embarrassed to discuss with her doctor the changes she saw in her own body that she did not understand.

I feel only tender compassion for her now, realizing she was only attempting to preserve my innocence, a child of the 1930's unsure of how to raise a child of the 1960's. In truth, there are times when I desperately wish to savor the innocence that still envelops my daughter, stop time and hold back all of the days.

Instead, I celebrate her childhood, adolescence and eventual womanhood, carefully and consciously weaving a web that cradles us both through all of our changes. We talk for hours about all of the issues that surround women and their bodies. We buy books that we read together and apart. The day she saw The Film, she rushed home to tell me about it.

Often, we walk together at dusk, leaving homework and dishes undone. We walk hand in hand through the foothills. She shows me the easy way to climb over fallen trees and how to cross creek beds without getting wet. We take turns teaching each other, and I realize this is how it was always meant to be, as my daughter lifts and rises, through days and dreams and night skies.

On this night, I answer my daughter's question about training bras. I tell her that whenever she feels ready, we will buy one. We'll make a special day out of it. Maybe we'll laugh together when I explain to her that training bras don't really train anything, and when we wonder how they ever got that silly name. I'm going to remember that day...for the woman she's going to be, and the girl I used to be.

I get to do it right this time, for both of us.

In the following story, the mother's unanticipated confidence in her daughter's ability makes the difference between failure and success.

Accident of Time

Stephanie B. Palladino

It was a week day. Maybe a Tuesday. You must have asked for a personal day at work in order to drive me to my college interview. We took the Massachusetts Turnpike, headed west. It was early fall, not yet cold enough to worry about snow or ice slowing us down. The sky was milky white, or perhaps pearl gray. The sun lay hidden throughout the day, peeking out listlessly maybe once or twice around noontime. There was a heaviness in the air, and we both felt it.

Neither of us spoke much during that two hour ride. I pretended to sleep to avoid conversation, hoping to keep a clear head for my interview later in the day. I remember feeling a quick panic in my throat as we approached Exit 8; the sign indicated Palmer, matching our directions. I fumbled for the coins and held them in my clenched palm. As you headed for the toll booth, I passed them to your outstretched hand and wondered what lay ahead for me. I held my breath as you met the greeting of the toll collector, a middle-aged, broad-faced woman. *Please mother, please don't tell her where we're headed. Leave the distance between her and us just as it is.*

You hesitated before speaking, and my anxiety teetered toward anger. My ears pricked like antennae, and I listened as your words tumbled out the window: *Fine, thank you. Is this the exit for Northampton?*

Like a prayer, I whispered in my mind: *Leave it there, mother. No more words. Enough.* Seconds passed, temples throbbed, the possibility of disaster sat between us. *If you announce our mission to this stranger, I wlll never forgive you.*

Maybe you sensed my silent threat, or perhaps you merely caught the reflection of another car in your rear-view mirror. In any case, I heard only her reply: *Yes it is. Follow Route 181 straight through to Belchertown. Take a left on Route 9 after the center of town. It'll take you all the way into Northampton.*

You thanked her and we drove off the exit ramp. I settled back in my seat, leaned my throbbing head against the headrest, and let my breath do its job. Long, slow intakes of air through my nostrils, followed by deliberate pushes from the diaphragm, and with each sequence a slight loosening of my neck muscles and clamped eyelids. I continued this meditation past the center of Palmer.

When I finally opened my eyes, we were passing through a one-street town called Bondsville. I caught sight of three teenage girls strolling along the sidewalk, their thin jackets open, revealing pointed breasts announcing themselves boldly to anyone who dared look. The girls' legs marched in unison while their shoulders bumped up against each other and their heads bobbed back and forth. I would have given anything to trade places with any one of them at that moment. The chasm between their fate and mine felt huge…their apparent aimlessness against my purpose was like a canyon threatening to hurl me over its edge. Again, I closed my eyes.

As we drove under the railroad bridge entering downtown Northampton, you spoke softly, and I listened while still feigning sleep.

If only I had known how to play bridge, or had a roommate from the start, it might have all turned out differently. Imagine, they put me in a first floor room no larger than a broom closet. Everyone else was upstairs on the second or third floor. Except the housemother. I was the only Jewish girl in Hubbard House that year, and the only freshman without a roommate.

Although I had heard this story before, hearing it that day triggered newly-hatched anxieties…was I meant to correct the injustice Smith had meted out to you some 30 years earlier? If I chose to follow in your footsteps would I regret it? And would I too leave at the end of my first year? How had such synchronicity occurred anyway…my applying to the same school that had disappointed you so?

Your discomfort at Smith must have been excruciating. Most of your classmates were high society girls who came with a confidence you lacked. Many already had experienced living apart from their families, having attended four years of private boarding school. Yours was a public school and you lived at home in the same neighborhood you'd known all your life, surrounded by relatives up and down your street. No wonder this loneliness drove you back home by the end of your freshman year.

Bridge. It always seemed so irritating to me…your fixation on my learning to play it. Though you nagged at me from the time I was old enough to learn the rules of Whist or Rummy, I never showed the slightest interest. I just couldn't see the point…for me, that is.

My breathing turned shallow as you turned left through the wrought iron gate with the words *Smith College 1875* engraved on its crest. A young woman was walking nearby, and you slowed the car to a full stop, rolled down the window and asked her directions to the nearest parking lot. I stared straight ahead as she leaned in and replied: *The closest lot is straight ahead, beyond this building here, and directly behind the next one, Hubbard House.* The convergence of your past and my possible future articulated by her few words left me lightheaded and suddenly overheated. As we approached Hubbard House, you held your foot on the brake, and pointed:

Look over there...through that window is the living room. That's where they gathered from early morning until late at night to play bridge. Some of the students even arranged their semester schedules around their bridge partners'. They had their own exclusive club from the start...

Recently I came across a transcript from your freshman year, attached to a letter addressed to your parents from the Dean of Students. From it I learned that you were on academic probation by the beginning of your second semester. Earlier in the fall, you had gone to the Dean to request a roommate, but your request was denied. You were told it was impossible to make any changes until the following year. By the end of that second semester, you were on your way home, defeated. No wonder.

Do you remember my phone call to you after my first three weeks at Smith? It was October, 1968. I had received an F on a Psychology exam. And I had missed the first freshman mixer at Williams College, due to a previously-scheduled weekend visit in New York City with relatives. I was wretched. It was early evening when I phoned you. You listened quietly as I whined: *Everyone here is so much smarter than I am. I just flunked a Psychology exam. I'll never make it. And I missed the mixer last weekend because you made me go to New York instead. Now all my friends will have dates at Williams and I'll be stuck here by myself. I don't know what to do,* I sobbed into the mouthpiece.

You might have said anything on the phone that night: *I know just how you feel. That's exactly how it was for me at Smith my freshman year. I think you should come home now. There are plenty of good colleges in the Boston area. I'll call the Dean tomorrow.*

I probably would have agreed, so desperate was I feeling at that moment. Later I would have blamed you for giving up on me, just as you had given up on yourself years earlier. I listened for those words that night, but you never spoke them. Instead, you told me that I was just as smart as the other girls, even smarter than many. *Just give it time. You'll be fine,* you promised. I took a few deep breaths, we hung up, and I stayed. You were right; I graduated cum laude four years later.

I just want to tell you now, Mom, from the distance of all these years since that phone call, *thank you...*for your words of encouragement, for your belief in me, for your refusal to yield to my discouragement that night. Though my years at Smith College were sometimes difficult, I have no regrets. I was compelled to complete your unfinished journey on that campus, to turn your defeat on its head, for your sake as well as my own. Had it been possible, had the accident of time not stood in our way, I might have offered you friendship, there, then. I can only offer it now. I want you to know that my graduation in the spring of 1972 was yours as well as mine.

4

Help is at Hand

Mom is standing at the sink, cleaning up from breakfast. The dishwasher door is open and the upper basket is pulled out for loading. Sophia, fourteen months old, ambles over to the dishwasher and climbs onto the side of the door, hauling herself up by grabbing the upper basket.

Mom comes behind her and moves her gently around to the front, saying,

"You'll have more room to stand on the front." Mom stays behind her, but does not impose her presence on Sophia's exploration.

When Sophia reaches for the dishes, Mom simply places china ones out of reach and puts plastic ones in front. Sophia moves the dishes around for a few minutes, then wanders off to another fascinating activity.

What has happened in this brief interlude is that Mom has seen what Sophia wants to do…imitate Mama loading the dishwasher…and has assisted her to do it successfully and safely.

What does it mean to assist someone? When we're taking care of another person, that question does…and should…come up with great frequency. The answer is different for each person…both for each care giver and for each care receiver, and it changes over time.

Sometimes the best assistance is support, as in the anecdote above; sometimes the best help is doing nothing. Whatever decision we make, the outcomes we need to try for are pretty clear: communicating love and respect; helping expand confidence, competence, enjoyment and independence; and assuring safety (to the degree that we're able).

In the following story, the mother helps her daughter by following the daughter's lead.

Holding the Reins

Mimi Moriarty

What is it about young girls and horses? A large percentage of adolescent females become enamored of these creatures and sustain a love affair throughout their lives with them. It usually starts after an innocent pony ride at a local carnival, so parents, beware! That pony could be the most expensive $2.00 ride of your lives. Once is all it takes. The bond is formed, the psychic connection is charged, and there is no turning back. She is hooked, irreversibly and unconditionally.

My daughter was a very shy, clingy child. She did what she was told and peace reigned in her little corner of our home. Until the announcement. She wanted to go to horse camp. I, of course, was appalled. Never mind the cost. My baby…away from home at age 11…with strangers…and large, sweaty animals? Absolutely not! This was our first really big disagreement.

She won, of course. Her only concession was to attend a camp of our choice and to pay for half of the expenses. A newly acquired paper route fulfilled the financial bargain. My job was to find an affordable camp in a safe, germ-free environment. After scouring the ads and speaking to a very kind, enthusiastic woman, we chose a small camp in northern Vermont. What could happen in Vermont?

Driving up to this camp in August, I was filled with anxiety. Driving into the camp, I was filled with horror. There, on a gentle slope, stood a ramshackle ranch house with children of all shapes and sizes spilling from the doors. Most of the summer was behind us, and we noticed as we unpacked her things that the sanitary conditions of the dormitory were on a par with those of the barn.

But the die had been cast with the non-refundable deposit, so we left her reluctantly and drove home. Happy reports from camp were our salvation, and two weeks later, when we returned, we found instead this other child. She occupied our daughter's body, but this independent, carefree girl was not the one we left. She had been transformed.

Many years later (and many summers of horse camp poorer), I stand proud of that moment when I let go of my child and put her in the care of another. I never could have helped my daughter develop into a horsewoman. (I have no interest in horses; in fact, I had a near-death experience on a horse and promised God that if he ever got me off in one piece, I would never climb back on.) We have only a few things in common, my daughter and I, but we enjoy each other's company and I marvel at her accomplishments. She is organized, hard-working, independent and fun loving. She would rather shovel out the stalls than shop at the malls, and her true love wears a leather saddle, not a leather jacket.

I asked her what it was that attracted her to horses. She was twelve years old at the time. In my naivete, I assumed that horses were a substitute for boys, and would be replaced in time. What she told me came straight from the heart.

"Control", she said. "I can control something bigger than myself."

And then I understood what it was about young girls and horses. She had two parents and two older brothers who called all the shots, made all the noise and set the agenda. She was the baby, the tag-along, the quiet one. When she found a way to control a part of her life, it made her strong and sure of herself. She learned to take the reins, not only of her horse, but of her destiny. I wish her a good ride.

Here, also, the mother helps the daughter by joining and following her.

Mood Shift

Anonymous

My teen-age daughter and I were really in a bad mood, both of us. I was down-stairs in the family room and I thought she was upstairs in her room. It was pour-ing rain outside. All of a sudden she came bursting through the door from the outside, absolutely soaking wet, saying that she had run out into the rain and that it had changed everything. On impulse, I got up and said,

"I'm coming out too".

We both ran outside and danced around, looking up into the rain. It was pounding on our faces and we got absolutely soaking wet, running around the front and the back of the house. After a while we went back in, and both of our moods had completely changed.

What I loved so much about her was that she could think of things like that. What I loved about myself was that I could get past, "Oh I don't want to get wet" and just follow her out. Also I think she realized what she had done…that she had changed my mood. That was so different from my own mother, whose mood I never could affect like that, no matter how hard I tried.

The mother assists her daughter, in this story, by letting her learn from experience, while staying actively involved and engaged.

On Probation

Sally DeFreitas

My feet are hot and my daughter Jodi is beginning to fidget as we sit at a long pockmarked table in the juvenile court office listening to a pinch-faced woman named Earlene. I am wearing my normal work clothes for January, a sweatshirt with corduroy pants tucked into tall snow boots. I would like to take the boots off but they have an elaborate system of lacing, and I want to look like I am paying attention to Earlene's instructions.

Earlene is a tall, angular woman wearing a short plaid skirt over purple leggings, and the kind of shoes my mother used to call pumps. My mind drifts and I wonder how it would feel to have an office job like Earlene's and wear short snappy outfits like hers.

The indoor job fantasy appeals to me right now as the distinctive odor of perspiration mixed with deodorant comes drifting up from inside my shirt. I feel a little faint from the smell, and want very much to get back outside into the weather I'm dressed for. Through the window, a glimmer of late sunlight on swirling snow turns the scene vaguely surreal, like a Fellini movie.

In a gravelly voice, Earlene explains the terms of Jodi's probation and then shows us the forms to be filled out each week. In a sidelong glance at Jodi, I see her masking boredom with a look of genuine concern.

My daughter, the actress.

Funny thing is, Earlene was a grade behind me in high school and boy, was she ever wild. If there had been a juvie court thirty years ago, she certainly would have been a regular customer. But that's pretty irrelevant now. The three of us are not here about Earlene's past indiscretions; we are here about Jodi, my pot smoking daughter.

To be perfectly honest, I was neither surprised nor horrified when Jodi came home from Eastern University and told me that she and some kids had smoked a joint in her friend Sandi's dorm room. After all I'm part of Clinton's generation and yes, I did inhale, so I won't be a hypocrite about this. I figured it was no big deal.

But it turned into a big deal. Because the dorm room party got busted by the campus cops, who took everybody's name and address and told the anxious participants that someone would be in touch. Jodi filled me in on the entire fiasco the day she got home from her college weekend. When an uneventful month went by, we began to hope that the whole thing would just go away.

But we were not so lucky. The campus cops did their duty and notified the local juvenile court, who in turn notified *our* juvenile court, and now here we are, sweating on a January afternoon.

I actually considered, very briefly, hiring a lawyer to get my kid out of this mess. But I didn't. Partly because lawyers are expensive, but also because I had always told Jodi she would have to deal with the consequences of her actions, whatever they were. And where she is sitting now is the consequence of something she did, six weeks ago and a hundred miles away.

So deal with it kid, you're on probation.

Earlene is talking about drug counseling and community service while Jodi and I nod like those little dolls with loose heads, eager to show that we understand. Finally we sign papers and are dismissed. Outside, we stand together in the ice covered parking lot and breathe deeply of the fresh cold air.

My watch tells me it's four thirty, but my work day is not finished. I'm a home care nurse and there is a diabetic lady who needs her blood sugar checked.

"Jodi," I say, "I've got to run. Start something for supper and I'll be home in an hour."

She gives me an awkward hug as I turn to climb in my Honda. "Thanks mom, for going through that with me."

"Sure, no problem," I say.

But what I'm thinking is, *yeah, sure, like I had any choice, right? You can't exactly resign from being a mother at this stage of the game.*

WEEK ONE

I am taking clothes out of the dryer when the thud of a back pack on the floor tells me that Jodi is home.

"Well, mom, you won't have to worry about what to wear to the honor society banquet this year."

That particular event had put us into a frenzy of preparation last spring, as we tried on dresses, searched for nylons and argued about whether or not my birkenstock shoes were acceptable footwear.

I look up. "No banquet this year?"

"Not for us. I've been kicked out of the honor society. Because of this thing…because it's a drug offense."

She seems calm, but I am crushed. "Oh Jodi, the honor society…I was so proud of that."

"Mom, it's no big deal." She wanders into the kitchen and I follow. "I was in it for a year, so I can still put it on my resume for college."

"Well, I guess that's true, but…." I struggle for words.

Jodi finds a granola bar and unwraps it. "Face it mom, the banquet was really the pits, remember…?"

Now I remember that we sneaked out early, high heels in hand. "Yeah, the speeches were pretty self righteous."

"They were pompous and boring." She is munching.

"But isn't this embarrassing, Jodi…I mean with Stephanie and your other friends being in it?"

"They're not really my friends, mom. Not any more." Jodi tosses the wrapper at a waste basket and misses. "And besides, I'm still an 'A' student and they know it…honor society or not."

Her resilience amazes me. "Okay, we'll boycott the stupid banquet," I tell her, "and take in a movie that night…as a protest."

"Good plan. I'm outta here. I should be home by six-thirty."

Jodi is off to her first drug counseling session at New Life Recovery Center which fortunately is within walking distance.

My daughter, the druggie.

I turn to the basket of clothes and start to fold, wondering why one kid needs six pair of blue jeans that all look pretty much alike to me.

WEEK TWO

"So what are these sessions like?" I am peeling ginger and Jodi is chopping apples for our secret recipe home made chutney.

"About what you'd expect, mom. They show us videos about the terrible things that drugs do to your body."

"Like the frying egg one…this is your brain on drugs?"

"Well, a little more factual than that. They use big words like synapses and chemical transmitters. And then we have these talk sessions with Jerome, the leader. Actually, Jerome looks pretty fried himself."

"Probably has a pony tail, right?"

"Yep, he's going bald and still wears a stringy pony tail. I don't know why."

"It's so you kids will know he's really cool, or hip, or whatever." I put the apples and ginger in a kettle and light the stove.

"Well, he isn't cool, or hip either one. He's just an old fart with a pony tail."

Jodi opens the refrigerator and finds a can of soda. She pops the top and leans against the kitchen counter.

"Anyway, Jerome leads these sessions where everyone is supposed to tell about their experience with drugs. How we started, why we did it, how it felt, and all that stuff."

"How many in the group?"

"Usually six or eight."

"Are you the only female?"

"No, Theresa comes sometimes. She's got a kid and she's an alcoholic. And then there's Joanie…she got caught selling LSD to a Narc."

"Not exactly the Brady Bunch, are they?" I stir the apples and add a handful of raisins, lingering to inhale the pungent steam.

"Oh yeah, and then there's Tony. He was locked up for a while. I don't know what he took, but for a while he thought he was a glass of orange juice."

"A glass of orange juice?"

"Yeah, and he still holds himself kind of rigid all the time. Like he's afraid he might spill over if someone bumps into him."

I'm not sure how to respond to this revelation so I don't say anything. *Maybe I know how Tony feels.* Lately I've been feeling pretty rigid myself, like something is waiting to spill over.

WEEK THREE

Jodi put off choosing her community service as long as possible. I offered to arrange work at the Cherry Blossom Nursing Home, where she could push wheel chairs and feed old people at dinner time. But she refused that, and finally got a spot helping the custodian for two hours after school on Monday, Wednesday and Friday. She cleans lockers and bathrooms for two hours, either four to six, or five to seven, and either shift is equally disruptive to our home life.

I had always made it a point for us to eat supper together, but now it seems like we eat late, separately, or not at all. Our weekday schedule, what little we had, is pretty much in the toilet.

But today is Saturday. I am savoring the quiet, the newspaper and a late morning cup of coffee when Jodi yells from the shower,

"Mom! I'm all out of Green Forest shampoo!"

"I'll get it when I shop Monday," I tell her. "You'll just have to use mine."

"But yours is gross!"

"So deal with it."

There are no further protests, so I assume she is making the sacrifice. Sometimes I think we could feed an entire African village with the money we spend on hair products…well, at least a large African family.

Jodi emerges with her hair wrapped in a towel and joins me at the table. "I used some of your oil treatment. It's got to stay on fifteen minutes…help me remember." She puts some bread in the toaster.

"Sure, I'll set the timer." I reach for the rooster-timer and set him for 12 minutes.

"Mom, I almost died last night. There was some kind of cheerleading practice, and I was cleaning sinks when Stephanie and Kendra came in to use the bathroom."

"Gruesome. Couldn't you hide in a stall?"

"It was too late." She butters the toast. "They looked at me like I was some kind of bug and finally Melanie said, 'Hey Jodi, what are you doing here?' like maybe I had beamed down or something."

"What did you say?"

"I just said 'community service' and kept on scrubbing." She sprinkles the toast with sugar and cinnamon. "It sort of took them a while to register and then they couldn't seem to say anything. I kept scrubbing so they only had one mirror between them, and pretty soon they left."

"Jodi, why don't you change your community service? You could still work at the nursing home. That would at least have some some dignity."

"Oh mom, I'm not good with old people. I might hurt someone." She extricates the comics. "This just seems like the easiest way out."

"Doesn't sound all that easy, it sounds kind of hard…I mean on your social standing anyway."

"In a way it's a relief," she says looking up from the paper. "I've been hating that popularity game for a long time…. and now I'm clear out of it."

"Because you're doing janitor work?"

"Right. I lost so many points last night I'm off the board."

"It sounds so complicated." I refill my cup. "Why can't you kids just be buddies, like in grade school?"

"Buddies? No way…high school is a total caste system. And I'll tell you the worst part, it's the teachers. They treat the jocks and cheerleaders like they're little gods."

"But Jodi, you always get such good grades."

"Nobody gets points for grades, mom. That just makes me a nerd."

I retrieve the comics and wonder, *when did high school turn so brutal?*

WEEK FOUR

Jodi and I are coping pretty well with this probation business, is what I tell myself on the drive home in the thin sunlight of a February afternoon. Then I walk into the house and she throws herself in my arms, bawling.

Bawling. Like a baby. This hasn't happened since she was eight and it puts me into automatic comfort mode. My nursing bag slides to the floor as I reach around her, tangling my rings in her long hair.

"What's wrong?"

"Mr. Mooney's not gonna let me do my play," she sobs. "He says I'm kicked out of drama club too."

This news from principal Mooney is so devastating that I'm ready to start bawling right along with her. You see, theater has been our life blood, hers and mine. When the divorce felt like a shipwreck we found a life raft in community theater. Our first show was *The Wizard of Oz*, starring Jodi as an apple cheeked munchkin and me as Aunt Em.

We sang together in *A Christmas Carol* and danced in *Aladdin*. I worked backstage with swarms of restless kids so she could be an orphan in *Annie* and a pickpocket in *Oliver*. When the theater group dissolved, Jodi was poised for high school drama class and the chance to be a student director. We were both crushed to learn that high school offered no such class, because the teacher had retired and was not being replaced.

Jodi coped. In her sophomore year she found kindred spirits and formed a drama club. The club created skits and performed for pep assemblies and holiday programs. The following year they became a renaissance troupe of jugglers and storytellers, a show that made the local paper when it was presented at the annual school board dinner.

But this year should have been Jodi's triumph, because she was going to direct her own play, a spoof on *A Midsummer Night's Dream*. In it, Jodi moved the entire plot of adolescent crushes and unrequited love to a high school at prom time and called it *A Midsummer Night's Scream*.

My daughter, the playwright.

The cast was chosen, the props were ready...and now this.........

"It's not fair, mom," she bawls, "and he knows it. I'm only on probation for ten weeks. If I were in sports I'd be benched for half the season. But there's no way to take away half of this…either I do the play or I don't. That's what I told him."

"And what did he say?"

"Oh the usual shit about having to follow procedures…that he didn't make the rules, he's only following them…he can't make exceptions and blah blah blah."

I slump into a kitchen chair, angry and disappointed, although I can't quite decide who to be angry at. "Jodi, why did you let this happen?"

"Give me a break, mom, I didn't *let* this happen. There's no reason for this except that Mr. Mooney hates me. He's a total fuck up."

I would like to tighten Mooney's neck tie and watch him turn blue. But I don't say that. What I say is something inane like, "Dammit Jodi, don't swear. After all, he's just doing his job."

"I can't believe this." Her voice gets shrill. "Now you're taking his side."

"I'm not taking anybody's side, I'm just trying to…."

"You're a jerk, mom…just like him, just like the teachers. You don't see how important this is…. you don't even care!"

I put my head down to hide the onslaught of tears. At times like this I literally fall apart. Why? Because Jodi is all I have, and I can't bear for her to be angry with me. Probably all my enlightened child rearing is just a facade…to cover the fact that I can't bear to lose her love.

It's my turn to sob. "Jodi, I don't want to be your mother any more. It's just too hard."

This puts her into comfort mode. "Oh mom, don't cry, I didn't mean anything." She hands me a tissue and rubs my shoulders until the tears stop. "I'm sorry," she says.

"Me too." The tension lightens and we manage to hug.

But now the killer headache that shows up whenever I cry has arrived on schedule. And from all indications, it is going to be an overnight guest.

I tell Jodi to make her own supper. In the medicine chest, I find a bottle of Tylenol with codeine tablets and wash one down with a glass of water. Then I rinse my face and collapse onto the couch.

I am still there, with a washcloth over my eyes, when Jodi comes in to start her homework. "Is it okay if I turn on the light?"

I mumble permission, the light comes on, and then I begin to ramble…probably it has something to with the codeine. "I don't understand this. School was easy for me, nurses training easy, so was French. Merde! Why do I find it so hard to be a mother?"

"Probably because it takes something more than memorizing facts."

I lift the washcloth and peer out at her. "Is this your life skills class talking?"

"Yep."

"So what is it I need here…this something beyond the ability to memorize and categorize?" *Great! I'm asking my teen-aged daughter for advice…on being a mother.*

Jodi nibbles her eraser. "…judgment, maybe…critical thinking."

"Ohhh, that sounds good…. how about wisdom? As in 'God grant me the wisdom of Solomon'?"

"Solomon…wasn't he the one that cut the baby in half…no I mean, the one who threatened to cut the baby in half?"

"Yeah, because two people were fighting over it."

"Right. That's what I thought." She disappears into her homework and I take refuge under my washcloth.

Two days later, I am filling out the weekly probation report and wondering why Jodi isn't home yet for supper. The report is a series of questions with boxes for me to check yes or no.

Does she observe curfew?

Does she attend class regularly?

Does she refrain from using illegal substances?

I am checking all yeses, of course. Would I do otherwise, if she had broken some of the rules? I don't know. She could be committing mayhem, but if I check the right boxes, she is having a successful probation. So in the end it all comes down to the mother. Would I lie for her, I wonder? *How much love is too much?*

Fortunately she hasn't broken any of the rules, at least not while I was watching. I sign the paper and place it in the thoughtfully provided envelope, but I have to add my own stamp. Then I remember where my daughter is…she's waiting for me.

Jodi is already eating corn chips with runny cheese when I arrive at La Senorita, the neighborhood Mexican restaurant. I know why she suggested eating here tonight, it's what we do when we're depressed.

Although we haven't talked about the drama club business, it's been on my mind since the night of our quarrel. Whenever I think about the situation, I get depressed, angry and just plain confused. Confused, because my motherly philosophy about accepting the consequences of one's actions has blown up in my face, because I really don't like these consequences…not at all.

Now I'd like to back up and start over. Is it too late to hire a lawyer? How about a lawsuit against the school? *Should I storm the principal's office, growling like a mother bear?*

"Do you want me to come in and talk to Mr. Mooney?" I ask, after the waitress has taken our order.

"Please mom, no." She sighs.

"But Jodi, there's got to be something we can do."

The sigh again. "Mom, just stay out of this. Okay?"

I fall silent and stare at my placemat, reading ads for *Lifetime Mufflers* and *Mike's Deer Butchering Service*. When the ads run out I change the subject. "How was the counseling session tonight?"

"It was okay." She starts in on her bean burrito.

"How about that guy who thinks he's a glass of orange juice? Is he making any progress?"

"Sure. Now he thinks he's a popsicle and wants someone to suck on him."

"Jodi, that's crude!"

"Well, you asked."

I can't tell if she's putting me on or not. Some of her drug rehab stories are borderline science fiction. I wonder if my daughter will survive these sessions with a bunch of wasted druggie burnouts.

Or will she come home one day convinced that she's a tootsie roll?

WEEK FIVE

"Your daughter is on line two." We don't have an intercom at work, the secretary just walks across the hall to tell me.

A little tightness in my chest. Jodi *never* calls unless it's for something really serious. Not that I've instructed her that way…it's just how she is. I pick up.

"Jodi…hi…"

"Guess what, mom."

"I can't. Don't make me try."

"Don't worry, it's good news. Great news in fact. I've still got a chance to do my play…a real good chance, I think. I'll find out for sure next week."

I move, in a heartbeat, from anxiety to elation. "What happened? Did you stage a demonstration?"

"Not quite." She laughs for the first time in a week. "You've heard about the power of the pen…right?"

"Sure, it's mightier than the sword and…look Jodi, I'm thrilled but I've got a call here from a doctor. Let's meet at La Senorita in an hour, okay?" We also eat at La Senorita when we want to celebrate. It's clean, it's cheap, it's cheerful….it's basically our all purpose therapy.

We get our favorite table, the one under the giant sombrero with a row of little mariachi statues serenading us. We both order the special because we are too excited to make any decisions.

"Okay, tell me how you pulled this off."

"Well, it's not for certain yet, but Mr. Mooney said I could choose three teachers to hear my case and he would abide by their decision."

"What caused this turnaround?"

"This." She passes me a copy of the school paper *Hart Beat*, opened to a story captioned, *Shall We Cut the Baby in Half?*

I read in bemused silence. "Solomon was wise enough to know that there are some things that cannot be divided. We are hoping that our principal will understand that this is the case with the drama club and our plans for the spring play. We either do the play or we don't and if we don't, a dozen students will have missed their only opportunity to participate in a full length theater production. Considering the attention given to sports in our school and our society, it seems little to ask that this independent attempt at the performing arts not be squashed…."

"Pretty clever," I say when I finish. "You used the editorial 'we'…you didn't make it too personal. You focused on the effects on others more than yourself, and invoked the support for the arts routine."

"Right, I didn't mention my probation or the drug offense or any of that."

The shrimp tacos with guacamole arrive and we dig in. "Is that what you were banging out on the word processor the other night?"

"Yep, our deadline was the next day. I kind of slipped it in at the last minute."

"Of course, this still isn't settled," I remind her, and myself, fearful that we're getting optimistic too soon.

"I know, but at least I've got a chance."

Three days later, when Jodi comes home from her janitor duties with a mile wide grin, I know she is bearing good news. Bubbling, she tells me that the panel of teachers heard her argument, and voted to let her direct the spring play.

After supper, we walk to the library, laughing as we kick our way through the soft snow.

"You know," I tell her, "I'm really impressed with the way you took on city hall and won. I could never have done that when I was your age."

"I had to, mom, I was fighting for my life. Putting on plays is the only thing that makes school bearable."

Her words sadden me. How can my daughter, who continues to bring home such great report cards, find so little joy in school? Reluctantly I ask "Are you saying that Hart High doesn't offer you much, Jodi?"

"Only what I've made for myself," she says, "And that's the drama club."

WEEK ELEVEN

It is not yet daylight and I've had no breakfast, but Jodi and I are loading flats for the play into a borrowed van the color of an old dishrag. We are heading for the Westlake College High School Drama Fest…a Saturday morning caravan of moms, pops, kids, props and costumes, driving north into a bank of clouds that could offer any combination of rain, snow and sleet.

But Jodi and her friends are so excited about this day that nothing short of a tidal wave could keep them at home. After a successful three night run in the school auditorium, *A Midsummer Night's Scream* is going on the road. The festival will feature plays from six high schools, with a panel of judges providing feedback and awards at the end of the day.

"Having fun, mom?"

I could say this is not my idea of a perfect Saturday morning, but instead I mutter and pull into the Wesco station for gas and coffee. When we pull out, the eastern sky is crimson and the coffee has quickened my pulse. "This came yesterday." I pull a letter from my jeans pocket.

Jodi unfolds and reads, "…your daughter has successfully completed her term of probation…". She lets out a whoop. "Hey, mom I made it. I mean, we made it. I'm out of jail. Thanks."

I tell her she can thank me by making sure we never have to visit Earlene again, and she promises we won't. The radio doesn't work, so we sing goofy songs we learned at camp, and then make up our own lyrics on the forty mile drive to the college. A drizzling rain has begun by the time we pull into the campus parking lot and I am relieved to see the other cars, with kids waiting to unload us. According to my watch, we have thirty five minutes until show time.

Nine hours later, saturated with theater after seeing five plays besides our own, I lean against gold embossed wallpaper and wait for the awards ceremony to begin. I'm standing because I got lost on my way to the beige and gold room and arrived too late to find a seat. Within twenty minutes, however, I am oblivious to my fatigue, because *A Midsummer Night's Scream* has won awards for best costumes, best actress (Hyppolyta) and a special award for Jodi because she wrote the play.

I am ready to collapse into an empty chair when I am approached by a tall, thin man wearing a corduroy blazer with leather patches on the sleeves. The guy has been around all day and I think he might be one of the judges.

"Mrs. De Lano?"

"Yes, that's me." I feel less intimidated now that I see his jeans and hiking boots.

"You're Jodi's mother?"

"That's right." We shake hands. Does he notice that mine is sweaty?

"I'm Ivan Sorensen from the Interlochen Arts Academy. I've been talking with your daughter and, well, we're hoping you might consider the academy for Jodi's senior year."

"Interlochen," I say, struggling for an intelligent response. I've heard of the place, of course. It's famous. "I thought it was just a summer camp."

"Not any more." Ivan smiles through his mustache and hands me a business card. "We've had a full high school program for eight years."

I stare at the card as though it might be able to tell me what to do next. "It must be expensive," I say at last.

"It is," he agrees, "but there's help available. Hello Jodi, we were just talking about you."

Jodi is at my side now, glowing. She slips her arm through mine. "So whadd-aya think, mom?"

"About what?"

"About the academy." She nods toward Mr. Blazer with Patches.

"Jodi, we'll have to talk about this later."

"Just call the admissions office and ask for an application." He scribbles on another card and hands it to me, then directs a conspiratorial wink at my daughter. "I think you really belong there, Jodi. It's a place that values creativity."

"We'll think about it," I tell him, and then, to Jodi, "We need to head home, it's starting to snow."

Driving into swirling snow, I listen with half an ear as Jodi critiques the other plays and talks about the kids she has met. But I know what is uppermost on her mind because it's right there on mine too.

I have told her we need to think about this academy business before making a decision. But as I drive, there is a part of me that knows already, beyond doubt, what the answer will be. That I will mortgage the house if I have to, in order to make this happen. Because Jodi has found the place where she needs to be.

And another part of me is struggling as I think about being left alone, and that part is scared to death. Scared of what I might become when I'm left by myself.

Afraid that I will fall back into the habits I overcame in order to set a good example for her.

Like eating too much. Or drinking too much. Or acquiring unsuitable men.

Still (I reason) I knew she would be leaving eventually...does it make such a big difference if it happens a year early?

I'm not ready! screams the imp lurking in the back of my brain.

Reading my thoughts in the dark, Jodi says softly, "Mom, it's only a hundred miles away."

Under the pale light of a cloudswept moon, we pull into the driveway and climb out of the ancient van. Jodi stops on the porch and turns to face me. "You know mom, I really, really want to do this."

There is no need to ask what she's talking about, because I know exactly what she wants. She wants to get away from the jock and cheerleader society at Hart High, she wants to forget she ever cleaned other people's toilets, and she wants to escape from teachers who don't value her talent and never will.

"But are you sure you're ready to leave home...?"

She answers without hesitation. "Mom, this is the chance of a life time. I would live with kids who are all writers, musicians, actors and artists. Just think what it would be like."

I think about it. I imagine it for myself at that age. "Okay, we'll go for it," I tell her, "but of course you have to get accepted first."

"I know. But I've got a good start. Mr. Sorensen said he would recommend me. And mom, thanks...this is just beyond belief."

We move inside, unwrap ourselves and put on water for tea. As she forages in the cupboards, Jodi says, "this feels like a miracle....the kind that only happens in books."

"It is pretty close to a miracle," I tell her, "and I'm happy for you, don't get me wrong...but..." I hesitate, unwilling to spoil the moment.

"But what, mom?"

"It's happening too fast. Right now, I almost wish you weren't quite so independent...."

"But gee, mom, it's your own fault isn't it?" She hauls out bread and peanut butter. "Independent is the way you raised me."

"Really?"

"Sure, and there's another thing. I think, maybe......I think I'm just a lot like you."

"Like me?" I look up in surprise.

"Sure." She opens the jar and butters the bread. "See, I knew you were wiped out after the divorce, but you never let on. You went back to school and got a decent job. You drive around in friggin' weather taking care of old people."

"But Jodi, that's just my job."

"That's what I mean, you do what you have to. And that's how I feel about going to Interlochen, it's what I have to do." She rescues the screaming teakettle. "So if I'm independent and ready to fly, it's because you raised me that way. You could say it's a consequence of your own actions."

I struggle to follow her logic. "So now I have to deal with those consequences....and that includes your leaving home?"

"That's what you always told me."

"Smartass." I feel the tears coming and reach for a tissue.

"It's only a hundred miles away," she says again as she wraps her slender arms around my larger form. "It's not all that far."

Jodi holds me and soothes me while my tears fall into her sweet smelling hair until finally I look up and see a blurry moon winking down at us through ragged, snow filled clouds.

In this poem, the mother assists her daughter by remaining always in connection to her while adapting gracefully to each new stage in her growth.

Loving a Daughter

Karen Ethelsdattar

Loving a daughter
means being big enough
to let her pummel you
with the fists of her anger
& not shrink away.
Means being a mountain for her...
that may be what she needs today.
Tomorrow she wants you invisible,
but making meals, supplying a bed
& clothes closet
& telephone
through which to speak
to anyone
but you.

Loving a daughter
is thinking you have begotten a stranger
& finding you have begotten yourself.
Is thinking you have given birth to yourself
& finding you gave birth to another.

Is seeing your own faults mirrored,
magnified.
Is having taught someone how to hurt you
the way you hurt yourself;
is learning to love yourself enough
that you can teach her
to love herself.

Is preparing to praise God
that she is able to get to her feet
& stand on them
& walk out your door
over & over & over again
till she can stand in her own door
& hold out her arms
& say, "Welcome."

Here, the mother actively comes to the rescue of her daughter.

The Rocker

Kendeyl Johansen

I stumbled with exhaustion, searching for the ringing telephone. Colicky three-month-old Max slept only two hours at a time, and my husband was away traveling again. My fatigued body ached. I found the phone under a receiving blanket and answered it.

My mother asked, "Is Max sleeping any better?"

"A little."

"You're not getting any sleep, are you?" She sounded worried.

My gritty eyes burned. "Not much."

"That must be so hard."

My throat closed. "Oh Mom, I'm exhausted! I can hardly think."

"I'm coming up."

Outside my window a December blizzard moaned through the darkness. My mother would have to navigate icy canyon roads to reach my house.

I said, "It's snowing hard here. Don't come. I'll be okay."

"I'm on my way."

She hung up. Tears of exhaustion and relief blurred my vision. My mother has always been my rock. The usual thirty-minute drive took her an hour. My mother arrived looking rosy-cheeked from the cold, snow frosting her reddish-brown hair. She took baby Max from my arms and ordered me to bed. I said,

"But Max needs to eat in the night."

She shook her head. "I know how to warm up formula. Go to bed!" Her determined look told me not to argue.

My soft pillow beckoned to me, along with my cozy down comforter. I headed upstairs feeling relieved, but lying in bed I couldn't sleep. Guilt overwhelmed me. I should be able to take care of my baby. At least I could have offered to help.

My mother wouldn't have let me, I realized. I heard her coo to Max as she climbed the stairs. Soon the rocking chair in baby Max's room creaked, back and forth, back and forth.

Suddenly I remembered my mother rocking me when I had the chicken pox. I was too big for rocking, but blisters invaded my throat, my ears, even the backs of my eyelids.

As we rocked my mother sang, "Rock-a-bye my big-big girl." The monotonous chant comforted me. I slept. When I woke in the night my mother offered sips of water, and laid cold washrags across my burning forehead. I slept fitfully, but in the morning the blisters had crusted and I felt better.

Now I could hear my mother chanting to Max, "Rock-a-bye my ba-by boy." Her monotone relaxed me, just as it had when I was a child. I slid towards sleep, knowing my baby was in capable hands. In the morning I'd hug my mother, thank her, and tell her how her love had rocked both Max and me to sleep.

5

With You But Not Of You

"AAAAAAAAAAAAAAOOOOOOOOOO!!!!!!"

bawls my two-year-old granddaughter, when her mother, upon bumping into a table, has said, "ouch!". That is empathy. She is literally feeling her mother's pain. Her empathy comes from her profound bond with her mother.

Empathy is born from intimacy. Another source of empathy is experience…when you see someone feeling something that you have felt, you may share her feeling vicariously.

The value of empathy to a relationship is that it enables a person to understand another's feelings, and thus respond in ways that say,

"You are not crazy or weird to feel that way".

However, to be most helpful, empathy needs to be accompanied by objectivity (at two, my granddaughter is not yet capable of that)…by objectivity, I mean saying to oneself:

"I understand what you're feeling, but I am not in your situation, so I can think about it from outside of it".

Empathy can also be sought after, as in the following dialogue between myself and my daughter, who was four at the time:

Julianna, angrily: "Marla was mean to me. She called me lots of names. What should I do?"

Mom: "Why don't you just ignore her. She'll stop after a while."

Julianna shakes her head, "No".

Mom: "Tell her she's hurting your feelings, that you don't want her to do that."

Julianna sits there gloomily.

Mom: "Say, 'Sticks and stones can hurt my bones but names will never harm me.'"

Julianna frowns. Mom tries a few more suggestions, with no luck. Finally it dawns on Mom that she has to present a response that will reflect Julianna's anger, so she offers the grossest reply she can think of, that is just short of being off limits:

"Tell her to go stick her head in the toilet and flush it!"

Julianna's eyes light up, she bounds off the chair and out the door. Mom hears no more about the problem, and Julianna doesn't complain again about being called names.

I had finally tuned in to my daughter's angry energy, and offered her something that was fierce enough to match her feelings, and thus validate them. Most likely, she never used that phrase aloud—she didn't have to, because she felt understood.

The stories in this chapter reveal mothers and daughters with sharp insight into each others' feelings and needs…mothers and daughters expressing empathy…and being objective enough to offer valuable assistance.

In this story, the little girl understands on some deep level her mother's grief and shame, and cuts through it with her love and her need.

The Keyhole

Diane Payne

Unlike before, the upstairs bathroom door closes tight and Mom says she doesn't want me to wash her back. I stand beside the door listening to rushing water fill the old four-legged bathtub, wondering how awful Mom could look...certain it's not bad enough to refuse my back washing. Since the mastectomy, Mom has quit getting dressed on top of the living room register, the only warm place in the house. Now she dresses in her bedroom behind a closed door. And when a bra commercial comes on TV, she runs into the kitchen bathroom crying. I know her breast is gone but I don't know what that means. At seven it's hard to understand the importance of breasts.

Quietly I bend toward the keyhole, relieved to find it isn't covered by a towel. The water has quit running but Mom hasn't got into the tub. I don't know what's taking her so long. All the sounds have stopped. If I hadn't seen her go into the bathroom, I wouldn't know there was anyone in there.

When I peek through the keyhole, I find Mom standing near the door, looking at herself in front of the mirror. I can see her fleshy back, sagging rump, and muscular legs, not her breast. The floor creaks as I move to the left a bit, trying to get a better view. Then I hear Mom crying. She lifts her arms over her head and squeezes her fists together, wrapping her head in a tight embrace. The more she squeezes, the louder she cries, yet it's a stifled cry, one that she smothers by sucking the side of her arm. This is something she doesn't want me to see. Something even she doesn't want to see.

Slowly she lifts her legs into the bathtub and sinks into the water, still crying. I remain crouched by the keyhole, staring at her missing breast, finally understanding the loss of so much flesh. Mom's skin is red and raw, crusted with wounds that will become thick scars. Blood drips from the stitches. She looks bruised and off balance, but not untouchable. I can see she'll never have another breast to replace this one. All that will remain is a bunched up scar and memories.

Mom's been cut off from her womanhood and now wants to be alone with her body, which means cutting herself off from me. But I want to scrub her back again. All I want to do is wash her neck and back. When Mom's naked, I'm a bit afraid of her. Her developed woman's body is so unlike mine. It isn't until she's naked that I realize how different we are in age. She's a woman and I'm a girl. With clothes on, we seem more the same.

When she was in the hospital, I could only wave at her through the window, since I was too young to be admitted as a visitor. And now she's home and I can only peek at her through the keyhole, unable to comfort her. I watch her cry and begin to cry softly, stifling tears by sucking my arm. I must be with Mom. That missing breast isn't enough reason to separate us. After my tears are wiped away, I open the door and Mom screams,

"I'm in here!" She holds a wash cloth over her missing breast. There's not enough cloth to cover the wounds.

"It's all right, Ma."

Nothing else is said. The wash cloth remains clenched over the wounds and I pick up the bar of soap and wash her back.

"Does that feel good, Ma?"

"Yeah."

"You can take that wash cloth away. I still think you're beautiful."

Tears roll down her cheeks again. "You're too young to see this."

"I saw it through the keyhole, Ma. It ain't that bad."

"Are you sure?"

"Yeah."

These two sisters join their mother in her connection to the coat; then she uses the coat to give them what they need.

The Raccoon Coat

Grace Reilly Tierney

This story is about a raccoon coat. They were a big hit in the 1920s. People were dancing the Charleston and wearing Raccoon Coats. Now, I suppose, there would be a protest about them, animal rights and all, but then they were the style.

The coat was much too big for my mother. It was October 1949 and I remember my mother going to the closet and looking at the coat. It was on a wooden hanger. My mother had very blue eyes and they sparkled like sapphire as she took the coat out and as we watched her try it on. It hung down to her ankles. My sister laughed. There was a rip under one of the arms, and we could see the flowers (they were daisies) on my mother's dress. She rubbed her hand along the fur. "Nice," she said.

We laughed. My sister was eight years old and I was ten, and nothing could be funnier than my mother in that coat. She pranced around the parlor, hauling the hem of the coat over our frayed oriental rug, and we laughed again.

Mom stood in front of the hall mirror, bunching the coat up around her waist and moving from side to side. The coat swished.

"Aunt Molly left me this."

She rubbed her cheek against the collar. Aunt Molly had visited from Boston once, and we knew how big she had been. I've often wondered why she gave my mother the coat. It was much too large to have altered. Yards of fur needed to be trimmed away.

When we mentioned bringing the coat to Mrs. Miller, who took in sewing, a look of sheer terror came on my mother's face.

"Oh, I couldn't cut this coat," she said. "It's too precious."

From then on my sister and I called it the "precious coat." Winter came and the precious coat stayed in the closet. Whenever our mother would open the closet door to take out her cloth coat, she would put her face against the fur of the Raccoon and breathe in deeply. It got to be a habit with her, and my sister and I started to do that too.

My sister and I shared a bed, and on the first cold winter night we shivered with the one blanket we had. Anne had reached up and was running her fingernail over the frost on our bedroom window when the door opened, and Mommy came in with Precious. She covered us up with the warmth of the fur. She tucked the raccoon around our shoulders and around our legs.

It became a ritual after that. Every night when we got to bed, we would hear the closet door open and the clank of the hanger as Mommy removed the coat. In my mind's eye, I could see her snuggling her nose against the fur. We would pretend we were asleep. The bedroom door would open, and then we would feel the weight of the coat being placed across our bodies. Then the tucking would begin, first our shoulders and then our legs. At the end of all this, we would giggle, and Mommy would lean down and kiss each of us on the top of the head.

Our mother died in 1980, and if I could have a wish, I would want my mother to come into my room and cover us with her old raccoon coat once more.

The mother in this story deeply empathizes with her children's passions and playfulness, and discovers the depth of connection that empathy has created.

Children: A Suspect Endeavor

Virginia Schnurr

The world is dangerous to me. I never wanted to bring children into it. Instead I wanted "to save the world" for other people's children. I'm not sure what happened. I fell in love. I had one child and then another. I like my children. I find them challenging, funny, and heartbreaking. I'm glad to have them.

I expect my children to speak their minds, face loneliness, be unpopular, be outrageous, be quiet, be shy. I am very controlling. My Southern manners require that my children speak when spoken to, etc. Once I let my first child be rude to a male. A fledgling novelist with an ego to match his height and weight visited us. Evidently, all his literary efforts tired his feet. He eyed my child's rocking horse, moved it for his footstool. I watched Hava's eyes flash with sparks of anger. From her place on her father's lap, she bounded toward the invader. She pushed harder than you would have thought possible for a two year old. She moved the horse beyond his foot reach. Climbed on. Rocked.

For once I didn't correct her rudeness. How could I be angry when a stranger had turned her Thou into an endless it?

For hours on end my child and her horse roamed the downstairs floor until the rockers wore down. The wooden rocking horse with painted red reins and patient eyes would be the first horse of many. A wooden horse owned and guarded by a girl child, a child capable of defending herself against the shoes of a careless man. A child destined to enforce boundaries. A child who taught me that an object can be a Thou in the profoundest sense of that word.

My second child had her own relationship to an inanimate object. Before Eva's nap in the afternoons I would help her put the farm animals in her Fisher Price puzzle. After the nap, I would find the piggy puzzle piece gone. The farmer, the sheep, the cow, the dog, the horse, and all the other pieces were carefully in their slots. But the pig was always hidden by Eva.

Eva would grin at me, look hopeful, wishing me success in seeking, in finding. So trusting of me, that I would get the joke, be able to put the piece back in place for her. As Eva became more sophisticated, more challenging in her hiding places, some days I could not.

I wanted Eva to have the freedom to lose her pig.

I wanted to always find that piece for her, to put it back with the sheep, cow and farmer.

After Eva outgrew her interest in the simple puzzle, I took it to the Amherst Survival Center hoping that it might be useful to another child; but, at the last moment I took out the piggy puzzle piece, put it in my jewelry box next to my mother's engagement ring.

When Eva's menstrual period arrived, I offered to buy her a gift, a token of her womanhood. Hava had selected an expensive maple box shaped like a horse's head. To my astonishment, Eva asked for the wooden piggy puzzle piece. With great reluctance, I returned it to her.

In the following story, the mother understands exactly what her daughter needs, and provides it.

Mama's Move

Cherise Wyneken

It was her call. Blind, arthritic, stubborn…it took her a long time to make it. A long time to admit that she'd have to leave her home before they carried her out in a box. Out of her little yellow house at the end of Mulberry Lane. A perfect Grandma place with a fenced in yard for Spunky…her four-legged companion. Pink Grandma roses bloomed on white pickets, red pyracantha berries on the side, a tall pine graced the back where squirrels played hide and seek with Spunky. A haven for stressed out grandchildren who came out to the suburbs from Berkeley or San Francisco to lounge on her scruffy sofa, pig out on chips and ice cream, enjoy a home cooked meal…relax.

It took me as long to discover that you can help people, hug them, alleviate some of their pain, but no matter how much you love them…you cannot live their lives for them. Ultimately each one must make her own move. Too late I found I was just a soldier in Mama's fight for life. My plans…like the jars and bits of leftovers in my refrigerator…had to be moved around from time to time in order to fit hers in.

Like aging itself, learning that lesson was a slow process. It began when the Bay Area Rapid Transit system took my parent's home on Hillside for the Walnut Creek station. Dad must have sensed he'd not live long. He instructed me to "find her a place near the church…close enough to town so she can walk." I was off and running…the dutiful daughter…trying to organize my mother's life.

Shortly before Dad passed away, my husband took a job in South Florida. Prior to our move it had been easy to run out to Mama's…take her grocery shopping or to lunch, tidy up the house, tote her to the doctor, help her choose new clothes. Fun stuff! Not necessarily needed.

Then…3,000 miles away…the slow deterioration began to escalate. Moving from cataracts to operations, from thick lens glasses to macular degeneration to a white tipped cane. From keeping house and crocheting afghans to hiring housekeepers and watching the evening news with her ears. Arthritis weakened her legs and knees.

I felt impotent being so far away…unable to pop in to clean the kitchen stove or untangle hangers in her closet. I often wished I could be the one to help her to her feet from the pew or the cafe bench instead of those "nice strangers." My heart ached as I recalled watching her take off her stockings one night…tying them to the bedpost so she could find them in the morning. Or I'd join her in a laugh as she told how she'd gone to Betty's luncheon complaining that her feet hurt. "No wonder," Betty said. "You've got your shoes on the wrong feet."

Airline tickets once used for her to come visit us were switched around. I'd enter the plane on my return, laden with new information I'd gleaned for my bulging Perrier box on the floor of our guest closet…spilling papers and manila folders. Like some giant rat building a winter's nest, I had been gathering leaves and twigs of data. A number for Karen ($7 an hour…call after 5). One from my son for Shared Housing (Ask for Jack). Shopping by phone. Clippings from Aunt Elsie on Reverse Mortgages. Sandra, next door. Adult "Day Care." Independent Living Resources. Meals on Wheels. Friendly Visitors. Alarm systems.

Time for action. Why bother my brother? He's got his hands full with his family. I can handle it. Since Mama loved company I concentrated on retirement places.

"Times have changed," I said to her. "There are places now where you can have your own apartment with housekeeping services, meals, entertainment, friends. I think you should move into one of those. Live in style."

Mama didn't think so. "What would I do with Spunky? I'll never give him up."

Lurking close behind that statement was her fear of being trapped in a high rise during a fire or an earthquake. No…she wouldn't move.

"I don't know what I'm going to do," I said to my best friend on one of my trips. "I feel so guilty. The kids and neighbors do more for Mama than I do. She needs more than friendly visits now. She seems so disoriented."

"Have you thought of getting a live-in…like we had for my mom?"

"Yes, but live-ins are expensive." I was forever juggling figures trying to make Mama's income last her to the end. What to do? I'd better start searching for a helper first thing in the morning.

As I cleaned up from supper, I flicked the "on" switch of the garbage disposal and heard a growl from deep inside. Then *plop*! The whole thing dropped out at my feet.

"Great!" I grumbled. "Just what I needed. A chance to waste my time looking for a plumber."

I flicked the switch to "off." Shoved the parts inside and closed the door. It was Sunday night...already dark. No point in doing anything till morning. I went to bed and repeated my well worn prayer, "Please, God. Help us find someone to take care of Mama." Before we were awake the next day, the telephone began to ring. Mama's neighbor.

"Do you know a plumber we can call?" I asked. "The disposal went on the blink last night."

"My friend knows a retired man who did some painting for her. She says he's good at fixing things."

He not only came prepared to fix, but he came with a list of prices, ready to go out and buy a suitable replacement. While he set about installing a new model I explained my predicament.

"By any chance do you know somebody who could come in and help my mother?"

He not only knew someone...she was also available on the terms and hours we needed. She was not only available...she was trained and experienced with working and caring for the blind. She was not only trained...she was sweet and loving and kind. Fred not only fixed Mama's disposal, he came back from time to time to paint and do the yard. Best of all, whenever he came to do a job, he made a pot of coffee first and stopped to chat a while. I had gained some time and peace of mind.

For a moment. Always new problems popped up. Another worry. Sitting back in Florida, trying to concentrate on a book, I'd see Mama climbing into the bathtub alone. What if she slips and falls?

Fred to the rescue again via an extended showerhead and a stool that straddled the tub. Using the bars he put up, she could lower herself onto the bench, pull her legs into the tub and...with the showerhead...have a nice warm bath. All by herself. This is where she started singing "Pretty bubbles in the air." And this is where she became the last thing on my mind each night as I went to sleep...feeling her vulnerability across the miles...asking God to watch over her.

"How I wish she'd give up the dog and move!"

"It's her life," my husband would reply. "Let her live it like she wants."

I wrestled with the idea of moving her to a place near us. But what about those hours I wasn't there? Mama had lots of friends. Her house was often filled with visitors. The phone busy with invitations to go out to lunch, church, Senior events. Would it be fair to take her away from that vital part of her life? I hesitated too, because her health insurance was not covered in Florida. She had a good deal on it from my dad's retirement.

My brother lived in Southern California where her insurance was valid. He'd been begging Mama to come live with them. She tried it once for a few weeks, but Spunky didn't like it.

After several more housekeepers I realized I couldn't handle this alone. The time had come to ask my brother for some help. He and his wife came up. We scouted out a nice Board and Care place nearby. As usual…Mama and Spunky won out. We hired another woman to help. Signed up for Meals on Wheels. Went home again. Physically and emotionally exhausted.

Then came the late night call from Mama's neighbor telling me she'd had it. In my stupor I didn't know if she meant herself or Mama…until she offered to call 911. A few days before, Mama had heard Spunky going into convulsions and decided it was time to put him to sleep. Her decision caused her to fall apart. I got up and readied for another flight…determined to bring Mama back with me…insurance or no insurance. Before I could make the arrangements she called to say, "I've decided to take your brother up on his offer. They're coming to get me this week."

She'd already cancelled her Meals on Wheels, so I called the hired woman and asked her to come in once a day and fix her meals until my brother got there. But as I was finally beginning to learn…I was not the one in charge. My cousin and his wife happened to be passing through in their RV. They packed Mama up, put her to bed in the back, and drove her to my brother's. The move meant shorter trips to California in which to give my brother and his wife time to get away. Time spent sitting on the arm of Mama's easy chair reminiscing, playing her favorite music tapes, reading aloud. Sad…happy times. Three years of more degeneration…physical and mental. Stress and strain on my brother and his wife. Until one day she looked at them and said,

"Take me to a rest home."

"There's one close to me," I said. "Would you like to come to Florida?"

"Yes. That's what I'd like to do."

A pleasant flight across the states, a night spent in our home, second thoughts taking her next morning to the Assisted Care Home, greetings, introductions, smiles, a happy, "See you tomorrow."

All shattered when I found her next day…completely disoriented, angry, frightened. She grabbed my hand and clutched it in wild desperation.

"Where am I? I thought you were lost."

"You're here in Florida…near me. Don't you remember? I brought you to the retirement home yesterday. You seemed happy when I left."

"Take me home with you!" she begged, clutching harder.

I caught my breath as though my heart had stopped. What have I done?

"Don't worry," the director said. "She'll calm down."

"It was your idea to come here, Mama...remember? I'm just a mile away. I'll be back to see you. We'll go out to lunch or church. I'll bring you to my house for outings."

Mama's moods rose and fell as she attempted to adjust to her new environment. I'd pop a can of cold Pepsi and a few bananas...her favorite treats...into a bag and feel my heart make a fist as I readied to visit her. What will she be like today?

Some days were pleasant. I'd bring my clipboard and pen and take notes while she told about her childhood. As we laughed and talked, the other residents' eyes filled with envy. Tiny smiles crept into the corners of their lips.

"Who are you?" Mama asked on one of my visits. When I told her I was her daughter she bombarded me with questions in open disbelief. "What's your husband's name? Your father's? Your grandmother's maiden name?"

"Come on, Mama," I said. "I'm taking you to church."

"What church?" she asked triumphantly, as though she'd caught me out. When I gave the right answer she relented and came along peaceably.

Another day I touched her hand when I came in.

"Cherisey...is that you?" she asked. "I'm glad you came. I want to tell you something."

"What, Mama?"

"When I'm gone, I don't want you to be sorry."

"Yes, Mama. I understand what you are saying. I'll be happy for you...that you're in heaven. But I'll be sorry, too."

She gave me a little smile. "You don't understand. Not yet."

Months after she was gone, I knew what she had meant. Don't feel guilty. Those times she had clutched my hand and begged me to take her home would have haunted me forever without her words..."Don't be sorry."

After that she went through a period of sorrow that life had nothing left for her. She began to ask me if I thought it was wrong to pray that God would take her. She talked about my Dad and her own mother...wishing she could be with them.

Not long after, she became bedridden. A growing peace developed. She no longer begged me to stay or take her home. It became a joy to visit her.

"You sound happy," she said one morning.

"I am. We're going on a little trip."

"How nice."

I took her hand in mine, prayed with her, kissed her.

"I have to go now, Mama. I'll be back soon. You've been a good mother to us. Good-bye."

We returned home late from our out of town weekend. The message machine was beeping irritably. I listened half-heartedly as I took notes. "Please call the Retirement Home" jolted me awake. I recognized the nurse's voice and knew.

The attendant told me they had overheard her prayer the day before. Naming each member of our family. Commending each into God's care. In the morning, after being bathed and settled in her bed, she closed her eyes and went to sleep. Mama's move.

6

Letting Her Know

Every human being demands self-expression. At birth, the neonate expresses itself by sounds, gestures, physical activity, facial grimaces, eye contact. As the human matures, the complexity of self-expression becomes staggering. Here is a very incomplete list of ways humans express themselves: glances, sounds, physical activity and movement, gestures, words…spoken and written, smiles, frowns, withholding love or approval, hugs, laughter, weeping, tantrums, trembling, singing, creating images and music, cooking, decorating self and environment, worshipping, touching, sexual contact, teaching…you can add to the list.

The following anecdote illustrates a mother encouraging her daughter to express her feelings.

Diana, nineteen, is home from college during January break. Since she has been away from home, she has been recognizing how unhappy she was as a child, when her mom's attention was wrapped up in a difficult marriage, a divorce, and a re-marriage. She asks her mother, Yolanda,

"Will you sit down with me and have a 'heart to heart' talk?"

"Yes, of course, honey," replies her mother.

Diana's sadness and longing pour out, amidst many tears and along with some anger. Yolanda listens closely, acknowledges and accepts Diana's memories, observations and feelings. Yolanda assures her daughter,

"My inattention was never because you were unlovable."

Yolanda takes lots of time with Diana, sits with her and is affectionate while Diana weeps. Yolanda occasionally weeps with her, and expresses profound regret that things were not as they should have been.

"We can have a conversation like this again, whenever you want it."

Diana ends up feeling closer to her mom, less guarded around her, and more grounded in the reality of her experience.

Yolanda has already reflected deeply on her own feelings about those difficult events in her life, and on her guilt about how that affected her children, both through therapy and by writing in a journal. So she is able to pay attention to Diana's feelings, rather than to her own…she has already given herself the attention that she needed.

In this chapter, mothers and daughters demonstrate several different ways of expressing themselves. Most of the stories are about the many ways mothers and daughters have of expressing love.

This mother let her daughter know she was always important to her mother by a very simple gesture.

Car Seats

Meredith Morgenstern

Like any three-year-old would be, I was insanely jealous of my baby brother before he was even born.

And why not? On the Saturday night rides home from my grandmother's house I used to be able to lay my head on my mother's lap and sleep. Once she was into her third trimester, that became impossible. Where I used to have all my parents' attention, the two of them were now focused on something called *Lamaze* that involved, to my young eyes, nothing more than Mom lying down and breathing loudly with Dad kneeling by her side holding her hand. Who wouldn't be resentful?

I was taken to the hospital to visit my mother the day after my brother was born and I saw him through the nursery glass. He looked like all the other babies to me, but everyone told me how beautiful he was. He was wrapped in a blue blanket. My mother wore her usual dusty pink terrycloth bathrobe. She smiled a lot, although even back then I could tell it was hard for her to walk. My brother was a difficult birth. One of my mom's sisters gave me a *Little Rascals* hat, and then no one paid any more attention to me. I hated my brother.

I had thought that my mother's pregnancy was hard on me. Once my brother was born those nine months seemed like a walk in the park. If I got little attention from my mother while my brother was growing inside her, then I got none when he finally joined us as a real person. Whenever I wanted my mother, she was busy making baby food, or breast-feeding, or changing a diaper, or putting him to bed, or bathing him. I missed my mother, then. She cooed over him and scolded me. He could do no wrong, I could do no right. Everyone thought he was adorable, I thought he was stupid and messy. My mother made up silly nicknames for him and talked baby talk to him. I was told to behave myself. I wound up retreating into my own imagination where my brother did not exist and I had my mother all to myself again. I now realize that this was probably the birth of my career as a writer.

Soon after my brother's birth I had to go back to preschool, to finish learning the alphabet and to finally discover, once and for all, whether or not that stupid prince was going to find Cinderella. (He did.) Every morning, as usual, my mom would drive me to school, leaving my baby brother at home with my dad. Every afternoon, as usual, my mom would pick me up and, with my dad now at work, my baby brother would be in the front seat of the car...my seat...in his stupid car seat grinning his stupid baby grin, and I'd have to sit in the back. This was 1979, remember, baby-seat-in-the-back issues weren't around yet, because I swear that if they were, then my mother would have put her baby in the back seat.

I never was able to reconcile myself to this new change in protocol. It didn't help matters that my brother had, as far as babies go, a rather sweet disposition and never cried. He would just sit there smiling at me as if he had been waiting all day for me to get out of preschool so I could torment him some more. The cruel Miami sun always made him sweat, too, which just made him cuter. He was fat. He had chubby baby cheeks. It was very hard to resent such a cherubic, perspiring, smiling little baby, but I managed.

One day my mother picked me up and told me that she had a surprise for me. I asked her what it was; she wouldn't tell me. I ran to put my box of crayons back in my cubby hole, put my art smock away, said good-bye to my teacher, and collected my Star Wars lunch box. My mom held my hand as we walked out the door. I asked her again what my surprise was. I was hoping that maybe Superman was waiting for me and we'd all go to Baskin Robbins, or maybe she was going to tell me that Wonder Woman was my real mother and I was going to live with her now. The reality was even better.

We got to the car and my mother opened the front door for me. No baby seat. I looked in the back...there it was! I turned to my mother and almost cried.

"Really? I can sit in the front?" I asked.

"Just for today," she told me.

I climbed in the front seat while my Mom strapped my brother into his seat in the back. When she wasn't looking I turned around and stuck my tongue out at him.

Better than Superman, better than Wonder Woman, was this magnificent token of love on my mother's part, both because it was so unexpected and because it was so unnecessary. I was perfectly willing to resign myself to a lifetime of taking a back seat to my brother, but with that one simple gesture my mother proved to me that I was not forgotten and that I would never take a back seat to anyone in her heart, ever.

Just for the record, as soon as he was old enough to get out of his car seat, I sat up front on all future drives anywhere. My brother never even had the decency to complain about it.

Here love is expressed by the mother, and experienced by the daughter, through shared experiences and learning.

Fourth-Grade Report on the State
for Roberta Maddox Scurlock

Marjorie Maddox

I didn't measure the miles
myself, calculate the highest point,
interview any farmer, collect coal, gather up
armfuls of carnations, but I breathed each inch in
from my mother's kisses.

At eight, I opened my arms
and her love fell out of a file
into my fourth-grade report,
her enthusiasm for teaching children like me...
before there was me...
stacked neatly on my yellow lined paper.

Even then, women were fired
for getting married, children
expected soon after, career
shelved quickly away. Still,
she quit to read me
Uncle Wiggley, Thurber tales, and state lore,
she and I curled together
tight as a buckeye.

Summer nights we recited rivers,...
Great Miami, Little Miami, Tuscarawas,
Sandusky, Maumee, Auglaise
(those tiny rain dances on the tongue) *Mohning, Walhonding, Muskingum,*

Scioto, Cuyahoga, Olentang (counting the slippery names
with our toes), *Vermillion, Black, Hocking, Huron*
(her hands unbraiding my hair into a great mass of cardinals
flocking away from our state).

Sometimes it was the *Seven Sons* on our fingers
and "One Daughter"...me...
origin, an extra charm for the Presidency.

It must have been cheating,
this mother's love,
stapling together place and placement,
home and home state,
hole-punched into a thick notebook
with flags and photos pasted so easily on the front.

Even without knowing
how my mother's arms stretched farther
than the 210 by 226 miles
of the shield-like state,
or the hills and valleys in her Ohio eyes,
my teacher scribbled "A++"
and, smiling like a mother,
gave me back my report
for keeps.

Here the daughter expresses her love for her mother through her actions; and her mother loves her back by her discreet response.

Marmalade at Midnight

Elisavietta Ritchie

In a Florida motel at midnight, I am peeling an oversized orange...Delicious...Hate to discard all this good peel....could crystalize, candy it...

Suddenly: texture, taste and fragrance plummet me back to 1943.

Marmalade!

My mother disliked sweets but loved marmalade. For her birthday, April 14, I wanted a special present. Anything from stores was too expensive on my dime-here-and-there earnings for chores, plus a dime for every A. One cupcake I could afford, stick in one candle. Not forty. Another problem: she dreaded that birthday.

Granted all I had ever made was Jello, under supervision, I would make marmalade all myself, surprise her when she returned from work. On her birthday, surely she wouldn't have to stay in town to conduct some radio interview at 11:00 p.m., surely it would not be the last train from Philadelphia, there would be no air-raid drill tonight.

This was World War Two. My mother...a pacifist at heart...was a career woman before the term was in vogue. Now, abandoning her musical and literary talents, she utilized her other abilities as a writer and promoter, handling publicity for the mid-Atlantic Red Cross Blood Donor Service. In peacetime a man had held the job, so she had to work twice as well and twice as long for fifty-nine percent of the salary. She herself donated blood regularly, more often than she should have.

Normally she caught the 7:30 a.m. train, after first braiding my hair ("the color of marmalade," she said), then preparing breakfast for my Russian grandmother. Babushka came to live with us in 1933, when my father, who escaped from Russia in 1920, finally earned enough to buy her an exit visa.

Now in the American Army, my father served four years overseas: England, the invasions of North Africa, Italy with the Fifth Army, France with the Seventh, and on into Germany. He rose from major to full colonel.

Babushka's contribution to the war effort was to roll bandages, crochet multi-colored afghans for wounded veterans, embroider layettes for orphans, teach Russian and French…and she taught me. She worried about and prayed for everyone: not just for my father on his several battlefronts, but also my father's sister, my unknown Aunt Maria who was not allowed to follow her mother from the USSR, instead remained inside Leningrad during the 900 Days of the Nazi Blockade. On one slice of ersatz bread daily, thousands perished. No letters got through. Later Aunt Maria wrote that by day she had constructed barracks from rubble, by night manned artillery, and also during and since the war, taught French and English. Like Babushka and my father, she spoke three languages impeccably, studied others. My Kansas City born mother spoke three, also read Latin, though she couldn't remember enough of it to help me decode the map of the lost gold mine in H. Rider Haggard's *King Solomon's Mines*.

Of my mother I saw little except at breakfast. One rare occasion I accompanied her to a baseball game. During the seventh inning break, she conducted a live radio interview with the legendary star Connie Mack, who obliged her with a statement supporting the Red Cross…then signed a hardball for me.

Although my mother may not have known the term then, she was also a civil rights activist. In that era, the "whites only" tradition was hard to breach, even in a Pennsylvania officially north of the Mason Dixon line. She was to interview a black minister, and not knowing of any other place, invited him to one of Philadelphia's best restaurants. Forewarned but nervous, the maitre-d received them properly. Over lunch she conducted her interview, made a friend for life in the minister, and coincidentally integrated that establishment.

Even during the War, a part-time housekeeper came daily because as my mother said, "Your Babushka does not know how to boil an egg." Before the Russian Revolution, Babushka had seldom set foot in the kitchen. After the Revolution, there were few eggs to boil. Now in America, she ate one daily. My mother, a vegetarian in principle, saved her meat ration for Babushka and me.

That April 14 the housekeeper was off. *American Woman's Cook Book* stood on the shelf. A rare bag of Florida oranges waited in the icebox to be squeezed for the morrow's breakfast. I peeled them as the cookbook directed: "free from blemish." The brilliant orange strips, and presumably some of the pulp, simmered and soaked the required "several times over." At the proper moment I added what the cookbook vaguely termed: "an equal weight of sugar" or "about 7 cups."

After several hours, the mixture became thick and tangy. Delectable. Babushka also approved. She loved sweets, of which she'd been deprived during her fifteen years under the Bolshevik regime. She was my co-conspirator and co-taster in the Marmalade Matter. We feasted on the pulp.

Every pot and pan was in service, but I found no Mason, jelly or other old jars in the cupboards. The only glasses were crystal. Though the paraffin leaked over the stove, no glasses broke.

By eleven p.m. (forget this was a school night), a dozen crystal glasses of marmalade, each girdled with a green ribbon, gleamed on my mother's Hitchcock table. I fell asleep on the couch.

After walking the darkened streets from the midnight train homeward during an air raid drill, my mother tiptoed into the house.

"Happy Birthday, Mummy!" I exclaimed sleepily. "Look at your present!"

She looked, and presumably deeply touched by my surprise, burst into tears.

Only later I understood: our entire month's sugar ration went into twelve glasses of marmalade.

This midnight in Florida, as I peel these oranges, I cannot remember the recipe, and that *American Woman's Cook Book*, now tattered and stained, remains on my shelf at home. It must have been my daughter who inked in after *Woman's*: "or man's".

One pot, one hotplate, in this motel kitchenette. I'll soak the peels, pour in tons of sugar, boil for hours. This may be an all-nighter…Naturally simpler to buy a jar of local product, but this is the eve of April 14, and to honor my mother's memory, I need *real* marmalade again.

This story, written by an eleven year old, is about the experience of her mother's loving presence.

Special Time

Rosie Simon

Rosie fidgets with her jacket and shifts her weight onto the other foot. It's Tuesday, the day when she and her mom go out to the Moosewood Cafe to get a brownie and some hot chocolate to enjoy while they sit on the squashy couch and read aloud from various books.

Finally Lynne, Rosie's mom, pulls out of the conversation she's been having and takes the car keys off the hook near the door, calling "Be back by five thirty!", and scooting Rosie out the door in front of her. In the car they talk about school, and Lynne answers Rosie's questions about space and laws and traffic regulation. They park across the street from the cafe, which is in a small shopping mall in downtown Ithaca.

In the mall there are about fifteen small shops. First, they enter The Bookery, which is a cozy little bookstore in the corner of the small plaza. Rosie, who loves books, breathes in the smell of the ink as they walk through the door, the little bell tinkling. Rosie and Lynne, who look remarkably alike, both head towards the children's bestsellers and start looking for a book to read at the Moosewood. Even though the store is quite tiny, there is a large selection of books to choose from, and finally they decide on *Toad of Toad Hall*, a fictional book about a bunch of animals who are friends.

They pay at the checkout counter, and then make their way down the long hallway to the cafe. When they enter, all the people recognize them, since they come every week. They plop down on the couch and pile off their winter coats. Lynne takes out the book, and starts to read. Rosie, who just got her brownie, takes a bite, readies herself for the fun and excitement of Toad and his friends, and snuggles deeper into the softness of Lynne's sweater. Around the Moosewood, things get a bit quieter as the staff and other customers listen to Lynne's kind voice carry the stories of Toad across the room.

This story was also written by an eleven year old, and describes the experience of being loved by her mother and of her way of loving her mother in return.

Bedtime With Mom

Elizabeth Feidelson

It is 9:00. The house is quiet. Only a couple lights are on. I am brushing my teeth in the stark, cold light of the bathroom, my feet flat and shivering on the hard linoleum.

"Hi."

She comes in, stretching her muscles away from the taut silence she has used, sitting with my sister until her warm breathing is slow and steady, until she creeps out and down the hall to me, to say that one word. I smile through my wash-cloth.

"Make sure to get all the way up to the hairline," she reminds, unable to stop being motherly.

I nod, squeezing out my cloth, wringing it's neck in one satisfying flick of my wrists. Done with the tedious washing up, I bound into my room and flop onto the bed. She follows me, tired. I pull down the covers and wiggle into their warmth, scooching over to make room for her. She makes do with a stiff red pillow, propping it up next to me and sitting down, her long legs almost to the end of the bed.

"Can we read?"

I don't really want to, and that's why I ask. I know the answer.

"Oh, I don't know."

She looks at the clock, weighing the time.

"Its late. Not tonight,"

She looks at me, wondering if I'll protest.

"Not tonight," I say.

Now comes the interlude, before I sleep, after I am resigned to bed. It's both of our favorite times.

"You know what?"

The introduction.

"What?"

The reply.

"In school Becky said." or "I can't believe." or "I wish we could."

One of us introduces a subject, always funny. The other will match the story with another, better, funnier. This trade of material will go on forever, until we are cracking up, my tousled head and hers almost joining as we double over in glee, wondering what Becky or her boss or Mr. Bush will do next. Or we'll be poking fun at each other, laughing at my morning grumps or her reaction when I wake up during the night, swearing we'll kill each other and enjoying every moment.

Until I unconsciously yawn, and she notices the time.

"Oh boy. In to bed. I have loads to do."

A little disappointed, but very tired, I curl deeper into bed. She stands and kisses my head, and flicks off the light. She stands for a moment, framed in the doorway. Sighing,

"I could talk to you forever."

As she quietly latches the door and walks lightly down the hall, I know it is true.

Mother and daughter have an intimate conversation around issues of emerging womanhood, and feel their shared affection.

Bonding

Elayne Clift

I had just crawled into bed with the New York Times Book Review…my reward for surviving a harrowing day of professional and domestic detail…when my daughter burst in on the scene like Sarah Bernhardt.

"I can't believe it!" she wailed. "I didn't get the part!" Her disappointment was as genuine as her shock. After several years of sailing into the lead role in children's community theater, we had both been complacent about the latest try-out. "They want me to be in chorus. Chorus! Are they crazy?"

"That would seem regressive," I offered.

"But if I pull out, they'll think I'm just a snob 'cause I didn't get the part. Besides, it was so much fun last year. Maybe I should do it. Or maybe I should try dinner theater. Oh, I don't know," she cried. "I'm so confused!"

After an hour or so of considered counseling regarding the professionalism of her pending decision, including its moral implications and practical consequences, I realized something more was going on when she flung herself on the bed with great heaving sobs. "I don't have a boyfriend, I'm too skinny, and my friends aren't paying attention to me!"

This apparent string of nonsequiturs made sense once I identified the theme as rejection. My daughter, I realized, was having her first bona fide adolescent crisis.

Suddenly, I remembered her as a baby, so sweet with rolypoly legs flailing around when I changed her diapers. In those harrowing days when child care consumed every ounce of energy I had, I used to imagine how much fun it would be to sit by my daughter's side as she suffered the pangs of puberty. How good I was in my fantasy…a patient and profound soulmate, pillar of wisdom and good advice. It would be such fun to share her agonies!

"You have no idea how much I've looked forward to this," I said after a respectful period of silence during her mourning.

The remark stunned her. "Looked forward to what?"

"Sitting by your side while you suffered," I explained, filling in the bits about my fantasies during her infancy.

"You did? Wow!" she said, viewing me with what I think was a certain amount of awe.

"I always imagined it would be such fun, and I'd be so good at it. But you know what?" I offered in solemn confession, "I don't think I'm very good at all, it's not exactly fun, and frankly, I just wanna go to bed. Maybe it's just that your hormones and my hormones are raging in opposite directions just now. Whadaya think?"

"Let's get those hormones in sync!" she said, breaking out in a grin, reminding me how very pretty she is when her eyes twinkle.

All at once, the scene seemed uproariously funny to both of us and we collapsed on the bed, giggling like schoolgirls at a pajama party. It was a good, good moment…even better than any I had dreamed. Then we talked. About guys and values and responsibilities and friendship. I saw that my baby was growing into a beautiful woman…someone I liked and was proud to be connected to.

The next day, she called me at the office, to report on her hormones, and to inquire about mine. "Holding steady," I said, "But can you believe it? That story I wrote was rejected. I'm behind on a deadline, and God, I feel fat!"

"You know," she said in tones of false mockery, "I always thought it would be so much fun to counsel my mother in a crisis. But you know what? It's not really fun. So shape up, kid!"

"You got it," I said. "See ya later."

"Love you."

"Love you too."

I smiled at the ritual of farewell which has been in place since she first talked. The bonds were strong then too. But this is different. This time, the heartstrings of womanhood are part of the glue binding us to one another. And no fantasy in the world can compete with that.

If you don't believe me, just ask my daughter, The Actress. Because when it comes to bonding, all the Bernhardts and Barrymores in the world couldn't hold a candle to her performance. It's a definite Oscar.

A daughter finds the ideal way to let her mother know how much she is loved.

Swimming Across the Lake

Susan DeFreitas

Certain summer days feel like they could go on forever. The kind of days when a quiet breeze sifts light through maple trees in front of our house, when the days are so long it seems like the sun will never set. When my mother, Ramona, is lying on the rusty old lounge chair in the front yard in her bikini, the grass unmown and unruly and climbing up around her. When the deep, sweet smell of Lake Michigan drifts through the air, hanging just below every breath you take.

This day would have been just such a day, if not for one thing: goldenrod. It was spreading.

At the beginning of summer where I live, goldenrod is easy to miss among the first great explosions of wildflowers. But by the beginning of August, where I found myself now, goldenrod starts eating up more and more land. At first it hides out all sly and sneaky in the tall grass in the field behind our house, then it begins to bloom by the side of the road, the mailbox, and up around the front steps. By September, there would almost be more goldenrod than grass.

I prodded the plant in question with my big toe from where I sat on the porch. It had sent down roots right below the drainpipe, and though I could probably have pulled it up if I'd tried, it wouldn't have made any difference. Goldenrod, like September, could not be stopped. Goldenrod reminded me of things I would just as soon have forgotten. Like the fact that summer was not going to last forever. The fact that school was only about as far away as the Big Lake to the west. The fact that I had to attend a sports banquet this afternoon in the high school gym.

And the fact that I was going to have to take Ramona.

"Mom!" I yelled across the yard. The pink-bikinied figure on the lounge chair didn't respond, so I knew that she was sleeping beneath the old straw hat. My Mom sleeps a lot because she has a disease called lupus. Before she got diagnosed, I used to just think she was lazy.

I walked barefoot through the high grass to the place where she lay.

"Mom," I said softly, touching her shoulder, "we've got to get ready."

She sat up a little and yawned, removing the hat. "Sure," she said, "I'll be there in a minute."

So I walked into the house and up to my room to do battle with my closet.

If I had my way, I'd never wear anything but shorts and a T-shirt in the summer. I hate dressing up, and the truth is, I'm not very good at it. But I had a dress I'd bought at the end of my sophomore year that was almost exactly like the dresses Lindy Carmichael and Melanie DiAngelo had, so at least I knew that was right. But…earrings? Shoes? Nylons???

Twenty minutes later, I thought I'd found semi-acceptable solutions to the first two, but the nylons remained an absolutely baffling prospect. The dress was blue. Should I wear black, white, natural, beige, navy, or taupe? (What on earth is 'taupe', anyway?)

As a last resort I marched downstairs to consult Ramona, who had dressed and was now watering the philodendron in the kitchen.

"MOM!" I blurted out, "You can't go like that!"

Ramona looked down at herself and then back at me. She had put a T-shirt on over her bikini, and you could still see the bathing-suit straps up around her neck. She was wearing yellow terrycloth shorts and a pair of flip-flops which I suspected were older than me.

"All right, all right," she said, "I didn't realize this was such a big deal. What've you got there?" This in reference to the multi-colored wad of nylons I held clenched in my fist.

The question kind of blew off whatever steam I'd built up. I opened my mouth once and then closed it again.

"I…I don't know what nylons to wear," I admitted, "What do you think, Mom?"

She looked me over. "I don't think you need to wear any nylons at all," she said. "You look great the way you are. Besides, nylons are always sliding down around your ankles and if you get the tiniest run they start to deeble."

'Deeble' was one of our private words. It means to self-destruct.

I really didn't know what else to do, so I took her advice. The big thermometer on our front porch had read ninety-two degrees since noon, and I hadn't exactly been looking forward to having my legs trapped inside that itchy second skin, anyway. Ramona took my advice regarding the white cotton pantsuit as well, and ten minutes later, we were out the door.

On our drive to school, we crossed the bridge over an inlet of Lake Michigan, one of the many locations my mother likes to swim. The places of sunshine through the cement grates swept over the car as we drove, and Ramona smiled.

"Remember the Buck Rogers bridge?"

Of course I remembered. When I was little we owned a tandem bicycle, and we used to bike up to the top of the hill by our house at night, get going as fast as we could downhill, and fly through the fluorescent lights on the inside of the bridge. It looked just like the beginning of the sci-fi TV show *Buck Rogers*, which we also used to watch together.

Ramona and I have a lot of things like that. Dad hasn't lived with us since I was too little to remember, but it didn't even really matter. Like Kurt Vonnegut says, we were a nation of two.

But the minute we stepped into that air-conditioned high school gym…with all the teachers and parents and grandparents and my whole softball team and all the other kids from school I hadn't seen since May…my heart slowly sank into my shoes. It didn't matter what direction I looked in. Every single girl in the entire room was wearing nylons.

I tried to cover the best I could, but I couldn't help but notice that nearly everybody else's mother had concocted some type of lavish, rich dessert to fill the sports banquet requirement, while my mother had graciously contributed a bowl of fresh fruit instead. It's not like she'd even bothered to squirt whipped cream on top of it or anything. Everyone kept telling me how great she looked for her age (54), while I just smiled and hoped they wouldn't notice that she wasn't wearing a bra.

Finally Mr. Minters, our principal, walked up front by the podium, cleared his throat, and launched into the obligatory boring sports banquet speech. He always said pretty much the same thing.

"Young people are the future, and how proud we all are to share our pride in this fine community, blah blah blah."

After what seemed like an hour and a half, he finally got around to handing out the awards. My name was about halfway through the list.

"Our surprise ace pitcher this summer, Raime Morrows, with honors in softball and track," he said, and I walked up to the podium to accept my award.

I smiled out into the sea of faces and hoped that my Mom would flash a picture, the way everyone else's parents had. But as Mr. Minters shook my hand, he put his other hand awkwardly close to my backside, and just to prove that it wasn't an accident, he left it there. The smile kind of froze on my face. I thought, does he do this to everyone who comes up here? Am I making a big deal out of nothing? How do other girls deal with this?

In the end, none of this really mattered. I just wanted out of there, away from those people. They always want me to be something, and I don't know what. They weren't really proud of me, the future of their community…they didn't even know who I was! I was suddenly glad that Ramona hadn't snapped a picture, because there wasn't anything special about my big moment up there at the podium, any more than there was anything inspiring about Mr. Minters' speech. It was as fake as the frosting on Mrs. DiAngelo's angel food cake. Ramona, somehow, understood all this, and we walked outside to the car. The gym door swallowed the applause behind us, and the heat outside was thick with the sound of crickets.

"Hey, kid," Ramona said, kind of quietly, "What do you say we go swimming?"

I just looked over at her and smiled. I couldn't think of anything I wanted to do more at that moment.

Rainbow Lake is fed by the inlet traversed by the Buck Rogers Bridge. Remote and lovely, it is my mother's very favorite place to swim. At this time of year, willow trees wet their hair at the water's edge, and the tangy smell of juniper hangs in the air like a dream you can't quite remember. I pulled a deep breath as we stepped out of the car.

There's a pair of bathing suits we always keep at my Uncle Robert's cottage for emergencies such as this, and these suits are bright green and red, just about the ugliest I've ever seen. The great thing is…out here…it didn't matter. Rainbow Lake wasn't like the public beach at Painted Waters where I ran into girls from school sunbathing and reading *Seventeen*. My Uncle Robert's cottage is one of about three on that side of the lake, and if anybody even lives in those other houses, I've never seen them.

Ramona and I stepped out into the water. The lake's smooth surface reflected the summer sky like an immense blue jewel with light suspended miles within the middle. This reflection broke up into waves as we moved, and eventually the waves traveling outward from my body and the waves traveling from hers began to intersect and form other waves. I, Raime Morrows, surprise ace pitcher with honors in softball and track, floated free in my ugly green bathing suit on that rippling jewel. And…for the first time in a long time…I found myself watching Ramona.

It was something I used to do a lot as a kid, I guess because I've never really understood Ramona's obsession with swimming. I mean, sure, it feels good to cool off on a hot day, but she takes the water in great, loping, graceful strides, strong and easy and self-assured. I remembered her when I was a kid, swimming all the way across Rainbow Lake and back while I sat on the dock and watched. Ramona swimming is easy to watch. Ramona swimming is ballet.

But on that perfect day in Rainbow Lake, feeling cool water like wind flowing over my skin, feeling my body so light and quick and effortless…feeling great, yes, exactly the way I was…I suddenly began to understand what it was my mother loved about swimming.

It was freedom.

Freedom from a blue dress that looked and felt like some one else! Freedom from old Mr. Minters and his groping hand! Freedom from worrying about Ramona's lack of a bra! Freedom from angel food cake with frosting three inches deep! Freedom from nylons!

In that bright, wet, sparkling moment, I decided to do something. Something to show Ramona that I understood about freedom. And that it didn't matter if she couldn't bake a cake for school or tell me what to wear.

I decided to swim across the lake.

Now, at the beginning of August when I made this resolution, I really had little or no idea how much work was going to be involved. I thought I already knew how to swim. What I really knew how to do was float. Which is good, of course, but it doesn't help you cover any kind of real distance, and I soon came to understand exactly how much bigger Rainbow Lake is than it looks. I swam everyday for two weeks straight and didn't even come close.

At first, this was kind of discouraging; I'd wind up floating for what seemed like hours, then spend the rest of the day with a sore neck and a bad attitude. But right around the third week of this routine, I came across my Uncle Robert's old flippers wedged beneath his little dock. When I put them on, I was magically transformed into an Olympic mermaid; they made the prospect of swimming across the lake seem a lot more realistic.

With each deepening August day that I swam, my admiration and sheer respect for Ramona grew as quickly as the goldenrod overtaking the land. Here I was, a sixteen-year-old trained athlete, knocking myself out to rival the accomplishment of a woman in her fifties. Maybe it was for this reason that I kept my daily training a secret from her. But maybe it was also because this act…this thing…this gesture I wanted to make, had somehow become more to me. There were always a lot of things I'd wanted to say to Ramona that I'd just never known how.

Finally, during one of those last, golden days of August (which, by some miracle, never seem to appear on the calendar), I could do it. Without flippers, all the way across Rainbow Lake and back. My lungs burned and my head felt like it was inflated with sky, but I could do it. I could swim across the lake. When I pulled myself back up onto Uncle Robert's dock that day, I let out a whoop of victory like nobody in my county has probably heard since the girls' varsity basketball team took State last year. I saw the curtains draw back on a few of the cottages next to my Uncle's, but I still didn't care. I wouldn't even have minded if they'd snapped a picture of me there.

The next day I asked Ramona, kind of casually, if we could go swimming at Rainbow Lake. I could hardly keep from blurting it out in the car, but I wanted to wait until we got there. When we finally did, the sun was glowing in the air like liquid honey, sparkling on the water like fairy dust. The sky was a smooth blue jewel. And the goldenrod that lay in every direction danced brightly, in a soft, quiet breeze.

"Mom!" I told her, finally, "I can swim across the lake now, too!"

And suddenly it was as if some thin cloud had passed over the sun. Ramona's brow furrowed, and the first drops of rain welled up in her brown eyes. I knew then that something was wrong. Rain does not easily wet my mother's face.

"Raime," she said, softly, "I…can't…anymore. This lupus makes my muscles hurt, makes things like that a lot harder."

I could see the deep lines by the sides of her mouth, set there by independence and determination. I could hear the willow tree beside us moving in the wind.

"I guess I'm getting older after all."

"I can't". Words I had never, to the best of my knowledge, heard my mother speak. I knew how much she hated those words, hated having to say them to me, the daughter she had always told she could do anything, be anyone. I also knew how blind I'd been. Ramona had been doing a lot less physically in the last couple years. It's just that she had been very good at hiding this fact, like the sneaky goldenrod growing in the field behind our house. Blind and stupid, and now it was too late.

Everyone knows that summer doesn't last forever.

Most stories, I think, would have ended right here. But not ours…as usual…it's a little different. Because out of the corner of my eye, I spied my Uncle Robert's old flippers, sitting in the bottom of his little boat at the dock where I'd left them. Ramona followed my eyes to where they lay, and we looked back at each other. It occurred to us then…in that moment…that there might still be a way.

I don't know, really, what it means to swim across a lake with your mother on one shining day at the end of August. All I know is that it was everything I'd been trying to say to her for most of my life. Feeling cool water like wind flowing over my skin, in my element, a mermaid's daughter. Somehow…out there in the middle of sun and sky and water…we were finally on common ground. Strong and easy and self-assured. Wet and wondrous and infinitely free. Equal in passing.

Flying. A nation of two.

In this story, mother and daughter exchange deep feelings with each other and learn about each other in the process.

Feet of Clay

Ann Leamon

My mother and I have grown up together...not just grown old. I am her first-born. I was a sulky, sullen, withdrawn child with imaginary friends...I loved long car trips because I could daydream. My younger sister, on the other hand, was a sunny, outgoing, happy kid who naturally liked the things Mom did...gardening, especially. People just liked Becky better. I was an acquired taste, like olives.

Mom was very much the dominant presence in the household; Dad worked and Mom ran the family. I'm not sure how it was that I grew up to feel that the worst thing in the world would be to disappoint my parents, but I did. We weren't beaten, ever...we were lectured. My siblings and I recall sitting around the dining room table and just dying inside as they said,

"What were you thinking?!? Nothing? What did the good Lord give you a head for, child?" We'd've taken a smack any day.

Mom, in those days, pronounced. There was a rock-solid moral certainty about her...she read theology for fun; she ran the League of Women Voters and did surveys with my brother in a carrier on her back; she could solve math problems in her head. She pronounced that living together was not an acceptable state. I'm not sure if she said as much or if I filled in the blanks, but any child of hers who did so would be exhibiting weakness of judgement.

I graduated from high school at 17 and took a year off in Sweden with Jude, a friend of Mom's. That summer was a disaster; I arrived full of 17-year-old angst and anger and tried to impose the rules of my upbringing on this much more free-wheeling household. When told that certain family members were used to having particular plates to eat from, I said breezily,

"Well, then I'll make a special effort to be sure they don't get them."

In the fall, as planned, I went to a friend of Jude's in the south of Sweden to care for her children. Speaking little Swedish, homesick beyond belief, completely broke...I had thought I'd be paid and was mistaken...I was miserable. For the first time in my life...aside from advanced placement calculus...I had failed at something I had set out to do. After a long talk with her kids, Jude came up with a plan...I'd care for her kids while she worked. And, I realized, this was a life buoy. I would be sensitive and aware and I would not pronounce. For the first time, I realized that normal is just what you grow up with.

This released me from thrall to the Word of Mom. I finally felt my grief and anger at the sense that I was second-best to my sister, that I had been the "little mother" to three younger siblings while Mom saved the world. I spilled all this out in a letter that must have simply exploded on the page…what Harry Potter would call a howler. I truly felt that I would be disowned when Mom read it. It broke all her rules, as I had thought they existed…it was irrational, emotional, angry, hurtful. No one could throw that sort of stuff at my mother and be thought sane, let alone loveable.

Mom's response knocked my socks off. Again, this was by letter; transatlantic phone calls were expensive in 1979 and my family had very little money. She was sad. She was sorry. She felt that she had saved the world but lost her daughter. At the same time, she had done the best she could. And she loved me, and felt I was so far away.

We talked. We incurred a $100 phone bill talking from Maine to Sweden. And we both learned that you don't have to be perfect to be loved. You don't have to be rational. Emotions are valid ways of processing the world. And in that interchange, I stopped seeing her as the Monolithic Mom. She became a person, fallible, well-meaning, kind, loving, clumsy, learning, wise.

It has been 22 years since that summer. My parents divorced a few years later, which put my mom in grad school at the same time as I was. We were job-hunting at the same time. I proofread her resume.

I married a man no one in my family had met, and, once they had, no one liked. After seven years, I understood why and him. Slowly, I put my life back together. Mom has listened, made suggestions, asked questions…one of the most profound being,

"You have forgiven your husband. But have you forgiven yourself?"

I have never felt judged or condemned. On my 36th birthday, the first spent separated from my husband, she sent me a pop-up card of Winnie-the-Pooh hanging from a balloon…I've always loved both balloons and Winnie-the-Pooh. "To my balloon child," it began. And it closed, "I like you, I love you, I respect you. Ma."

Sometimes I look at people whose parents are still together after decades of marriage, living in the house they grew up in, pillars in the institution of marriage, and I envy them that rock-solid foundation. It is a shock to discover that your parents are just like you, looking for jobs, seeking the answers, turning over stones to find the truth. But the discovery that those gods of your youth have feet of clay gives you both the freedom to search together. They're free not to have all the answers, and you're free to supply some of your own.

A mother loves her daughter by means of a story.

A Reminder

Janine Roberts

Natalya, my daughter, had recently turned eighteen and had just moved to Boston. She was taking "a year on" and working in City Year, AmeriCorps, in a poor neighborhood in the southern part of the city. One night she called me. She'd had a particularly challenging day. One of her students' mothers had just died from AIDS, and another student who had been a crack baby was crying all day because he was in such pain from stomach problems. She was questioning her own strength and capabilities to offer something in such situations.

"Read to me," she said through her tears, "from that book of memories you've been writing about me."

I had told her shortly after she left that whenever I was lonely for her, I had started to write down different memories about our eighteen years together, as a way to wrestle from the quietness of the house the vitality that had reverberated within it as we talked about and shared our lives.

"Just a minute," I said, and I went and got the wooden covered book with the photo of her and me on the front of it dressed in purples and oranges.

I leafed through it. Which memory to read…the one about Natalya at age 13 getting her violin out in the back seat of the car, bow bumping into the ceiling, because she wanted to play for me some new music that she "loved" that she had just learned in orchestra…or how Natalya adapted at age 11, when we traipsed off to St. Petersburg, to living with three Russian boys and staying with them each day while I went off to work…or the nightmares of the lion chasing her that Natalya used to have each night after her father and I separated when she was six?

I settle on reading what I had written about how adaptable Natalya was in Russia, learning Russian, ferreting out the rules of games to play with the boys, and navigating with them as they travelled around the city in the huge subways.

As I read over the phone, I hear Natalya's breathing deepen and slow down. "O.K.," she says, "I can do this. I have experience learning how to be in lots of new situations."

Once again the stories, the writing of them, the telling, help us to lean together into our memories, sturdy like lichen-covered New England rock walls.

This mother and her two daughters let each other know everything important and have created a deep intimacy through conversation.

Talking

Jean L. McGroarty

Talking is such an elemental part of a relationship. We talk about love, the weather, our aches and pains, our feelings. Through talking we learn to like or dislike each other. We decide which side to take. We laugh over the little nothings, and scream for joy or weep over the big somethings.

Talking to and listening to my children has always been important to me. Perhaps it's because I don't recall ever having a heart-to-heart talk with my mother. Perhaps it's because it's the right thing to do. Perhaps it's because, through talking, I've learned to love them, to take their side, to weep or shout with them.

My mother and I must have talked a lot. I was the youngest child, and by the time I reached high school my sisters and brother were either married or in college. When my father worked the swing shift, we went to dinner together, or ate potpies or frozen pizzas at our kitchen table. But I don't remember any big conversations, any words of wisdom, or any outpourings of pride or pain. I do remember my mother's lips pursed in disapproval when I mentioned a boy I was dating. I remember her wondering why I got that "B+" that kept me from the "A" honor roll. I remember her telling me that my IQ was 139, and I really should be able to understand algebra.

I know she loved me, and yes, we did talk. But now, ten years after her death, I wish I could remember the big and small joys that we surely must have shared. I vowed that my daughters and I would talk, would share happiness, and would be proud of each other. Though sometimes keeping this vow seems tedious and petty, most often it's a pleasure.

My twin daughters have always been very verbal, talking early, arguing with each other in babyspeak. I talked to them and they talked to me, even though some of us might not have made much sense. When they were old enough for nursery school, I was blessed with a flexible work schedule, and was able to be there when they came home from school. We talked about their day.

"I don't like Michael," Nora said to me when she was in kindergarten. "He hits."

How could I respond to that?

"Good for you, Nora. You don't have to like kids who hurt each other."

Or maybe, "Give Michael a chance. Maybe he's really a nice guy who doesn't know how to be nice to others."

I was learning through these conversations, and so were they. I was learning when to be generous, when to be firm, when to just let it go. They were learning that talking to Mom was OK, that I would listen and try not to judge. They were learning that respect for others isn't always easy.

As they grew older and plunged into that miasma of pre-teen hormones and little-girl reactions, there were times when I thought they wouldn't ever stop talking! Yes, I wanted them to talk. Yes, I wanted to be the one they talked to. But did I really have to listen to all the minutiae of their every conversation? That's when I learned not to listen to every tiny little thing. I heard about the teacher who supposedly threw an eraser at a student, but I knew there must be more to it than that. I heard about the girls in their class who were sneaking off to kiss boys in seventh grade, but having done the same thing myself, I didn't care to throw stones from my glass house.

I did listen to their pain at being in middle school. I ached for their lack of athletic ability in a school where athletics were everything. I nearly cried with them when boys were mean to Haley or girls didn't invite Nora to parties. I sighed when they decided they didn't like volleyball or basketball anymore, because they didn't like being yelled at by coaches or hated being berated by others who were better then they were. When did games stop being fun for them? I hugged them when they made the honor roll, "A" or "B".

There came a time when, once they were home from school and had deposited their backpacks in some inconvenient place in the middle of the floor, we just sat in the living room and talked. We laughed about silly things, and examined serious issues. Nora started bringing home questions and comments about the day's news, wanting my input. Haley was concerned about a misogynistic remark by a teacher, to which I responded with a letter to the school superintendent. I enjoyed their company. We discussed abortion, presidential politics, and the antics of our local community leaders. I appreciated their thoughtfulness and their concern for the goings-on in the world.

I think they listened to me, too, when we talked about drugs or sex or any of those topics that make us all squeamish. They are nearly grown now, academically on target, ready to head to college. They don't touch alcohol and dating is more of a friendly get-together than a passionate wrestling match. They have goals, which they communicate to me without hesitation. They plan to reach those goals, without succumbing to the distractions that independence may throw in their way.

We still talk. I still listen. Nora now tends to corner me when I'm playing games at the computer. She knows they really aren't as important as she is. Haley is more easily impacted by hormones, and often vents her frustrations with tears and bitter words. I hug her and kiss her and hope this phase passes before she goes away to school.

Talking has been so important in my relationship with my extraordinary daughters. I feel that we respect each other so much, and have so much in common. They turn to me when they need advice, but also comfort me when things look bleak. We are on each other's sides. We love each other. We appreciate those little nothings and big somethings. We will for the rest of our lives.

In the following story, a daughter expresses her gratitude and love to her mother, in words.

Follow Your Instincts

Catherine G. Bamji

Two years ago on a cold, brisk, February afternoon I was overwhelmed with the need to see my mother. She had been battling cancer for a couple of years and I did not get to see her as often as I wanted. But this feeling was different from the typical need to call home. I lived almost 500 miles away and had two small children. I was busy with schools, nursing, keeping my house running smoothly. These were all excuses for not wanting to face the inevitable. Mom was dying.

I spoke to a friend, who when finding out about my nagging need, did not hestitate a second. Her response was, "What are you waiting for! Pack those kids in the car and go. There are obviously things you need to say to her."

So I did. The boys and I packed the car and were away the next day. The entire trip, when there were peaceful moments of reflection, I continued to think about what it was that was driving me so hard. Why now? Why this unbelievable need to go home? What was I going to say? I kept remembering the advice my mother gave me upon hearing the news that I was pregnant for the first time,

"Follow your instincts."

She believed in me. She knew beyond all doubt that I was going to be a good mother, that I could handle whatever came my way. Well, if ever there was an example of following my instincts, this was it.

After nine hours of driving with two kids under the age of three I was worn to the bone. I unpacked the car, chattering on and on about all the latest happenings with the kids, the highlights of the drive down; anything not to discuss my real reason for coming to visit.

The next evening, no longer able to put it off, I wandered into my mom's bedroom, as I had done so many times before. There she was, sitting in bed, reading glasses on her face, covers pulled to her waist. I can feel the softness of her sheets and the warmth of her heart. I began to cry as I do now. She looked at me and asked what was wrong. I opened my mouth still unsure what was going to come out and said,

"Thank you. Thank you for teaching me how to live, for being patient, for being there whenever I needed you, for teaching me how to be a mother, without judging me. Thanks for loving me even when it was difficult, when I lied to you, when I said I hated you. Thanks for teaching me how to love a man for who he is and accepting people, trusting people and facing the world head on. Astonishingly enough you have not only taught me all these things, you have now taught me how to die."

My mom never once uttered the words, "why me," never once cried or screamed as the toxic liquid filled her veins. She faced each treatment, each stack of pills, each new food, the nausea, the pain, the lack of oxygen, with complete acceptance. This was her fate, her destiny, perhaps her reason for living. She was teaching others, teaching me, how to live a good life and to die fighting, proud of who we are, the life we lived, the lives we created.

7

Courageous Love

"You never let me do what my friends do; it's not fair; noone else's mother is so strict", wails Alma, as she stomps into her room.

Alma, sixteen, is a warm and responsive young woman. She sometimes wanders through the house with eyes cast down, not looking at anyone, being unconnected and emotionally absent. Alma's mother, Ginny, has come to understand that at those times, Alma's full of uncomfortable feelings that she doesn't want to feel, doesn't want to pay any attention to, but that she can't shake off.

Usually, she'll try to get away from her feelings by asking to go out with her friends. But Ginny has also learned that if Alma does go out, it's as if she leaves at home the part of her that is feeling miserable, so when she returns, she gets right back in it…she's still sullen and inexpressive. What seems to be most helpful to Alma is when Ginny says "No" to her request to go out and then accepts Alma's eruption into a storm of protest and tears. Instead of going out, Alma "goes in" and feels all those uncomfortable feelings. After the storm, Alma seems fully restored to her usual interactive self.

It takes wisdom, courage and love to become a holding tank, a container, for a daughter's tumultuous or chaotic or miserable feelings; to maintain just the right amount of pressure, so that she has to notice what is going on in and around her; to arouse discomfort sometimes by expecting, and even insisting that she reach towards a goal that you know she deeply wants, but will come only with concentrated effort; or to protect her from harm, while allowing her to face the consequences of her choices and actions.

This kind of interaction is the most complex of all…it includes all that are described in the preceding chapters. It requires a mother to be sensitive, strong and flexible…much like the earthquake-proof buildings that hold together because they can "give" just the right amount in a temblor.

Daughters need their mothers to be such containers for them…it helps them develop an inner focus; it also helps them to build their own containers as they grow older. Occasionally, daughters can even be containers for their mothers, though that is *not* a useful long-term role for them when they are children. It can be, however, a reasonable role for an adult daughter.

This story is a light approach to courageous love.

Best of Friends

Aloha Brown

Sunlight flooded the living room windows and the storm door screen making isolated heating pads of areas of the Early American rug where Gwyn and Moy Moy were playing. Both were nine months old, and they were the best of friends. Gwyn had been walking since she was eight months old so she toddled while Moy Moy pranced daintily as they played. Gwyn thought Moy Moy was a little girl, and Moy Moy thought Gwyn was a Pekingese puppy. As they stood at the screened storm door looking at the outside world, Gwyn with her white-blond hair and Moy Moy with her white fur, they looked like sisters…if I squinted. After all, Moy Moy meant "little sister" in the older Chinese dialect.

"Ready for a biscuit?" I called from the kitchen. For the last few months, I had tried to get my two little ones into a routine because then I could do work without checking to see if they were in mischief, at least for the time they were eating their biscuits. When I brought the biscuits into the living room, Gwyn and Moy Moy were in their usual self-chosen position, in the center of the rug, side by side with bottoms touching. Every morning, same position…at biscuit time. I gave Gwyn her zwieback biscuit, and I gave Moy Moy her doggie biscuit. Both girls were happy. They began to eat their biscuits. I left. Usual routine.

I stood immobile in the kitchen, fighting the intuitive feeling that I should return to the living room although the laundry was calling to me from the room next to the kitchen. Yielding to Mother Instincts, I tiptoed through the dining room so I could see "my girls." What I saw made my mouth drop open!

Gwyn was smiling as she munched the doggie biscuit while Moy Moy eagerly gnawed the zwieback one. Obviously, *they* had had *this* routine for some time. I sneaked back to the kitchen to ponder how to handle the situation. I decided to let them finish eating their biscuits.

The next morning before ten…the usual "biscuit time"…I sat Gwyn at the table with cookies and milk. Moy Moy had to be content with a doggie biscuit on the kitchen floor. It's called Tough Love.

The mother in this story is able to let her daughter struggle through to triumph, without rescuing her.

Flying Lessons

Gwyn Johnson

Kelsey wants to glide, twirl, leap, and fly. The only problem is, she can't let go of my hand long enough to let it happen. I sometimes grow impatient with her. Not the physical act of hand holding. I want to wean her of the emotional hand holding, if only a little. I understand her fear. When I was six I believed that I would fall while ice skating, the tip of my skate blade embedding itself in my forehead, killing me instantly. My understanding doesn't lessen my desire for her to occasionally strike out fearlessly. It magnifies it. Thankfully, Kelsey's fear is tempered just enough by her desire, for her to plead with me to take her ice-skating.

We've come to the outdoor ice skating pavilion near our house. It's a swarm of activity. Dozens of people, missing from their weekday jobs, bundled in winter garb, blowing puffs of their breath into the crispy, sunny December air. Voices mixed with canned music, laughter, shrieks of delight, and thuds of all-sized bodies hitting the wooden sides of the rink.

"What do you say we try the single blades today?" I ask her.

"No, double blades are better."

"You know, when you go to take lessons, they aren't going to let you skate on double blades, so you might want to get used to the single ones now."

"Double blades."

She looks straight ahead to the rows of skates waiting to be used, sneakers, boots and other footwear holding the place of skates out feeling the ice.

Kelsey finds a seat squeezed in between a mother with her much younger than six child and an older man. She sees that the much younger than six little girl's mother is easing single blade skates onto the much smaller than Kelsey's feet. Her eyes lower for a moment with a touch of embarrassment. I bring both my rented skates and her double blades to her, not even reaching her before she speaks.

"I'll try the single blades."

I suppress the urge to hug her or in some other way express my glee at her finally leaping off into the world of single bladed skates. If anyone saw my insides they would see me dancing, arms in the air in victory.

"OK" I say as I turn, hiding my enormous smile until I'm sure my back is to her, hoping the face on the back of my head that she believes is there is completely stoic. Inside I'm singing at what I perceive as Kelsey's arrival at a place where not succeeding the first time out is acceptable.

The skates are on and we move out onto the ice. Fear is plastered all over her face. I feel a fleeting tinge of guilt at having even suggested single blades, but then banish that guilt by telling myself that Kelsey needs to take more chances, be less tenuous about life.

The music is tinny. If it were warm, it would feel like a carnival. The outdoor pavilion wasn't designed with acoustics in mind, but the sound just adds to the freedom that skating outdoors brings, telling us we aren't surrounded by anything other than the winter air. For me, it's reminiscent of skating on frozen ponds, being careful never to get too close to the only sort-of-frozen edges and the ever-present concern of falling through. For a moment I long to fly around the rink, gathering speed, feeling the cold wind I create with my own movement. The activity surrounding us holds me back, feeding the remnants of a protective urge I feel for Kelsey. Older, bigger, faster skaters whiz past unaware of the girl with the long blond ponytail clinging to the wall.

"Please hold my hand."

"It won't help......It'll make it harder and we'll both fall down."

"Please......Bring me one of the buckets." She nearly shrieks. She looks like I've abandoned her.

I grab one of the large buckets, turn it upside down on the ice for her. She bends from the waist clutching it, her savior, her rescuer when her mom refuses to be. We circle the rink this way several times, each turn taking at least fifteen minutes. Kelsey is exasperated with me; she looks close to tears and quitting. She moves toward the entrance. I'm sure she's going to sit on the bench and cry. But then, something inside of her rises up and she pushes the bucket off the ice, suddenly angry with it. It tumbles over and rolls a little way before coming to rest near one of the seats, making no noise because of the rubber padding on the ground to protect the ice skate blades. For an eternity she grips the wall, squeezed into a tiny space to allow people to exit the ice. My heart screams for me to go to her, take her hand and run the risk of both of us ending up in a heap on the ice. Her face stops me. She steels herself against her fear. She slowly begins making her way around the ice, clutching the wall like a rock climber who can't find the next toehold, but knowing the only way to escape her predicament is to continue moving forward. It seems like forever for her to make a single pass around. My legs are stiff from following so slowly.

"I'm going to skate around a couple of times, OK?"

"Sure."

"Are you OK?"

"Yes."

She concentrates on some invisible point on the ice, not looking up. Off I go. I glide, I fly. I don't try to twirl or leap. Mostly because I can't do either. I catch her eye, filled with a combination of admiration and envy. I can hear her talking to her friends.

"My mom skates really fast." Only the admiration left, the envy hidden from view.

I pull up to the wall to catch my breath and I see her clear on the other side of the oval. The long side. She looks at me, locks eyes with me. Her face is a master-piece of determination. Then she starts out toward me. She's bundled in a winter coat that is a little too big for her, purchased so that it would last more than one season. It makes her body look so small. Her cheeks are flushed...maybe from nerves, or the cold, or just maybe excitement at what she's doing. She is moving straight toward me across the longest part of the oval. She doesn't smile or look up at me. The concentration is so deep in her eyes, mouth and muscles that I'm sure it will never leave her even if she does reach me. She wobbles, stays standing. She's oblivious to the skaters going with the normal skating traffic. She's like the mother duck that simply believes the cars will stop to allow her across the busy street. Crossing against the flow of skating-proficient humanity around her. She moves ever so slowly, inching her way along like the inchworms of summer. Unlike them, however, she doesn't stop and wave her head around wondering what to do next. She seems to know what to do next, not in the mechanics of skating, but in the idea that she must move forward. I want to go to her. I'd say

"You can do it Kelsey."

And I'd skate beside her. Or, I'd go to her and crouch down in front of her, holding her tiny body.

"Do you need some help?"

I don't do either of those things. She's my baby bird, going on her first little flight, probably a little shakier than I'd like, but insistent that this is the time for flying.

This single moment epitomizes Kelsey to me. Always hesitant until she believes she'll be perfect, a trait I have for so long wanted to rid her of, daring her to jump in and perhaps fail, perhaps appear foolish, but to jump in nonetheless. Trying endlessly to make her see the pure joy in just trying, regardless of the out-come. Then, when she is sure perfection is hers, quietly, determinedly, pushing forward. She's moving closer, halfway across now. The lump in my throat feels big enough to be seen by everyone. A lump of pride, of fear that she might fail and not try again for a long time. A lump of knowing that similar dramas will be repeated over and over again in varying forms until she is finally what we define as an adult and will fly from me one last time. I'm overwhelmed by what I see as the much larger meaning of what she has undertaken.

At the same time she's teaching herself, she's teaching me…that she'll know when it's time to let go of my hand, but until then I should hold it as often as I can, because it won't be there to hold forever. She reaches me, beaming. I wrap her in my arms, bursting with pride.

"I'm so proud of you." I whisper in her ear, feeling the coldness of her skin and hair mixed with the warmth of her. I want to cry…I do a little, so little that she doesn't see. We take a few more spins around the rink before calling it a day. We start off skating side by side…slowly, haltingly.

"Whaddya say we hold hands?"

She says nothing, but simply places that little six year old hand in mine and smiles.

Maybe we get to hold their hands even after they've proven they don't really need it. Maybe we get to hold their hands when they've done something so amazing to them that they want to, need to, connect with us to make sure we understand. Whichever it is, or if it's something else entirely different, there is nothing like the feel of a little hand in a bigger hand, gliding, twirling, and leaping. Suddenly it's so clear, that we must hold their hands if they are ever to glide, fly, twirl or leap, or even just try.

This mother also had the courage to let her daughter struggle with painful emotions.

You Must Stay

Marianne Preger-Simon

My mother was a remarkable woman. She was progressive, fun, charismatic, interested in all kinds of people and all kinds of new ideas. She loved music and art and poetry, had lots of friends, loved to go dancing and to entertain. She was a devoted mother...both protective and permissive. When my brother and I started school, she did too, and obtained bachelor's and master's degrees in early childhood education and in psychology. She taught children, then became a school psychologist, a psychologist in the New York City criminal courts, and finally formed a private practice. All this, in the first half of the twentieth century.

Unlike my mother, I was shy; and I did *not* like to be away from her. The summer of my ninth year, my brother, who was older and much more independent, was a camper at Raquette Lake Camp in the Adirondacks in New York State. At the beginning of August, my parents and I went to spend some time at the guest hotel in the camp, while visiting my brother. During the day, I played in the girls' camp, ate with my age group, napped with them, swam with them, and joined my parents in the evening and at night. This was very pleasant and worked very well.

After a week of this arrangement, my mother announced firmly:

"We are going home and you are going to stay with your new friends in the girls' camp."

This announcement came at naptime. I dissolved in tears, begged her to take me home, and after she went back to the hotel, wrote her and my father the most pathetic letter imaginable, confessing myself the most miserable, most unloved, most pitiful child in the universe. Here are some quotes from my letter (my father saved it for posterity!):

"Mother! You have lied to me and you have broken your promise....I am very *un*happy here...I still love you very very much. Most of the people are not nice to me...I am crying all the time and I *don't* have a good time! Please please please take me home...I know you don't want me to be happy. love, *Poor* Marianne"

How this kind, soft-hearted, protective mother managed to resist such blandishments, astonishes me to this day, but resist she did. Away they went, leaving their poor unhappy daughter to her dreadful fate.

I wept my way through the last weeks of August…but the following summer, I happily went off to a new camp, only a bit anxious, but mostly very eager for the adventure, and free from fear and self-pity. It had been a painful but effective action. Her strength and confidence paved the way for mine to grow.

In the following story, the mother's total sensitive engagement with her daughter's healing, while at the same time holding back from being indulgent in any way, enables her daughter's remarkable recovery.

Anniversary

Ann Clizer

We're bouncing down Rapid Lightning Road in the Jeep before I think about the date: September seventeenth. My fifteen-year-old daughter, Maya, sits in the passenger seat fingering a tube of black lipstick. In the rush of getting out the door this morning, she forgot to apply it. At our first stop, she will wrench the rearview mirror to her side and correct this oversight. I think of the task as another opportunity to practice fine motor skills with her left hand.

"Do you know what day it is?" I ask.

"What?" As if she didn't quite catch what I said.

This is her regular answer to my questions. I wonder how many of the "whats" come from her age and how many from a slightly reduced rate of information processing.

I wait. After half a minute, she answers.

"Somebody's birthday?"

This isn't the answer I was fishing for, but I say, "Hmmm, in a way, yes." I give her another minute. Maya is watching alpacas in the field alongside the road. The herd is mostly white animals, with a few brown, tan and black ones sprinkled in. On other days, we have stopped and walked up to the fence line to admire the animals's liquid dark eyes fringed by long lashes.

"It's the fourth anniversary of your injury."

"Oh."

I know I'll sound corny, but I'm going with the birthday theme. "That makes it a sort of a birthday, don't you think? On that day you became a new person, completely different than you would have been otherwise."

"Yeah, I guess."

Maya doesn't care to explore the subject. She gets the look on her face that says, "Oh geez. There she goes again."

"I'm proud of all you've done since then," I tell her.

"Huh," she answers, staring ahead at the bare ski runs of Schweitzer spilling in wide swaths down the slopes of the Selkirks. I wonder if she is thinking about the times she skied there, whizzing down Vagabond with a cold wind burning her cheeks, back in those days when she was someone else. Maya's clipped response is typical, but these days she's fluent when the subject interests her. Her resilient brain has learned to negotiate scrambled circuits until the uninformed listener would have a difficult time distinguishing her speech abilities from any other teenager. For me, the anniversary triggers a flood of memories.

On that bright September Sunday four years before, I stood in my kitchen washing chicken for a barbecue. We'd invited some neighbors over. Maya had been working with a black Morgan gelding named Deno, teaching him to pull a wagon. The horse had been entrusted to my daughter by a cousin who was spending a year on the East Coast. I watched them pass along our driveway on the far side of the lawn and disappear onto the dirt road that led to our back-woods cabin. A neighbor girl, Tianna, rode in the wagon with Maya. I remember smiling as I set the chicken to marinate.

Seconds later, I heard screaming in the yard.

"Call 911...Maya's hurt bad!"

I snatched the cordless phone and punched the numbers. Racing out the door and toward the road, I hit the end of transmission range, lost reception, and reeled back until the buzz faded. Trees blocked my view.

"Maya's hurt bad." The words scrolled through my brain as I bolted back and forth, relating a series of directions to the dispatcher so the ambulance driver could locate our remote property. *Bad, bad, bad.* My throat clenched up, and my feet kept aiming me toward Maya. I forced myself to focus on the task of giving clear instructions. *How bad was bad?*

Finally I punched the off button and burst past my boundary. A knot of bodies, including Maya's father, Chris, clustered over her. She lay unconscious in the dust, blood seeping from both ears. People moved aside to let me in. I sank down onto the rough ground and laid my hand across my daughter's chest so I could feel her breath, her rhythm, her life force. I offered my own heartbeat as a beacon, hoping to ground her so she wouldn't drift away into some unknown place where I could never find her.

"I don't want her to die!" Tianna screamed. She sat on the road bank, crying and hugging her knees. In a distant part of my mind, I felt relief that Tianna hadn't been hurt. Maya's face had gone white, and splotchy freckles stood out on her nose. Dark lashes lay still against the delicate skin below her eyes.

Eighteen hours later, in Kootenai Medical Center's ICU, Maya suffered a massive stroke caused by damage to the carotid artery. Speechless and paralyzed on the right side, she drowsed in a light coma for the next three days. She was alive, but in what condition? She could breathe on her own; an IV sprouted from her left arm. Chris and I agreed that keeping Maya alive with machines violated our beliefs, and prayed we would not be faced with that decision. But we also knew that without modern medicine, we'd have already lost her. Doctors hedged their bets, proposing and discarding courses of action to save her from the swelling inside her brain.

Chris and I alternated between kicking ourselves for allowing Maya to train an animal that outweighed her by twelve hundred pounds, and soothing each other. It was all our fault. It was nobody's fault. We hoped Deno had run deep into the mountains to die so we wouldn't have to shoot him ourselves. We hoped someone would find the poor horse and take him to a safe place. We would never let Maya near a horse again. We hoped our daughter would be physically capable of riding again.

At midnight of the fourth day, a nurse roused Chris and me from the couch in one of the private lounge rooms set aside for family members.

"Dr. Dirks needs to speak with you," she said, then backed away and let the door click shut. We looked at each other, knowing that Maya's neurologist being here in the middle of the night was not good. A moment later, the doctor entered the room, hardly taking time to greet us before he got to the point.

"We're going to have to open up Maya's skull," Dr. Dirks said. Chris had been more successful at controlling his emotions than I, but the prospect of surgery blew his composure.

"Open up her skull!" he yelled. "What do you mean, open up her skull?"

"I mean drill through the skull in four to six spots. This will relieve the pressure. If the swelling isn't controlled, it will kill her." Dr. Dirks showed no sign of alarm at Chris' outburst, and I detected a deep sorrow in his eyes as he watched us absorbing the news. "I have children of my own," he said, and I nodded at him, but I didn't believe he understood how it felt to discuss the *opening* of your child's skull.

The room smelled of fear, a scent so strong it overpowered the ever-present disinfectant. Tears coursed down Chris's face, and he went silent. Inexplicably, I felt calm. "Are there any other options?" I asked.

Dr. Dirks hesitated. "There is one thing I'd like to try. Sometimes pure oxygen will reverse swelling."

Panic rose in my throat.

"Your daughter has gone far past the normal turn-around for swelling to begin a decline," said the doctor. "Maybe she just needs a tiny nudge. But I'm only willing to give it an hour. If there's no improvement, we'll have to do the surgery."

"How do you give the oxygen?" I whispered. I already knew.

"Respirator. I'll get the technician on it." Dr. Dirks turned on his heel and pushed through the door into the ICU.

A wave of nausea washed over me. Would this be the first of a host of artificial devices? I hugged my husband's heaving shoulders, knowing how Chris hated to cry.

"Can I do something?" I asked.

"I need to talk to my mother," he said. "But I can't call." I picked up the family room phone, dialed in our calling card numbers and woke Chris's parents across the Cascades in Washington State. I explained what was happening, and Chris spoke with his mother. The connection restored his sense of balance, and together we slipped into Maya's room and took our places beside the bed. My eyes focused on city lights outside the window while the accordion-like tube snaked down her throat. I settled in to watch the monitor over her bed, a mantra pounding in my head: "*Come back to us, Maya, come back.*" At fifteen minutes, a nurse checked for response, and found no change. Chris and I looked at each other across the bed, and I wondered if he was picturing Maya's head shaved, her chestnut hair lying in two-foot strands on the floor. He adored his daughter's hair.

I saw by the clock that thirty minutes had passed, and I reached out to stroke Maya's head. Any minute a nurse would be back to do another test. I thought of Maya's soft baby-skull at birth, how organic and right the fontanel opening had felt as it shrank each day. And how wrong a set of perfectly round holes drilled with a tool would be. At the thirty-minute check, there was still no change.

I reached across Maya and Chris took my hand. We both closed our eyes, but held on, feeling the easy rise and fall of our daughter's chest. I listened to the perfectly spaced breaths being pumped down Maya's throat, counting and praying.

At forty-five minutes, Maya responded to the pinch-test, and her pupils contracted. In honor of the oxygen, I drew in a deep breath and smiled at Chris as Dr. Dirks announced the surgery would be canceled. Maya slept on, and my horror at the tubes receded exactly one smidgen.

The next morning, Maya opened her eyes and offered up a crooked smile. The composure I'd managed to hang onto the night before dissolved, and I felt all my strength drain out with the tears running down my face. No one knew what functions in our daughter's brain had been destroyed, but when I looked into her blue eyes that morning, I saw something I could understand. Besides her obvious pleasure at finding us beside the bed, there was a subtle fierceness to her expression. She gazed down along the right side of her body, and I saw muscles on the left part of her face set into a look I'd seen during soccer games, just before Maya blasted the ball through a knot of opponents. I'd seen it when she taught her Labrador retriever, Hershey, to pull a sled in the snow. My daughter fixed the recalcitrant muscles on her right side with a look that said, "Give it up; I'm going to win on this one."

Silenced by damage to her speech center, Maya fought aphasia, a condition common to stroke victims. Words and meanings were jumbled in her brain; she couldn't spell or write letters correctly with her remaining functional hand. Although a third of her brain was damaged by the stroke, her memory and intelligence remained intact, and I can only imagine the enormous frustration she must have felt with her lack of ability to communicate.

All the muscles on Maya's right side were affected, and so not only was she unable to speak, but she had lost the ability to swallow. Three weeks later, she would nod emphatically when I said, "Enough drooling. Let's fix that." An entire weekend would be spent with me prompting, every fifteen seconds, "Swallow." In the space of forty-eight hours, Maya reinstated her swallowing reflex. But at first, she ate and drank via a tube that ran through her nose and down to the stomach. Greenish nutritional fluid oozed in a continual stream from a plastic bag that hung from a rolling stand. Even so, Maya's eleven-year-old body shrank each day. Nubby adolescent breasts melted away, and I tasted bitter sorrow at the prospect of her womanhood receding into an uncertain future. Unused muscles began to atrophy and hipbones poked against her hospital gown. Only her eyes appeared to grow larger.

On the eighth day after her injury, Maya was discharged from the Intensive Care Unit and transferred into Pediatrics. The move told us our daughter's life was no longer in danger, and shifted the focus toward recovery. We waited four days in the pediatric wing while arrangements were made for Maya's transfer to St. Luke's Rehabilitation Institute across the state line in Spokane, Washington. Speech pathologists helped us test methods for silent communication: one-handed signals or gestures, alphabet boards, pictures and symbols representing people and activities, chalkboards, pencil and paper. Pictures and symbols were manageable, but seldom showed anything she wanted to say. Nurses taught her universal signals for important concepts. When she needed to use the toilet, she formed a fist.

Formerly right-handed, Maya struggled to shape letters with the left, then threw her pencil at the wall when I failed to decipher incorrect spellings of the simple words she tried to write. As Maya stared out the third floor window, the upright back of the hospital bed bracing her position, I studied her face. Slack muscles on her right side made its shape asymmetrical, but to me her beauty was untouched. My daughter's blue eyes became my passport into her mute world, and she wielded the power to suck me into the depths of that labyrinth. I wished a thousand times I could suffer this for her: let it be me buried in the confusion of mixed signals, burdened by the dead weight of unresponsive limbs and unable to answer the people around me who were talking, always talking. It seemed to me Maya grasped larger concepts, but the qualifiers slipped by her; she understood, "I'm leaving," but missed "for just a minute." Her speech therapist warned me how severe the damage could be.

"In some cases of aphasia, the patient assigns opposite meanings in her brain to words without even realizing it." She gave me a book to read. The illustrations showed old men and women in wheelchairs with thought clouds above their heads, picturing squares when the nurses held up circles. I refused to believe Maya's brain could work that way. My baby would never think I meant "up" when I said "down." After the therapist left, I staged a test.

"Look at the pretty snow on that tree," I said to Maya. I pointed out the window at vibrant red maple leaves fluttering in sunshine.

Maya widened her eyes at me and wiggled her left eyebrow. I nodded at her and smiled. She frowned, and pointed with her left hand at the tree, then shook her head, *no.*

"You don't see the tree?" I asked.

She nodded again, then shook her head once more, fluttering her fingers through the air in a falling motion.

"You see the snow?" I asked. She shook her head, then smiled her crooked smile at me, with a glint in her eyes that told me she was on to the joke. I laughed, my voice edged with hysteria born of relief. I knew she got "tree," and "snow," and on that day, it was enough.

As the days wore on, Chris and I talked to Maya as we always had. Nurses and attendants spoke to her as they would a toddler, and she rolled her eyes at their backs when they left the room. I knew she often fell short of full understanding, but I couldn't change my approach.

After the transfer to St. Luke's, our world shriveled to a private hospital room and a half dozen therapy rooms. To keep Maya out of the impersonal stroke ward housing hundreds of elderly patients, her doctor chose the smaller brain injury unit, which we shared with eight or ten others of varying ages who had suffered head traumas. Some of the patients were unpredictable, and entry and exit doors were kept locked at all times. Patients wore a bracelet that set off the alarm if they drew too near the door without an attendant to key numbers into the code pad. Maya triggered the siren three times while practicing maneuvers in her wheelchair. Finally a nurse removed the bracelet, muttering, "That's ridiculous, a little girl like you! There's no need." But the ward was usually a quiet place, with minimal foot traffic; brain injury victims have difficulty with excessive stimuli, and so it was ideal for Maya's recovery.

Days were crammed with the business of rehabilitation, and Maya's schedule revolved around meals, therapies and tests. Chris returned to work in Idaho, visiting us some evenings and for a few hours on the weekends. I slept on an easy chair that folded out into a strip of lumpy cushions, positioned a yard from my daughter's hospital bed. The walls, blank and colorless on our first day, soon grew cluttered with cards and letters, posters and drawings that rolled in from school, home and friends. The windowsill bristled with stuffed animals: bears, puppies, cats, a frog, and a pale pink pig with a corkscrew tail.

A carload of children from Maya's class came to visit one day. The room filled with voices and motion, and I watched my daughter carefully. Helium balloons bumped against the ceiling, two kids tossed a tennis ball back and forth, and Maya's teacher, Thomas, presented Maya with a gift from the class. Maya endured the onslaught, huddling under her thin blanket, flattered and overwhelmed. After twenty minutes, I signaled Thomas, "Enough." The class departed. We watched them go, laughing and pushing each other, back to their busy lives. The gift they left became Maya's instant favorite: a stuffed horse covered with silky fur the exact shade of Deno's hide, frozen in a flat-out gallop.

Nobody would tell us when we could go home. Therapists talked about physical goals, and doctors discussed how long Maya might need injections to thin her blood. At night all the doors leading out of St. Luke's Rehabilitation Institute were locked and guarded by uniformed security officers. When I lay in bed courting sleep, I thought about the noises I would hear at home: the hoot of an owl, wind nudging lanky lodgepole pines, a chorus of coyotes, or rain pelting the metal roof. At St. Luke's, I listened to quiet shift talk among the nurses, faint sirens on the streets of Spokane, the whoosh of vented hot air, and "phhtt, phhtt, phhtt" from the tiny pump feeding green liquid into Maya's stomach. I napped during the two-hour intervals between vital sign checks.

Maya begged me with her eyes to understand her needs. I learned caution, the art of touching the surface to glean her simple requests, guarding my strength and purpose for the job of advocate. In the first three weeks we spent at St. Luke's Rehabilitation Institute, Maya and I honed our silent exchanges to a cutting edge, developing an intricate language composed of facial expression, eye movements and hand signals. I knew when she wanted to shift her body, when she couldn't reach the remote control, when she craved another chapter from *Stormy, Misty's Foal.* After she began to eat again, I could tell by the way she set down her fork if she was still hungry, and I'd cruise her wheelchair through the cafeteria line for thirds. On shower days, the angle of her chin told me she was worrying about getting chilled when the hot water shut off. Restless fingers tipped me off that she wanted yet another game of Rummy, the tilt of an eyebrow said she'd had her fill of visitors, and a glance at the windowsill told me she was ready to feed her fish.

My reserves dwindled. When I paced hallways, I longed for the trails on my mountain, rocks and dirt underfoot, the press of a half-buried root wad against the sole of my boot. Early mornings, I would slip outside and tip my face to the city sky, suck in deep breaths of chill air, but always the intensity of Maya's need drew me back inside. I knew she would wake and look for me beside her bed, reach out for my hand, and gift me with a serene smile I had never seen before her injury. But my emptiness grew. I hadn't slept beside my husband in more than a month.

I needed to go home. Other children in rehab spent nights with only nurses in attendance, but I couldn't bear to think of leaving my daughter that alone. I arranged for my mother to take my place for one night.

"I'll get your sweat pants and those blue shorts," I said. She could wear her own clothing, but needed pants without zippers, things that were easy to get on and off. Maya turned away from me, her mouth set in a frown and her left hand clenched on the television remote control.

"Do you want your pillow? Your art tablet? The time will go fast, you'll see."

Secretly, I hoped it wasn't true.

On the two hour drive home, heading deeper into the mountains of North Idaho, I worried that her grandmother wouldn't understand the language, wouldn't know when Maya wanted to work her jigsaw puzzle, or which set of felt-tip markers was her favorite. But the tightness in my chest disappeared when I nosed the Toyota into the clearing around our cabin. I stood in the driveway for ten minutes, inhaling crisp mountain air and listening to the staccato of a woodpecker drilling the cedar that guarded our compost pile. I grabbed an armload of firewood from the shed before I headed inside, feeling the familiar weight and press of rough bark against my muscles. I sighed out a breath deeper than I knew I'd been holding.

On that afternoon, waiting for Chris, I crawled around in the garden, digging dahlia bulbs and reveling in the grit of rich dirt beneath my fingernails, the dampness against my knees. Withered pea vines and brown strawberry leaves radiated a pristine beauty, and the sounds of my neighbors passing on the road inspired feelings of safety and belonging. I searched Maya's room until I found a beading kit. I filled a leather pouch with natural treasures from outside the cabin. I snuggled against my husband's chest with only moonlight filtering in through our uncurtained window. I listened to trees creaking in the wind. I slept.

Somehow I restrained myself from calling Mother until morning. When I woke in the upstairs bedroom of our cabin, I stared out the window at the wall of forest marching up to our south border, but I couldn't keep my hand off the phone long enough to get out of bed. Chris heaved a deep sigh when he woke to my voice asking for the Brain Injury Unit. In room 305, my mother answered the phone.

"Somebody's got something to say to you."

Great! I thought. *I don't want to make a decision about medications now.*

"Maya," came a whispery voice over the line.

"My baby!" I shouted. Beside me, Chris jerked upright.

My mother came back on. "She just started saying her name this morning. I've been wishing you'd picked a different night to go home, so you could have been here."

"I'm leaving this second!" I leaped out of bed, throwing on whatever clothes came to hand. Tears streamed down my face. *My daughter was coming back*! She'd spoken the first words of her new life, and I was much too far away. The drive stretched ahead of me, a hundred and twenty minutes before I would hear Maya's voice in person.

On the trip to Spokane, my speedometer told me I was doing sixty, but it felt like twenty. I blasted the radio and sang along, hoping to distract myself from the reality of how long two hours was. Finally, I was galloping through the hallways of St. Luke's, loaded with goodies from home.

"Look what I brought," I said to Maya, when I'd settled back in beside her. I opened the leather pouch and laid each piece of my collection on the over-bed tray: a pine cone, a papery curl of birch bark, a handful of the grey moss that hangs from tamarack limbs, a chunk of white granite peppered in black, the tip of a hemlock bough, a heavy clod of clay earth, a sliver of cedar from the kindling pile, and a gray Stellar's jay feather. Last, I pulled out the only item I'd had mixed feelings about bringing, a wad of coarse hair from Deno's mane.

Maya handled everything, sniffing the cedar and balling up the moss. She rubbed the horse hair between the thumb and forefinger of her left hand. Her eyes filled with tears, and she whispered, "Home. Home."

"Yes, baby," I said, closing my hand around hers. "Home is still there, waiting for us, and we'll make it back. You can be sure of that."

She wiped her eyes on her sleeve and stuck the horse hair deep into her pocket.

Maya relearned the task of forming sounds over a period of two weeks, and she built her voice from a bare whisper to audible tones. She spoke into a microphone on the computer, matching graphed voice patterns to retrain her throat and tongue. When people addressed Maya, she turned toward me, begging me to answer. I discovered how adept I'd become at speaking for her. Still battling aphasia, Maya could never be sure if the word she wanted to say would be the one that popped out of her mouth when she began to talk. Conversation came hard when she spoke to anyone but me. With my understanding of her silent language, speaking for my daughter was easy, and sometimes I did. But with ever-increasing frequency, I bit back my responses. Maya's face twisted in frustration as she searched for the right words, and her fight for fluency pained me more than her halting steps as she learned to walk again. When Maya glared at me for my silences, I reminded myself how angry she would be with me later if I prolonged her dependence. Each week we checked off the goals she'd accomplished and knew we were that much closer to going home.

Nine weeks after her injury, Maya was released. On a gray day in November, just before Thanksgiving, we arrived back on our mountain. It was everything we'd dreamed of all those nights in the institution: the warm, cluttered cabin, rich with familiar smells, our own things all around us. Outside, the woods were settling in for winter. Maya stamped around the yard, kicking at rocks, tripping and laughing and clutching at my arm. We landed at the fence, staring into an empty pasture.

"Mom, when can I get my own horse?" Maya asked. Deno had merged with a herd of six horses my sister kept about a mile up the road.

"You have lots to work on right now," I said.

"I know. But I'm going to ride again."

As much as I hated the idea, I knew she meant it.

The scaled-down schedule of three therapies a week alarmed me at first, but we worked into a routine of home exercises, and Maya went back to school part-time. Verbal confidence returned in the same gradual manner that her body moved once more toward womanhood. As she gained back lost weight, my daughter approached puberty for the second time, and I marveled at the resiliency of human flesh.

Nearly a year passed before Maya was brave enough to make her own phone calls. Early efforts took place with Maya pressed against my side, her limp right arm wrapped through mine for support.

"That wasn't so bad, was it?" I asked after her first solo call. She needed to know business hours for the Panhandle Animal Shelter, where she planned to volunteer, and I had refused to do the job.

"It was terrible!" Maya said. "I sounded dumb. I'm never calling anyone again."

"You sounded fine," I said. "Your voice was smooth and you only hesitated once, just for a second. You asked a question, and you learned the answer. Next time it will be easier."

Sixteen months after her injury, Maya ordered her own birthday meal at Panhandler Pies Restaurant. Savoring bites of Mud Pie for dessert, she celebrated her thirteenth year and her official status as a teenager. By April of the following spring, I coaxed my daughter into standing up at our book group meeting to propose selection of the first adult novel she'd ever read, one she felt sure could help our friends understand some of her experiences after the injury. I choked back tears when the group unanimously voted in *The Horse Whisperer*, Nicholas Evans's tale of a young girl damaged to the core in a horse accident. Maya's smiling face flushed crimson, just as it used to when she searched for elusive words, only this time the color came from pride.

On a sunny September day four years later, I drive through the Selle Valley toward Sandpoint, a day of errands and shopping ahead. Tamarack needles glint with the promise of gold, and yellow birch leaves litter the roadside. The Selkirk Mountains, velvet-shouldered in elegant green, slope down to meet Sand Creek along our southerly route.

"Mom, can we stop at Wal-Mart?" Maya asks.

"I was planning on it; we're low on dog food. What do you need?"

"A watch. I washed mine, remember?"

"Sure, you can look at watches," I say. "But you're buying."

"I *know*," she says, rolling her eyes.

I smile. My daughter's frugality is a frequent issue between us. She guards her resources like a sow bear protects its cubs.

I leave her at Wal-Mart's jewelry counter. When I come back from the pet department, she's chatting with a clerk over two watches laid out on the glass.

"This one's kind of big, but I like the band best, because it's cloth. Metal irritates my skin," Maya tells the clerk, who nods without speaking. The woman is wearing a delicate silver watch with a metal flex band. Maya's choices are men's watches, big and bulky, with buttons to push and buzzers to beep. The one with the cloth band also features a velcro fastener.

"Go for the one that feels good," I tell her. "You'll get used to it being bigger."

"I *know*, Mom," she says. The eyes roll again, this time toward the clerk, who smiles at me in sympathy.

In the Jeep, Maya straps the watch on her left wrist with her teeth. Using the knuckle of her right thumb as a solid point to push against, she jogs the side button until she has set the time and tested the alarm. Maya's right arm and hand functions remain limited, with no fine motor abilities. She walks with a slight limp, and is prone to falls. My daughter can't ski, but she can ride a bicycle or a horse; she buzzes around our mountain on a four-wheeled ATV with reversed hand controls, and she earned her driver's license a few months ago. She can't put her hair in a pony-tail, but she writes a readable script with her left hand, talks on the phone until her ear throbs, punches computer keys, trains Jack Russell Terriers, and mows lawns. She runs a crew of younger cousins each spring, uprooting Canadian thistles with a shovel while the kids pull and bag the weeds. Maya still wrestles with her share of frustration, but she is quick to laugh and finds joy without a map.

The anniversary isn't mentioned again. In the evening, Maya comes asking for a screwdriver, and I see the same fierce look in her eyes I remember from that day at the ICU. Not content to wait for her father, she takes the paralyzed front doorknob apart in search of a quick fix. It's a long way around to the back door for Maya to hustle her Terrier pup, who sports a hair-trigger bladder. I hear her worrying the latch mechanism with the screwdriver, and I know my daughter is having a serious conversation with that doorknob. At this time in her life when she speaks for herself and seeks the independence every teenager craves, I know more than she wants me to know. I lower my eyes, and pretend I know nothing. Maya works the latch, and pretends her thoughts are hers alone.

I squelch the urge to help her. My hands scrub carrots and peppers, and my feet remain planted in front of the sink. The doorknob doesn't stand a chance.

In this story, the mother's insistence opens up a lovely interaction with her daughter.

Cleaning and Chatting

Anonymous

I'd been wanting to talk more with Gillian while she was having such a hard time in her life. Her room had been a mess, and had been for months. Every time I'd ask her to clean it, she wouldn't want to, though at Christmas, she said,

"I don't want any presents. I just want someone to clean my room".

From this I knew she really wanted a clean room.

I said to her (and I usually don't do this), "We're going to spend this week-end cleaning your room".

She said, "Well, maybe, if I've got time".

But I insisted on it because I felt that her room was really affecting her mind and vice versa. It ended up being really wonderful. We worked about six hours on Saturday and three hours the next day. We did a great deal of talking while we were cleaning up her room. We talked about how similar we are to each other. One of the things Gillian said was,

"Oh I know people always say adolescents go through all this stuff, because they're adolescent, but I look at you and your friend Amy, and I see you still go through the same stuff".

I replied, "Well, I think people who are sensitive and creative and thoughtful never allow themselves to be comfortable, but always go on to the next challenge. So I expect you will always do that in your life, just as I have always done that".

It seemed that doing a project like that and spending all that time together for a reason, started to release some things naturally, instead of making a special time to talk.

Here the mother allows her daughter to face the consequences of her choices and actions, with salutary results.

You're On Your Own

Phyllis Woolf

Jekki hated public high school. When she was in ninth grade, she decided she must go to Northfield-Mt. Hermon, a prestigious area private day and boarding school. She applied and was rejected because of her poor grades. It was clear she would have to work hard at her studies if she wanted to get in the next year. But one day, I was shopping downtown, and met her, hanging out and cutting school. I got very mad, and for the rest of the year I would drive her to school, watch her go in the door, and pick her up after school and take her to my workplace, where she would sit in an office and do her homework until I was ready to leave. As a result, her grades improved radically and she was accepted the next year when she applied to Northfield-Mt. Hermon. However, it wasn't long before she became disillusioned with that school too, and despite my insistence that she keep at it, she managed to get herself expelled.

Since she was already over 16, she got a job at a restaurant, and to my astonishment and delight, she was incredibly dedicated, serious, competent and effective. She would arrive for work early and stay as long as she was needed. When the restaurant closed after a year, Jekki said,

"I love this work. I need to go to cooking school. I need to go to the Cordon Bleu school in London."!!!

Eagerly, we cooperated, and sent her off, with all kinds of arrangements with friends for being a mother's helper, room and board, etc. True to form, it wasn't long before we heard from our friends that Jekki was cutting classes and hanging out in pubs.

"Your daughter needs to come home", they announced. And so she did.

At this point, we'd had it. We said,

"Jekki, you're on your own. Whatever you want to do, you will have to be financially responsible for".

I would help her in small ways, like if she needed a pot or a spatula, but no longer pay her way or direct her on her path. Clearly our old expectations had to go by the boards...we got that. No Radcliffe, no traditional path for this girl.

She decided she wanted to attend the New England Culinary Institute in Montpelier, VT, applied and was accepted, drove out there by herself, found a place to live, and loved it! It was just the right place for her…she worked hard, had to get meals out every day, and she was wildly successful. She supported herself, enjoyed her many interneships, and was even able to tolerate the ones she hated! That was great progress.

Her last interneship was in Napa Valley, CA, as was her first job after graduating from the Culinary Institute.

Then came a major turning point. She got carpal tunnel syndrome and could no longer use her hands. She, who was only happy when she was working, could no longer work. She quickly realized she was not prepared to do any other kind of work. There was no authority near her to say, *Do this*, so she made her own decision and enrolled in a Junior College. To her surprise, she found out that she was a very good scholar, and that she loved math and was excellent at it.

She determined to enroll in the university at Seattle. She needed a French course in order to be accepted at the university, and would receive the assignments by mail, do them and mail them back. She soon recognized that with the slow mails, she would never finish on time for the Fall semester, so she drove her Volkswagon bus to Seattle, settled in a campground, living out of her bus, and would do the work, deliver it, and pick up the next assignment. Every ten days she was required to leave the campground for a day. So she'd stay in a motel overnight, phone home and report on her progress, and then go back the next day for a new ten days. Once in the university, she got a job in genetics and discovered she loved that more than math, and that is the work she's been doing ever since.

Our relationship became very close again, once she found her own way and began enjoying her independence.

What she needed, for her particular path, was to be responsible for herself, for her decisions and for the consequences of those decisions. She was young for such responsibility, but she handled it well and succeeded.

8

Forever Connected

Every woman is a daughter, and every woman had a mother who birthed her.

The bonds between mothers and daughters are mysterious and profound. People can try to explain them biologically, psychologically, astrologically, energetically, relationally—but they remain beyond our capacity to fully grasp.

Those bonds can be tight, loose, peaceful, confused, conflictual, benign, malignant, erotic, uplifting, invigorating, liberating, imprisoning…the full range of human relationships is possible between mother and daughter.

There are mothers and daughters who remain or become very close; there are others who remain or become distant or disconnected; whatever the outcome of that relationship, the essence of Mother and of Daughter is deep in all women's souls, and on some level both are eternally connected to each other.

The poems and stories in this chapter illustrate some of the deep ties that exist between mothers and daughters.

These first two poems express a mother's anticipation of the pain of separation that her daughter's growing independence will bring.

Magic

Barbara M. Simon

Already, sometimes I try
to make you not here,
gone like summer or the flame
from the golden maples sheltering
our street in rich golden light.

This loving I feel for you
frightens me. I try
to time travel myself
into the future
beyond the years of your leaving,
the morning I wake
to wave good-bye to your strong
shouldered back, your perfect
blond head faced to your future
and me, behind, heart
clenched like a fist, tears punching
from my eyes. No words.
My arms empty, the loneliness
real and the years of your growing,
mere illusion.

Child,
sometimes I have to disappear you
so that when it happens
I'll get it right
to let you go.

Learning to Read

Maureen Flannery

Sprawled across the couch like an afghan,
still in flannel nightie, auburn hair
disheveled from tussling with dream demons,
she calls me over. I expect perhaps to be shown
an almost invisible fairy hovering
above a leaf in her picture book.
Listen, she says, with the authority
of one who knows she knows something.
There was on, onk...once a k, king...
She's memorized this, I tell myself.
with a love, lovely and dis, disob...ede...disobedient...
She gets a foothold on *disobedient*
and climbs over it like a sturdy stone fence
never meant to keep out neighbors.
dag, dag...ter, daughter w...wom, whom he wished
Future muscles in, elbowing out her babyhood.
to mar, marry a prink, prince of his own choos...ing.
This changes everything. Her early childhood
gone on the air with the breathy giggles
that chased the rabbits around the yard. Now Plato,
Dante, Shakespeare can whisper to her soul...
and so can many others with so much less to say.
Nutritional info on cereal boxes will complicate
her breakfast. Moving marquees outside banks
will conduct their unilateral dialogues with her
daydreams. *National Enquirer*s in the grocery store
will spit their sibilant lies into her nights.
Traffic signs won't seem like ruby crystal slices
or designs the color of black-eyed-Susan's.
The Shell logo won't remind her of the seaside.

Now everywhere she looks someone I do not know
will be telling her what she should want.
I hold her on the couch and we laugh and cry
for we can't bring back the knight's shield
that from now on will only denote highways.

Following are four poems about the depth of connection beyween mother and daughter.

Regal Birthday Girl

Maureen Flannery

I've brought cupcakes for twenty-eight
to celebrate her half-birthday in first grade.
Mr. Moore crowns her before the room,
ties the velvet cloak around her shoulders
as crinkled auburn locks cascade across
royal blue folds of its high collar and
she surveys her subjects, eyes avoiding mine.
The children sing, *There's a birthday today,*
their fleshy faces transfixed
while their voices trail behind her as if
following torch flames through Hibernian glades.
They no longer fidget in little oak chairs.
As her teacher tells of the star child's descent,
she sits straight-backed, fire-eyed,
Diana before the hunt,
Hildegaard recalling mandalas,
Elizabeth with her armies,
Joan listening to high commands.
Gold stars gleam from her foil-paper crown.
I sit, Juliet's nurse, awkward in the back
in the too-small chair, held captive by her hair,
feeling barely worthy to bake her cupcakes.

Woman-Child, Elephant-Girl, Bird-Daughter

Karen Ethelsdatter

My daughter is edging over to warm herself at my hearth
hypnotized by the fire outside her
the tongues of flame which dart from her poet-mother
toward sheet after sheet of paper, retreat
& cast forth again, aiming, aiming

She feels & does not feel her own flames flickering
gathering within her
knows to seek sun & fire
yet does not know it for her own

Woman-child, with heart & hearth & warmth
burning your fingers which glow with their own light
in your mother's fire
the infant in you still strains with her whole being toward me
screaming with rage when I vanish from the room
Your breasts are ripening, they are fuller than mine,
    though you deny it
Your menses are flowing…you cannot dam them
    with the thumb in your mouth

Child of mine, Elephant-Girl, searching out the Elephant Mother in me
knowing well she is there
the one who holds her child in her womb for two years
who would hold her child for a life-time if she could

Bird-Daughter, burrowing into the grasses of the nest,
hiding from the Bird-Mother, the wise one
who drops her eggs easily
lets her little ones fight & claw their way out of their shells
thrusts them out of the nest
letting go, letting go, letting go

Daughter who peers in my drawers
fingers my earrings
tries on my clothes
tells me of lands in the East
where to admire is to be given anything you covet
oh you would be forever in my debt
dangling from your birth cord, tangled in it
what's mine is mine
& I remind myself it is well

You sound an alarm in my heart
I remember *my* mother
lover of wild rabbits & deer
who could never put up fences
& knew ravaged gardens with slender harvests
letting her gypsy daughters steal into her jewel boxes
weeping only when *they* stole away:

one chose life, one chose death, she chose
to be cozy with walls against the wind
& roof against sun & stars
leaving only the door slightly ajar
for a glimpse of a wild doe, a glimpse of the gypsies,
& dreamed night after night
year upon year
of being raided.

A Dozen Years After I Rounded With the Seed of Her

Maureen Flannery

we choose cherry pie over chocolate cake,
perhaps because she wants change, or because
it is August and charming boxes of cherries
sang us their sour song at the farmers' market.
In the white porcelain bowl, they are round and smooth,
like she, too lovely to mar with pitting.
They are plump as the breasts that assert themselves
to the forefront like new ideas, red as the nurture
sleeping in her womb waiting for life
or the moon dark flow that will accompany
her into the fullness of possibility,
tart as the sorrow that will follow her youth
as surely as tides the moon, and inviting
as life is on the early side of its discoveries,
its duties, its unexpected sadness,
and surprises of small beauties like
this twelve-year-old girl and the waiting bowl
brimming with unpitted ripe pie cherries.

French Braid

Dianne Smaniotto

Each morning before school, when my daughter dusts herself
through the narrow hall to my room, I catch the long sweep
of her hair in my hands and begin to weave it
around my fingers and up into the nape of her neck.
She holds the how-to-book still between her knees
and calls out each step, rehearsed like a slow dance.
Although most days we talk quietly, others we just hum or sing
with the easy brush of the willow tree in the wind
through the red walls of our beating hearts,
and feel the rhythm of the push and pull,
the steady patience that comes
with the back and forth of being so close,
sacred on its own.
Her hands folded under her chin, bowing her head
of crowning glory for me, she whispers the words
of a prayer she is reciting, committing it to memory,
while the last fruit of autumn drops outside our window.
A warm peach mist hangs from her limbs,
and the skin of ivory blossoms from her milk bath,
spinning me in a slow fragrant spiral, the lips
she will raise towards mine and kiss me with
when its all done, flavored in strawberry gloss.
I think about how many mothers have done this before,
this sweet tug-of-war, the tangled rope I must let her climb,
resisting the urge to pull her back,
before the early run to the crowded bus,
before the long walk, holding on to that last moment,
before I turn her over to the circle of the world,
folding each strand in and out of each other,
learning to work together,
knowing as many times I've tried,
and practiced, having it fall in my lap,
only to gather it all up and try again.

I manage to spray the last pieces undone
up into the curls breaking free, and
stretch my arms around her, holding her
like a silk band tying loose ends together,
this is the best I can do.
She turns on one heel and smiles
with her face held in my hands,
catching a glimpse of her reflection in my eyes.
With such beauty staring back at her,
she is happy and content
with what has not slipped through my fingers.
She never asks for more than this.

The next five stories and poems are all about staying connected while being separated.

Hearth-Tending

Maureen Flannery

So this is what it means
    to hold the space,
to be the one that stays behind
    and is returned to,
that rises, singing,
    only slightly off the ground
on air currents around
    another's wings,
the one left to pick up the mess
    and sit down alone
in a quiet room reading
    offered journal entries,
to get the gown cleaned
    and stored away,
keep the papers, posters, pictures, junk,
    keep the space open
in the center of her life
    letting nothing extraneous
cave in upon it. This must
    have been the void
inside the keeper of the hearth,
    the fire tender,
as the warriors rode away.
    I never felt it before,
this staying back, and I'm not sure
    I've grown into it.

It calls for more grounding
    than I have yet acquired,
this new vocation that asks of me
    to stay and hold the space
and wait.

Partings

Margaret B. Blackman

This was not the way it was supposed to happen. I was rocking back and forth on the john in a soothingly appointed "luxury suite" hotel in Rhode Island, cradling my head in my hands, tears spilling down my face and onto my arms. On the other side of the wall, Ulpian, my unsuspecting boyfriend, was sprawled across the bed, tuned into ESPN and cheering on the Huskies as they trounced Miami.

I seldom cry. I have gone a year at a time without crying, and only once in the span of our six-year relationship has Ulpian had to contend with my tears. I'm neither deliberately stoic, nor particularly private about my emotional states, and I have even unsuccessfully tried to cry when I've been sad or hurt or just depressed. Which made my nonstop tears and sobs, offered up in an anonymous hotel bathroom, all the more disturbing. I moved from the john to the warm refuge of the shower, and cried until the bathroom was socked in in a steamy fog. One thing I've learned in my infrequent bouts of crying…sometimes you have to keep moving to deal with the pain. I toweled off and headed for the only other sanctuary the hotel room offered…the bed. Instinctively I curled into a fetal position and pulled the covers over my head. Another great wave of sadness lodged in my throat, and the tears began anew.

Halftime. Ulpi noticed the lump in the bed, pulled the covers back. He put his arms around me, tried to comfort me. "You poor kid," he soothed. His words hardly mattered; I felt as if someone close to me had died, suddenly blurring the shape and purpose of my own life. "Hey, she's not dead; she's just gone to *college!*"

She had. Just that afternoon. Twelve miles away from my hotel room my college freshman daughter was settling into her new home, putting up her Ani DiFranco and Salvador Dali posters, chatting with the roommate she'd met just hours before, getting acquainted with the people down the hall. That evening they would go to their first dinner on campus, attend a freshman rally in the quad, stay out late and go for coffee with new friends at the expresso bar on Thayer Street.

This was everything I had wanted for Meryn. A year ago I pored excitedly over the piles of college literature that flooded our mailbox. I arranged our summer and fall excursions to prospective campuses and I envisioned Meryn in each place we visited. As the decision letters started arriving, I think I was at least as excited as she when the coveted acceptance came from the Rhode Island School of Design. We made a quick summer visit to RISD after that, inspecting the residence halls, eating in the dining hall, walking through the studios so we would know what to expect when she arrived as a freshman in the fall.

It was a brilliantly sunny and mild September morning when we pulled up to the brick freshman residence hall complex. We were waved into a line of parked cars, and before we had even turned off the engine, a small squadron of smiling upperclassmen volunteers in black "RISD" t-shirts approached our van. In minutes they had unloaded the suitcases, the box of books, the mirror, the window fan and stereo, and most importantly, the goldfish in his travelling styrofoam cooler-aquarium. They put masking tape tags on each item with the dorm and room number. The fish got a nametag as well: "Moby 215 H."

As the squad of student porters ferried the gear through the tunnel and up the ramps to the second floor of Homer Hall, Ulpi went off to park the van and Meryn and I negotiated the seven stations of required stops set up in the mezzanine of the student union. In no time we had her student ID and room keys; we'd opened an account at the bookstore and filled out the required form for computer network services. When the three of us had reunited at her room, the fish cooler and all the gear were stacked in neat piles outside the door. Moving in was going at such a breakneck pace I feared we'd be done and on our way before the appointed hour of departure. Luckily, putting together a bookshelf and getting the computer configured proved challenging enough to command our services until well after the lunch we shared with Meryn and her roommate in the student dining hall. Then, just about the time the jumbled contents of the unpacked boxes and suitcases began to resemble her room on an ordinary day at home, it was time to go.

Colleges today seem more attuned to the potential trauma of parent/college freshman partings. Some schools plan joint parent/student fun events, host last minute information sessions and tours for the parents, and cleverly orchestrate the parting of parents and offspring. Savvy college administrators have even written guidebooks for bereft parents on handling that monumental goodbye and other crises of the college years. In a weak moment, I bought such a book, but I haven't read beyond the goodbye chapter. The Rhode Island School of Design arranged it so that the new students trotted off to a required residence hall meeting just as their parents were invited to the president's reception for (grieving) parents.

"Make a rapid, graceful exit! Have the meaningful conversation and tearful good-bye before you leave home." No parent wants to lose it in front of the new roommate, the RA, and the smart alecky 5-year-old brother of the girl down the hall who has planted himself on his scooter in your daughter's room, so I followed my guidebook's instructions: "A quick hug and you should be on your way."

An hour and a half and 12 miles later I had unraveled in the privacy of my bathroom at the Crown Plaza Hotel. I knew this parting would be difficult. This was *it*...the emptying...or as my therapist dubs it, the "exploding"...of the nest, one of life's big transitions. Leaving home to begin life as a college student (and being left at home by the departing student) ranks right up there with the likes of births, graduations, marriages, and deaths. As an anthropologist, I have an intellectual familiarity with these "liminal states," their rituals, symbols and meanings. As a friend, I have listened to many versions of sending children off to school; some marked by great sadness, others by great relief. My own mother has often reminded me of her reaction to my departure to college.

Like every other big event in our family, my father recorded my inaugural trip to Miami University on our movie camera. There I am in our driveway, dressed in a carefully chosen matching print skirt and blouse, hair sprayed into a perfect flip. I pack the last box into the trunk of our new 1962 Chevy convertible. My 12-year-old brother waves gleefully at the camera, probably cheerily anticipating his new "only child" status. Two hours later, in the heat of a southern Ohio September, we are unloading the trunk and carrying the gear ourselves up the three flights of stairs to my freshman dorm room. But no one made a movie of the return home and of my mother opening the refrigerator door. At the sight of the half-eaten bowl of cereal I'd left in the fridge that morning, she dissolved into tears.

I don't know if her tears were quick and bittersweet or if they took her to the place where mine took me. I cried so hard, I wondered if I would stop. I cried so long I wondered if I would ever feel like me again. I even began to wonder who "me" really is without this child who has subtly and not so subtly defined my life for the last 18 years. The empty nest seemed just...Empty. And it was. I would now have my 10-room house all to myself. After my divorce from Meryn's father when she was in the 8th grade, I made a new life for the two of us in a rambling Victorian home on a quiet street in the Erie Canal college town where I teach and where Meryn had spent her entire life. I immersed myself in rehabbing and redecorating our new home, giving our tiny household a permanency I knew it would never really have. In the course of ten years, I had gone from a household of four, to three when Meryn's older brother...my stepson...went to college, to two, and now, to one. It had been so long since I'd lived alone, I'd forgotten the rhythms and the shape of single living.

But living alone was only one piece of my life. Professionally, I'm an anthropologist with research interests that have many times taken me to the Pacific Northwest and Arctic Alaska. I was an anthropologist long before I was a mother, and that career could stretch well beyond my active motherhood. Coincident with my daughter's departure for college, I have a full year's sabbatical, a writing project, and a semester in residence at the University of Alaska awaiting me.

Consoling myself with these reminders helped not at all. Instead, I was Alice tumbling down the rabbit hole, Alice shrinking and growing, Alice watching the world before her shift. I cried myself to sleep in my Rhode Island hotel room, dreamt of moving from party to party unable to engage any of the people I met in conversation, dreamt of having a dinner party at which I hosted a dying guest. The dream was almost as bad as the reality I had escaped from in sleep. Only later would I understand that my tears, my nightmares, my loss were my passage through this liminal state.

When Meryn was 14 months old I knew just about everything a parent could possibly know about a child, including the precise content of her vocabulary (104 words). But there came a time when instead of knowing more, I began to know less. By the time she was ready for college, it seemed I hadn't learned enough about her, nor known her long or well enough to let her go.

As with that doyenne of Anthropology, Margaret Mead, like me a first time mother of a daughter at age 38, my professional training guided my mothering. I chronicled Meryn's development with the dedication of an anthropologist at work. I videotaped her, interviewed her, and wrote about her in a journal I began keeping when I was five months pregnant. My joy in my young daughter was boundless.

March 4, 1983

You have passed the three-month mark. And still I cannot stop looking at you, laughing with you, drinking in your smiles. I look forward to getting up each morning to feed you and I like to hold you until you fall asleep in my arms. And, as if this weren't enough, I photograph you incessantly…in your swing, propped up on your elbows, lying on your back. Each time I go away from the house without you I look forward to returning to you. And rather than leave you behind, I prefer to take you wherever I go. I take you, too, from room to room as I move about the house. Sometimes I lie down beside you on your sheepskin as sleep overtakes you and often I return to that position so you can awaken to me. Perhaps when you are ten months old I will be comfortable relinquishing you to day-care three days a week, but for now I could not bear the thought of being apart from you for the span of a day.

I am in love with you. It is not the fragile love of a man and woman, but a love so powerful that it began before your birth and gathered force as I nurtured you those months from womb to world. A love powered by your total trust in me, by the privilege I have of seeing you develop as a person, and by so much more. It is one of the ironies of life that you can never feel the same love for me that I feel for you, but that, I guess, is the nature of mother/daughter relationships.

There are many things in life I wish for you, my darling Meryn, and one of them is this special love that I, my mother, and doubtless her mother before her, have had the good fortune to know.

The journal ends sometime in middle school when it became difficult to chronicle at such close range our growing separation, Meryn's fierce indepen-dence, and my sadness that something irretrievable...something akin to inno-cence...had been lost in the process. But Meryn continued to exist under my anthropologist's gaze, which, in the end, probably drove her to increasing secrecy. In the field, in northern Alaska, I had watched her each summer play with her Eskimo girlfriends, speak the village patois, and become for all intents and pur-poses a village kid. Now, suddenly, my "informant" was leaving the "field"...for college. I was losing my most interesting subject, and could only write of her, as I am now, from a distance.

My grieving didn't begin in that hotel room in Rhode Island. It had been coming on for weeks. All summer I had looked forward to a hiking trip Meryn and I planned in Ireland for early August. Our holiday abroad was all I...all we...hoped it would be; we had a wonderful time together, and suffered not a single argument nor tense period. But when it was over, so was Meryn's child-hood with me. She was getting ready to leave. In the days that followed, from time to time I would be overcome by a pang of realization that grabbed at my chest and took my breath. That "Oh-no-it-can't-be-true-but-it-is" pain. It would come upon me at the oddest times. Once, when I went for my usual morning bike ride, the tears had already begun before I got out of the driveway. I cried my way nine miles north, turned around and cried nine miles south.

I shared with Meryn some of my difficulty. "I'm having a hard time with this separation," I confessed to her. "I know," she empathized adding, wickedly, "Mom, after I leave you're not going to do anything weird like hang out in my room and sniff my sheets, are you?" I laughed...with her...for the moment. But I knew that, just as much as I was mourning our impending separation, she was fervently wishing for it, eager to leave this house, this small town for the promise of some larger, more exciting life.

One reviews the oddest things in approaching such separations. Once Meryn mentioned offhand that her best friend who is attending college locally has a cell phone, only because her mother had a monthly plan where the second phone is "free." I thought of our single cell phone, purchased for emergency use, and shared between us. It's a three-year-old clunker that looks like it should have a rotary dial and that you'd never want to be seen using. We don't even know the phone number. I had been reflecting on my parenting one afternoon when I asked, out of the blue, "Did you feel deprived without your own cell phone?" Meryn looked at me like I had two heads.

Now and then a good healthy anger also took hold of me. Like the late August day I spent on the phone straightening out Meryn's medical insurance and new banking account while she and some friends took off for a rock concert in the city. I insisted that, before college, she go through the childhood and teenage possessions she was leaving behind, pare them down to a volume her room could reasonably handle, and archive the remainder in boxes in the attic, but she had barely begun the task. She had also promised to complete an IOU Christmas present to me, a drawing of a bicycle. I was hopeful of receiving it when she went so far as to buy the drawing paper, but her only artwork in those last weeks were a portrait of a friend and one more of the endless self-portraits that seem to be her major *oeuvre*. Yes, I reassured myself, it was time for her to leave.

There were many lasts as Departure Day approached. The last dinner and movie together, the last night she would knock on my door at 1 am softly announcing, "Hi Mom, I'm home." But the last night was the most difficult. The van was packed except for one suitcase that would hold the last load of clothes that she was washing, and the precious Moby who would be netted out of his glass aquarium and deposited in the styrofoam cooler in the morning. "I'll probably be up very late tonight," Meryn had announced at dinner. Sometime after midnight, unable to sleep, I went downstairs to be the good mother and offer my help. We could fold and pack clothes together and have that mother/daughter "this-is-a-wonderful-and-important-moment-in-your-life" talk that we had never had. I followed the sound of her whistling to the laundry room where she was draping wet wool socks over a towel rack to dry. "What are you doing up?" she asked. "I thought you might need some help," I offered. "No thanks; I'm doing fine." She moved to the kitchen to retrieve the bowl of popcorn she'd made from the microwave, and settled in to finish watching the MTV music awards while she folded the last of her clothes. My "talk" probably wouldn't have been very coherent anyway. "See you in the morning," I padded back to bed.

We were on the road by 9:30 the next morning. The gear fit nicely into the capacious, aging van, and Moby's styrofoam container was within easy reach. For the next 300 miles the fish sloshed back and forth as we bumped over the expansion joints on the freeway. Meryn periodically lifted the lid to check on Moby's condition. "The fish is freaking out," she announced at one point. It mattered greatly that I deliver the fish alive to Rhode Island. I had dark thoughts. I imagined the fish, exhausted, gills heaving, then floating lifeless on the surface of the water in his styrofoam tomb. I imagined Meryn speechless with grief, hugging her pillow in the back seat. And it would all be my fault since I had insisted that Moby was to go to college.

Somewhere along the New York State Thruway I asked Meryn, "What will you miss most about home?" She thought for a moment, then replied, "My friends, my bed, and my car." Late the night before she had sat for one last time behind the wheel of her Dodge Neon and then she had taken a photo of it. The single message she left for me, held fast to the door of the fridge with a magnet, was a reminder to change the oil in her car. "Won't you miss me even a little," I queried. "Sure, Mom," she grinned.

We stayed that night with Meryn's great aunt Charlotte in Connecticut, three hours outside Providence, just the right distance to make a midmorning arrival on check-in day. I have one especially fond memory of that Connecticut afternoon. After six hours of road travel we decided we needed some exercise, so we went running along the old railroad bed that connects the small towns of Lakeville and Salisbury. This was a first, the three of us out for a run together, and an unlikely combination we made: Ulpi, the former college sprinter, Meryn, the former high school cross country runner, and me the bicyclist who occasionally jogs. It was a warm, sunny afternoon but ancient trees shaded the path and for much of the time we ran together. Near the end, Meryn said she felt like sprinting. I watched her run on ahead, her arms pumping, her gait smooth and effortless. The dappled sunlight danced about her shoulders and I knew that in the days and months ahead she would be fine.

I was OK on the long drive home from Rhode Island, and all the next day, and the next and the next. Ulpi, with some relief I think, headed back to his home in Ohio and I headed off to Maine for a biannual reunion with my three best friends from high school. Five days of talk and laughter and blueberry pie and lobster, five days of strolls through small Maine coastal villages, and hikes in Acadia National Park did much for my soggy spirits. I called Meryn one day from our hotel as I had told her I would. Her phone was out of order, and still not working the next day. Finally I phoned Public Safety at RISD, not because I worried about where she was but, I told myself, because I was paying dearly for this college education and the phone damn well better work. Finally, I got through to her. No, she wasn't aware that the phone hadn't been working. In the middle of our conversation my friend Susie grabbed the receiver from me: "Meryn, this is your mom's friend Susie. Her friends just want you to know that we don't blame you a bit for unplugging your phone for two days!"

It has been a few weeks now since that trip to Rhode Island. The other day I opened the door to Meryn's room, just long enough to decide not to clean it yet and to grab one of her self-portraits, which I placed on the living room easel. Since returning home, I've discovered that I haven't had to leave any notes regarding my whereabouts nor had to worry about hers. The house is too quiet, of course, but it's neater and all messes are mine. Eating meals alone is my least favorite activity, but they go down well with a good book and the evening news, and I've managed to eat a few meals out with friends and to have dinner guests. I've taken in a concert and the movies. The phone rings often enough (I changed the outgoing message to reflect my daughterless status) and every message left on the machine is for me. I reserved space on a biking trip to Italy next summer. I still have a life. I think I'll make it.

Synchronicity

Gelia Dolcimascolo

Gypsy sparrow swings
on a seed-bell
while Wheel of Fortune
spins the color TV
with no remote-control.

The sparrow disappears,
returns with a friend.
They peck and sway
above the fire-escape
landing, then fly away.

I laze about
my daughter's house,
awash in the clutter of
art books, phone books,
and piles of dirty towels.
Surprisingly tidy shelves
display clayworks
and other passions:
The Joy of Cooking…
Masters of Drama…
SYNCHRONICITY: The Bridge
Between Matter and Mind.

The sparrow reappears solo—
a reminder of sweet moments,
letting go, and coming
together in Baltimore.

How To Let Go Of Your Daughter

Barbara A. Rouillard

I sit with you on the wooden planks that make up a pseudo-porch right outside the front door of the house, the duplex, you've rented for the summer. It's a dump. We both know it, but it's yours for the next few months. On this "Appalachian" stoop, I say to you, "Well, I think I'll have a cigarette and then take off."

I've already helped you move your last belongings in my old, beat-up station wagon from your dorm room to your new summer residence. I've already seen your new room. I've already spread the eight paintings I've done since the last time I've seen you on your threadbare lawn. There's no room in your apartment for you to see my work, the chaos of moving day, so we use your old blue plaid sleeping bag, lay my paintings on it, to exhibit my work, my latest art, for your review.

Like a meteor that streaks across the sky, I see a child lugging that sleeping bag to a friend's for an overnighter. The vision is a flash, and then gone in a flash, but the same feelings are there, that empty feeling, that heavy, oppressive weight on my chest. Don't leave. Don't go. Stay with me.

You love my paintings. I give you yours. It's an abstract oil and collage that I've entitled *Amherst*, your Rouillard college town. It's you, how I see you, a streak of blue, your favorite color, a patterned collage, you through childhood and now onward. I point out me in the painting, a small dot of pink, my favorite color, with a collage arrow that points to the continuum of oil that makes up you. You know what the inclusion of this small dot means. I know you know. I've already told you I'll be there for you, always. You trust this knowledge. I know.

You really love your painting and promise not to hang it between the *Michelob* and *Budweiser* signs, the previous tenants' contributions. We laugh. Your sense of humor is so like mine, a dry wit, a sophisticated, intelligent humor. Mine is seldom understood. Is yours, daughter?

Now I've already pointed out the other paintings' titles and meanings for you. I've done a self-portrait, a more confused abstract. It's called *Varina*, Barbara, in Greek, what I wanted to name you when you were born. You've heard the story a million times, how I was convinced not to name my daughter the name I had chosen.

We pack up my car with my paintings, *Adhesive Adolescence, On Visiting, Sisters, Daughters, JBottom Peace, Patterns,* and *Varina*...minus *Amherst*. You talk about an art gallery in the area you want to take me to the next time I visit, and I'm having that cigarette before I take off.

I look at your face. You look so young, like twelve, your round face, your flawless skin, a baby face to me. I ask you when the last time was that you went to the dentist and you look back at me quizzically, a bit perplexed, confused. The question's out of place in our dialogue of art and culture. You reply, "I dunno." I tell you to talk to your father. He has you on his insurance. I'm embarrassed by my question.

I ask you if you have any money. You never ask me for a thing. You must prove to yourself that you can be self-reliant, just like your mother. I know. I understand. You skirt around my question, so I write you a check to hold you over until you get your first paycheck from your summer job, and you are grateful. I can tell, relief passes briefly across your face. I want to make your life easier. I'd actually prefer to make the rest of your life painless, but know I can't.

I'm on my second cigarette. I look into your clear, hazel eyes. A baby's soulful eyes and hesitantly ask, not wanting to sabotage our little remaining time together, but not being able to help myself, "Have I taught you enough about sex, drugs, alcohol, AIDS, getting into cars with people who have been drinking?"

You answer, "Yes." You're more grown up than a year ago because you don't roll your eyes or get angry. I don't sense anymore your back bristling with impatience or annoyance. A simple "yes" answered with compassion and love in your eyes for your mother.

Somewhere along the line, this year, we've agreed to an unspoken pact. To accept each other. To help each other. To encourage and love each other. I don't know how it happened. I couldn't pinpoint an exact day. But our pact is there, stronger than any treaty ever signed, the best present two friends could ever give each other.

It is cemented, goes one step further with each visit, each phone call, each extended conversation. We both feel a growth, an extension and a confidence that this pact won't be severed. Ever.

Now I've crushed my second cigarette into the loose and scant gravel of your parking lot. I'm standing by my car door. I say I'm leaving. I hug you tight. "I love you." You say it back freely and hug me back. As I get into my car, I watch you walk towards your new home.

I start to back up my car to leave your driveway. I forgot. I wanted to ask you one last question. I beep the horn, but you don't hear it. You're already in the house with your friends, so I just drive away. Were there any smoke detectors in that tinderbox? I didn't notice, don't remember.

I don't put on my radio or tapes. I drive in silence for quite awhile, so quiet, all the car windows rolled up. Alone. You really are gone now. Not like when I left you at the dorm at the university last fall. That was a safety-net existence, compared to your living on your own now, even if it's just for a few months.

I haven't been able to write my story about you yet and I write a lot, every day. You're too much in my soul. Your story is too hard to get out of me. As I'm driving home, I decide your story.

I'm real "hip"…the artist, writer, potter me. I'm real "hot"…the pretty, body-builder, weight lifter me. But I'm Rachael's mother, just like any other mother…

I'll have to buy a smoke detector before my next visit.

Monsoon Reunion
for A, again

Davi Walders

Forty-eight hours by plane, train, and *tuk-tuk* to reach the last lap...a leaking long-tail boat sputtering between rocks, squalls and swells. It coughs us on to sand where dark hands of island gypsies pull our salt-crusted limbs from the Andaman Sea. The body, searching for the damp scrap of a Sanskrit address, tells the tale of transit. Swollen feet, muscles taut from lines and lugging, the ache of locked bowels and trapped intestines. Lungs expel stale air and squalor; a heart pounds loose from tight moorings.

More than a year of waiting. Calls crackling, the sudden flood of the familiar trailing off into night silence. Flimsy blue letters, blurred photographs, hunting for the scent, the touch of a daughter's life. Now, the path leads up from the foaming sea, up limestone cliffs to coconut palms, a school, a hut cut into the jungle. Yellow beaks, red-striped wings dart between the green. Light and heat swallow the air. *Continue 28 days after exposure. Avoid sun*, reads the doxycyline bottle. Glasses steam, a hat wilts in the island's glitter and glare.

Shaky legs carry me up the cliff path. Higher, a shadow looms. Ridiculous, I whisper, warding off gibbons, rats, elephants, untying the thread of letters fingered like worry beads through long seasons. White tinged clouds roll in from the sea. I push my glasses high on my head, focusing on the shape growing taller, tanner than memory. A sudden breeze frees a figure from the web of dreams. She is running, trailing orchids and lotus blossoms. Jumping and laughing, we bang into each other. Bones and flesh meld. Crushed petals sweeten our scents. Claps of thunder, falling drops. High above the sea, we are wet cheeks and sheets of water, a mother and daughter wrapped in the damp of each other, the monsoon washing us in its warm cocoon.

The next two poems express a daughter's connection to her mother.

Scones

Gelia Dolcimascolo

from The Bread Market...
microwave-warmed, electrically crisped,
then coated with margarine
and last year's leftover preserves...
slip down easily this wintry morning.

My breakfast treat barely compares
with flashbacks of your homemade
black-currant butterscones
piping from the porcelain
gas-heated oven, spread
with seedless raspberry jam and
topped with hand-whipped heavy cream.

On the cordless phone
I traverse the distance,
sharing the tender Sunday-morning
memory as you near
the wavering perimeter
of your life.

In My Mother's Kitchen

Gelia Dolcimascolo

I brought my own dressing this year,
even fixed a sweet-potato souffle
she didn't count on.

She can't always count on me;
I'm the one with delusions,
panics, night-dark voices
too black to fathom...
sometimes they make me hide
in my halfway existence.

She is worn out this Thanksgiving Day...
weary of plodding through motherhood,
roasting turkeys, simmering gravy.

After I arrived, she packaged
her homemade dressing,
stored it in the freezer
so we could relish mine.

We stirred the gravy
side by side at the stove,

returning us to a time
we thought we'd lost.

Here is connection across four generations.

Where I'm Headed

Gelia Dolcimascolo

I never saw my grandmother naked.
She stood tall, *zoftig*,
well-corsetted, buttressed
by bones, hooks, and eyes.

My mother's pendulous breasts
hung nearly to her navel.
Her shoulders blazed scarlet
from the abrasions of her bra straps.
I had to help lace her girdle
as she dressed each day
for work in sales.

Ruled by unruly hormones,
my own breasts waxed
and waned monthly.
Pregnancy pushed me to 38E.
I nursed for six weeks
before shriveling up.

My daughter, the sculptor,
brought me three nudes
she's moulded in clay:

a fertility vessel,
a pregnant woman,
a drooping old lady.

I know where I'm headed.

A story of a daughter's deep, though not soft, connection with her mother.

Her Dream Enacted

Anita Paltrinieri

The relationship with my mother was a good one, basically because I fulfilled my mother's dreams. She came from a pretty affluent family of wine merchants, and this explains why she never drank any water. During the war, when wine and money were scarce, she used to drink water mixed with vinegar. When she was eleven, her father died and she was taken out of school and put in the house to take care of cleaning and cooking for a family of ten.

Since I can remember, she used to say that she hated cooking and she wanted to throw pots, pans and dishes out of the window rather than wash them. Of course she cooked and washed dishes every day of her life. When she was eighty, I asked her why she hated so much something she had been willing to do all her life. She looked at me with her keen intense gaze and answered that, at eleven she wanted to go on studying, and instead found herself confined to the kitchen.

She always pushed both myself and my sister to study and get a real education (for her it meant a college degree), in order to be able to get a job and become economically independent and not to have to rely on marriage as the only option. She used to say that, had she had the choice, she would not have married. So, when she realized that I was inclined in that same direction, she supported me and helped me and approved of my choices, that would have been hers had she had a chance.

I never had a serious quarrel with my mother. She liked to take us dancing, she pushed us to wear high heels, to use make up, to wear a bikini. One day, over twenty years ago, I went home with my hair dyed shocking pink. She looked at me and said it was nothing special as she had already seen somebody with pink hair on the telly. She definitely was very cool. She was also strong, independent; she liked to earn her money and not be dependent on my father, and she always managed to do so.

When my father left home, she split her time between myself and my sister, but she preferred to stay with me. Even though she did not like to be left alone, she did not oppose my decision to move to the US. When, after twenty years, I decided to come back to Italy, she expected to come and live with me, but I was not ready for it and she resented it. There came the day when she could not live by herself and had to go to a nursing home. She never forgave me for it, but she actually liked being taken care of, living with other people. She actually would not have come to live with me as she hated the country.

I will always be grateful to my mother for her support and closeness, even though it was unexpressed: no kisses, no sweet words, but a deep real love. She gave me the greatest proof of her love when she died. She had had problems with her legs for some time and was confined between bed and wheelchair. The day she realized she was not going to get better, she decided not to speak and feed herself. For one month she did not utter a word, but just expressed herself with looks, bites, head movements; she was fed intravenously. Two days before Xmas I went to visit her. The doctor told me she was much better and was sleeping. I went to her room, took her hand and called her softly: she opened her eyes, didn't say a word, looked at me very intensely, closed her eyes and died. I am absolutely convinced she waited for my visit in order to die.

Again, separation and connection.

My Hands Are Full

Karen Ethelsdattar

The earth
as I turn it over with a spade,
a pitchfork,
but most of all my fingers;
lovely, dark, moist & loose.

These little dry seeds I plant
will thread roots into it;
from it will rise flowers.

Mother,
your roots delving in my heart,
blossoms emerging from it.
My tears,
good like the rain.
My fingers
knowing the earth as yours did.
Seven weeks after your death,
I your daughter am also become a gardener.

Your hand,
fingers clasping & unclasping mine
those last days
as though they were guiding my hands
into the soil.
My hands, my hands are full.

9

Shifting Perspectives

It was ten minutes before the end of a workshop for mothers and daughters, and participants were writing in their journals. Suddenly Margaret burst out into loud sobs. Everyone became still, and waited to find out what had happened. All during the workshop, Margaret, who had attended the workshop without her mother, had described herself as a person who had been deprived of mothering in her childhood, and who still could not get close to her mother, or even touch her, even though she knew that was what her mother wanted. This situation was very distressing to her.

When she had calmed her weeping enough to speak, she told us that she had just recalled a memory from her childhood, one that had been previously occluded. She was nine years old, at church with her mother, and she observed her mother and her mother's best friend holding hands with each other.

"You're queer," she said to her mother, not knowing what the word meant, but knowing somehow that it applied to this scene.

When they got home, her mother gave Margaret a lecture. Whatever the words her mother used, her facial expression and tone of voice conveyed embarrassment and discomfort. Suddenly Margaret felt very ashamed, and deep inside, below the level of thought, she drew the conclusion that it was wrong for women to touch each other. This decision remained with her and became a guiding principle in her life, depriving her of the capacity for intimacy and physical closeness with women, and especially her mother.

As she regained this memory, it dawned on her that her whole concept of her life story was turning upside down: she was not just a helpless victim of an unloving mother. She was an agent of her own destiny, and could therefore change it! It was she who had withdrawn from her mother's affection, because she had interpreted her mother's embarrassment as a condemnation of closeness between women. Now she was free to think consciously about that early unconscious decision. In doing so, she could begin the process of altering it, to one which could

170

allow her to get what she wanted…some closeness with her mother, and all her women friends. She now would have the opportunity to stop blaming her mother for neglect in the past, and to stop blaming herself for her inability to get close to her mother and other women in the present.

A shift in perspective can be triggered by a variety of events: a question someone asks, a book, a movie, a story someone tells, a comment someone makes, an observation of an interaction between people, a memory suddenly returning. If the time and situation are ripe and you are ready, the shift can come in a flash.

In that moment, it is as if the story you have been telling yourself all your life about why you feel and act the way you do, suddenly dissolves around you. In its place arises a new story, broader, more comprehensive, more liberating…one that allows you to notice more choices, to breathe in more love, and to breathe out more understanding…one that allows you greater freedom to create a greater life.

In the stories and poems that follow, mothers and daughters describe many small and large ways that they have experienced shifting perspectives, both in themselves and in each other.

This little story, and the following poem, show a mother's shifting perspective on her daughter.

Fire

Phyllis Woolf

One morning, when Jekkie was six years old, I came into the kitchen from outside, and found her standing near the stove with her hair on fire. You know that second while you're trying to understand what you're seeing? Well, in that second she realized that her hair was on fire, and she very calmly figured out what to do about it, and did it. In that second, she slipped into a logical mode: *Oh, my hair is on fire! Oh, I'll put my head in the sink and turn on the water.* And she did it so fast I didn't even have time to panic, or say a word.

At that moment, I became aware of how powerful her mind was, and I developed great respect for it.

Turn-over

Maureen Flannery

The body is assigned to replacement,
daughters coming into plum of upright stature
with perfect perpendicular thrust of breast buds
as mothers take pains so as not to shrink and bend.
Against strength of rooted women's supple stalks
girls, in iris unfolding, seem precarious lest May wind
or the weight of their succulent petals bend
the watery stem that holds them to the ground.
Bright blossoms predict vine-melon fullness.
Their vermilion flow into fresh fertility offsets
earth tones of their mothers' menopause.
Why am I struck at being dumb-struck
by her new, oblivious beauty, the rich tone
of flawless taupe skin, cinnamon colored hair?
I feel alone. *Why do you stare at me like that?*,
she demands, convinced of my disapproval.
Oh, nothing, I say and turn away.

With her daughter's love as a transformative agent, a mother realizes she can change.

Illumination

Sybil Smith

We swam across the Connecticut River, my daughter, my sponsor, and I. It was August first, and I had not crossed the river yet that summer. The water was as warm as it would get. We'd had day after day of brilliant sunshine.

My daughter, Celia, was wearing a black bathing suit which was lined with red; it was reversible. This added to its worth in her eyes, though she never used the red side. At fourteen, material belongings still give her intense pleasure.

The current was strong that day. We rested on the New Hampshire side of the river, our feet planted uneasily in the mud. The river can be scary. It is not clear, the bottom is not sandy, and as we crossed the middle we knew that beneath us lay a dark world where five foot pike undulated through the stripped carcasses of huge trees, above the pale shapes of cow bones, cinder blocks and empty bottles. Still, it was refreshing. We could see my house on the other side, shaded by an ancient pine tree that angled out over the water. It looked neat and whimsical, like a cottage in a fairy tale. My sponsor, Ann, who is some ten years sober, waxed rhapsodic over the delights of water and the buoyancy of flesh. She was, I knew, trying to reassure me that swimming sober could be every bit as fun as swimming while slightly looped. I was more than ready to believe her, despite the fact that recently I had noticed that the only reason I swam at all was when I felt too drunk. I believed that quick immersion in cool water could noticeably lower the blood alcohol, thereby (presumably) dropping it into a functional range.

This was handy when my boyfriend, Peter, was about to come home, or when I had to drive my car. Clearly, it was a theory fraught with danger. The research, though extensive on my part, had not been confirmed in vitro.

I had always had a reckless streak. I seemed to be invulnerable. I had never been physically hurt. I had not been in the hospital except to have Celia. I was rarely sick. Admittedly, a few years ago I had turned an odd sulphuric yellow, and began peeing what looked like coca cola. I had gone to the hospital and found out I had the dreaded Hep C. I was frightened enough to make numerous resolutions, which I promptly didn't keep. I did give myself shots of interferon, however, and my body had once again come through. My liver functions returned to normal, and my viral count went negative. My G.I. specialist was impressed, but predicted a relapse. He continued to test me. My viral counts stayed negative and my liver functions stayed normal. At my last visit he dragged me out of the examining room into the hall to show me off. Every time I had a negative test he said the same thing, "boy, are you lucky."

And it was true, I was lucky. I was tough as nails. I could take a hit and get up without missing a beat.

On the other hand, when it came to writing, I was convinced I wasn't lucky. Here I was, at the age of forty five, a minor writer. I had decided against getting an MFA when I was younger, because I had a suspicion that if I did I might become effete. I embraced nursing and real life with earnest vigor.

Effete was looking good to me now. I had published numerous poems and stories, had written a book and made a movie, but fame and wealth eluded me. In fact, getting sober was a last ditch attempt to change my karma. My sponsor, who had known me for ten years and who had watched me relapse innumerable times, had convinced me that sobriety was the missing piece of the puzzle. I had stopped drinking July 15th.

After resting we started back across the river. It was about five o'clock. The current was even stronger. I knew the gates at the Wilder Dam were open, because the demand for electric power was peaking as people got home from work. I could picture them turning up their air conditioners and making sophisticated drinks, ones that I had never gotten to try. What was a Gibson? What was a Manhattan? Was it possible I would never know?

We realized we couldn't fight the current, and that it might in fact be dangerous to do so. We simply swam and let the river pull us downstream as we worked our way west, to Vermont. This meant that we reached the opposite bank a few hundred yards south from my dock. We walked up on shore, onto the mud flats and started home. By this time Peter had joined us, in a kayak, offshore. My daughter went ahead and stirred up the water, having spotted baby crayfish. She looked perfect in the dappled sunlight, tall and slim and golden, like a girl who might inhabit the fairy tale cottage.

I was walking ahead of my sponsor, enjoying a small, darting moment of contentment. I reached a snarl of driftwood on the beach, and a low-hanging pine branch. I turned to my right and with one smooth movement launched myself into the water. It was a shallow dive. The bottom dropped off sharply there. The muddy verge was a narrow lip, and the river bed fell off like an ocean shelf.

Writing about it now I can recall exactly what it was like. My eyes were closed for the dive. My head had just hit the water. There was a brisk low noise, and my brain went bright, like it contained one of those lights that were turned on by clapping. I felt my body stop dead in mid-dive, and noticed a gritty sensation in the front of my skull.

This is how quickly the world changes. This is how the concerns you were just mulling over vanish as if an eraser had scrubbed across your cerebrum.

"Bad," my brain screamed. I popped up out of the water and clapped my hand to my head. "Help me" I said. Peter immediately knew something was wrong, because I seldom used those words. He levitated out of the kayak and ran towards me.

I turned towards shore. I walked. This was good. I turned my head. This was better. "My neck's okay," I said.

I don't know how I knew that. It might not have been true. I might have turned my head and felt my body disappear forever, exiled by a slice of bone. I might never have held my daughter again. Celia, who was the first to reach me. Who saw the deep gash on my forehead, extending far up into the hair, gaping open, revealing the secrets of adipose tissue, follicles, capillaries, and bone; secrets that are best kept hidden.

"I'm sorry," I said.

Ann tells everyone the same thing. "She never cried."

I'm crying now. Yesterday an agent who had written me after seeing a story in *The Sun*, and who had asked to see my work, wrote again to say she didn't want to represent me. These are the bald facts. I could soften them with flesh and hair and skin, but underneath is the hard word no. "Observant writer, great command of language, no doubt you will blah blah, but…"

And that's not why I'm crying.

My daughter led me home with my head bleeding. "I'm sorry," I kept saying. "It's okay," she reassured me, "it was an accident." She was calm. We went to the emergency department of the hospital where I work. The nurse suggested she might want to leave the room, because it would be hard to watch the suturing. But Celia said no. She stayed by my side. She patted my leg. She scolded me when I got up and walked to the bathroom, with blood pattering around my feet. She moved the light for the plastic surgeon, as, stitch by stitch, he recreated me.

But that's not why I'm crying.

A month has passed. I have a scar and a bald spot. I have not, as I informed the plastic surgeon, returned to my former state of pulchritude. I haven't had a drink.

But that's not why I'm crying.

I'm crying because last evening, when Peter and I picked Celia up at school, she pranced towards us in her pleated hockey skirt, and proudly told us she had run two miles. I said nothing. She talked about drama class and singing. I said nothing. We went to the store and I stayed in the car. Inside the store Peter told her about the letter from the agent. When she came back out she slid into the back seat and told me she had bought me Ben and Jerry's ice cream. She reached forward, rubbed my neck and said, "You are not a failure, Mom." And I didn't move, when I could have. I didn't reach up and touch her hand. I didn't turn. She rubbed and rubbed and I sat there like a stone.

I'm crying because she believes in the simple comfort of touch. Because she knows what matters, when I lose sight of it. Because I've forgotten the lesson so soon, the lesson written on my forehead in indelible pink.

I'm crying because now I know I can get up, walk downstairs, and hold her in my arms.

A step-mother and daughter gain new perspectives on each other.

Meeting Amelia

Deborah Bogen

Day One:

She's the only clean thing in the room. I try for a casual lean against the door. "You're my Dad's new girlfriend, aren't you?" The voice is flat, the eyes blank.

Beyond her I see the mattress on the floor surrounded by magazines...*Cosmopolitan, Mademoiselle*...piles of clothes and twenty or thirty votive candles vying for a chance to torch the curtains. A mirror leans against a dresser stickered with the *Grateful Dead, Amnesty International, Have a Good Day*. In the window sill a dead science experiment. In the corner of the room, amid dust bunnies, two plastic horses...the kind horse-girls collect. The dresser top's a buffet: nail polish, hair brushes, eye liner, scarves. She's decorated the walls with fans and a Swedish shelf heavy with more makeup and tiny porcelain animals. This one's a manifesto for the cosmetic industry, fifteen, bleached and blushed to match the magazines. Her nails have been chewed to the quick.

"Yes," I say, "I guess I am." We stare. Take stock of each other, weigh the options. I'm aggressively plain in jeans, my hair-dying days long gone, contact lenses abandoned. But I'm no less vain. I cultivate this look. There's nothing easy about long hair in middle age and my jeans are the same size she's wearing. Nothing easy about that. It's a different party trick, but a party trick all the same. She's just doing her version. I feel the old twinge...another daughter. I've been raising my two, Sarah and Jessica, and we're doing okay. Can I do it again? Is there enough juice left to field more phone calls, enforce curfews, talk about sex and talk her down from this incredible fashion high? School books still in the backpack catch my eye. Another round with the high school? And what about driving lessons?

Her perfume launches a full frontal attack. "So, do you like my Dad?" "Yes," I answer, "I do. Do you?" "He's okay, I guess. He's actually pretty cool, but he's a swinger, you know. He's had a lot of girlfriends." "Yes, I know." "You're like number 27 or so." "I know." "And he really has a temper, ya know?" "Yes, I know that too."

Her hand is running through wet hair, she turns on the hair dryer, continues to talk, pushing it. Trying to piss me off. Reading her back, I think she could do it. Then I remember how she looks when she goes riding, when she washes her face and pulls her long hair back into a braid. She doesn't know I've seen that, seen it from my car parked outside the stables, trying to decipher this possible daughter. She doesn't know I've seen how she sits a horse and the warm calm she brings to the currying. Gooseflesh. For a moment I can see more of her than she can…a small part of her dream world touches me…the connection molecular, instantaneous. She turns to look at me, checking for irritation, feels the tug then looks away. Turning off the dryer she says, "So, you're really gonna marry my father?" "Yes," I answer, "I really am." "You think he'll really do it? Like actually get married?" She moves to the mirror, starts the eyeliner.

"Your hair's beautiful." I say. "Your father says that you're a dancer." "Oh that, well, yeah." "It shows…the way you carry yourself." "What?" "Oh, nothing, I was just thinking out loud." She turns, opens her mouth, says nothing, bends back to finish the other eye. "Well, I gotta go now. My friends are picking me up." "Ok," I say and it slips out, "Call if you'll be late."

"You know," she says turning at the door, "my Dad's had a lot of girlfriends."

Wedding

Increments. That's the only way I can do things. All my big steps are actually 60 or 70 small ones…so small sometimes I can convince myself I'm not really moving at all. Everyone thinks this is fast, a big step. A wedding, new husband, new daughter, new town, new job. The small steps to this place have been going on for years in Phil's life and in mine. So small that at first I couldn't see them myself. By the time I could, I was careful not to talk too much, sorting out impulses, ideas, desires like clothes from the dryer. My mother saw more than most, so much she knew enough not to ask. Once as I was leaving an elevator a man whispered conspiratorially, "You look like a woman on the move." I whipped around, finger to my lips, "Shhhhh!"

A hundred small steps that got us to the springboard, the vaulting ramp, and now it's show time. The wedding. This ceremony is all about the daughters, his and mine. It's all about the parents, his and mine. It's not about Phil or me, it's not about us. We've been "married" for months, but we know this ceremony matters. Not to us…to them.

We want them all to see it. Forced witness. This is for real, for keeps. Nobody's leaving. And now it's time. I look at Philip. He's beaming and I'm suddenly wonderfully calm. I have never been this sure of anything. The minister says "for better or for worse." We look at our daughters scrunched into rental chairs in their wedding regalia…"Get it?"

Afterwards the grandmothers, our mothers, circle, balancing teacups and small plates of wedding cake. The rules of hospitality are rigidly enforced, but each wonders if her granddaughters will suffer from this marriage…each has said as much. We were dumbfounded. How terrible for these poor girls, we said to each other late at night, to live with parents who are happy, who love each other and who love them.

Phil and I have courted, moved, set up house, started jobs with the girls in tow. We've interrupted romantic weekends to track down daughters who have blown their curfews, to drive daughters to youth group dances, to watch daughters receive student awards and to rescue daughters from their other parents. Now, the daughters have been farmed out to uncles and aunts for a week. This is our week. When we get back we will start "regular family life". School in three weeks, dance classes, sports, the whole thing. We're in this together now. The girls have decorated the car with balloons. We take this as a good omen.

Tango

She wants to live with her mother. Understandable people say, but I know they have missed the point. Amelia doesn't really want that. She hates that house. She wants not to live with us…where there are parents in charge. She's used to equal odds, one on one. We're married, united, suddenly formidable.

The fight is terrible, one on one, Amelia and me. She's furious and shaking and clearly afraid. That I won't like her? That she won't get her way? And I'm afraid, oh boy am I afraid. I'm stuck. I'm screwing up. And I'm scared. Mothering's my thing. I'm supposed to be able to do this. I can hear Philip in the kitchen cooking dinner, trying to let me handle this. Amelia says this is just not what she's used to. She does not want to be "one of the girls". She's not ready for rules, big dinners, sisters. But something's not ringing true, that's not really it. I'm missing something. I can't get it, can't make the right connections. Desperately I say all the wrong things. I say what I really think. "You need me," I say, my voice escalating. "I could teach you things, I know things you need to know." It's hard to go farther wrong. She's screaming, "I don't need you, you're not my mother! I don't need anyone." Phil takes my arm, leads me toward the door. She is sitting on the floor of her old room, before me, before us, before the need for a bigger house, before change. This is her world and I have forced her out of it. "We're going for a drive," he hollers back through the screen door, but when we get outside, around the corner, when she can no longer see me I fold up and collapse on the driveway. My stomach hurts. I'm clam-shaped and cramping, rocking back and forth, groaning. Phil stands by, not hurrying, not telling me to get up, not worrying what the neighbors may be thinking. Just watching. "Labor pains," he says.

Detente

Amelia pulls up in her mother's car. She has her license. I hear the car door slam and in a flash she's in the kitchen. "Hey Barb! Wanna go for a ride?" I sip my coffee. "Oh boy," I think. "Another driver." Sarah's had her learner's permit for a couple months and she's positively frightening. The junior high parking lot, empty on Saturdays, was even scary. The first time I took her on the freeway I nearly threw up. The only thing that got me to do it was the sure knowledge that if someone was going to die when she got up to sixty-five, it should be me. And here's Amelia with another opportunity for terror. I force enthusiasm, tell myself I love parenting.

We get in, laughing. She's triumphant, I'm nervous. This is a test. We both know that. This is a test and she's in charge. I buckle up, she does too, readjusts the mirror, releases the emergency brake, then yanks it up again, checks the mirror again, re-releases the brake. She turns her head checking for traffic, signals and pulls out onto the road. So far so good. The morning's sunny, the street quiet, tree-lined, wide, wishing us well. We move smoothly to the intersection where she stops, looks both ways and moves out into heavier traffic. My hands relax their grip on my coffee cup ("she died true to her caffeine addiction," they could say in the obit). I notice she keeps clear of the car ahead of her, signals when she changes lanes. "Oh my God," I think, "she's good at this. She's a good driver, she's wonderful." And she is. Better than I am, better than Phil, waaaaaay better than Sarah. She can do this. We're safe.

"You're great," I effuse. "Yea," she says, "funny, huh. This is my kinda thing. I love this. I'm just good at it." Suddenly we're both laughing again. But out loud and with gusto. We've been waiting for months for something to agree about…and for heaven's sake…it's driving.

Ice Cream

We're excited, Phil and me. Amelia has been over for dinner. Now, all three daughters have voluntarily gone for a walk together. They're talking, we think. This is how things should be, sisters. Talking. Doing the dishes we are buoyant. Neither of us mentions the fact that all of our daughters have gone out together on their own. We're trying to pretend this is normal. We're trying to pretend it is no big thing…but good vibes reign. I don't mention that he's missed a spot on the dinner plate. He doesn't remind me to be careful putting the platter away because I've broken both the others. Tonight all is forgiven, everything's possible, the girls are Talking.

Phil puts the *Grateful Dead* on the CD player. We kid around. "The girls" really think this is old people's music we say. We are carefully casual. It sounds good, "the girls." They have been gone for an hour. What was the soft dark of evening has deepened to real night. We smell the jasmine flowers opening outside the kitchen window but, we aren't worried, it's safe here. We know they like to stop at the park and swing, great big high-school women that they've become. Then we hear steps on the porch, and voices, shouting, angry. Three scowling teenagers invade the living room. There's no space, no air, they are huge in their anger and loud enough to silence the *Dead*. I ask what's wrong. Sarah and Amelia both talk at once. Jessica, two years their junior slumps back in the futon crossing her arms on her chest, looking like she wants to move to Zimbabwe. Someone said something, we hear, and then someone said something, and then someone said something. And then someone pushed someone. I stand up. Demand silence. They sulk. We try again, Phil and I, totally unable to figure it out. Then Amelia stands up. She's had enough, she says. She cannot be treated this way, she says. She flounces out into the night. Sarah's face is dark and blank...she's giving me the garage door look. Whatever I say now she has closed up for the evening. She's dropped the garage door and if she's back there, behind it, we will never really know. I have seen this look before. Amelia's long gone, Jessica's miserable. I send them off to bed.

Philip puts his arms around me. "Ice cream?" he asks. We head out for Baskin Robbins, neither of us talking. We do not say "God, I hope she drove home alright" or even "God, I hope she went home." We drive in silence, our hands meeting in the dark on the emergency brake. We squeeze and drive. "Real sisters do this too" I say finally. It doesn't help. We park and walk up to the door. They've just locked up. A kid is sweeping and hanging the chairs upside down on the tables. The man at the cash register counts money. He sees us. We beg silently, pleading, and he is miraculously moved to pity. He unlocks. "You folks really need a scoop?" he asks. We confess, "Our three teenaged daughters have just thrown a communal fit. We need chocolate." He laughs, scoops doubles and we sit on the steps outside his relocked door in the moonlight. The traffic is loud, the street alight with Kentucky Fried, Supercuts, PizzaHut, Nails are Us, but the moon's still up there shining too. Phil kisses me, his tongue cold and chocolately, his breath warm and close. "We keep trying," he says.

Horsegirls

Her leg is broken. Badly. She was thrown by a rogue horse, a horse no one should have ever let her ride. But they did and this really happened. She's in the actual hospital, ropes and pulleys slung across the room like a cat's cradle. Amelia was made to be in motion; she will hate this.

Sarah's not happy her step-sister's in the hospital, but she's excited to have something dramatic to talk about at school, at dinner. Sirens, ambulances. She was there, Amelia's horse protege. A compound fracture isn't pretty. I shiver, imagining Amelia screaming in the dirt, the bone jutting through skin and clothes, Sarah running for the stable, for the pay phone, dialing 911.

By the time we found out what happened they were both at the hospital, Amelia on drugs and Sarah looking like she wished she was.

For the next few days Philip and I take shifts with Amelia's mom, reading, making up news, trying to make it all less awful. It's hard on everybody, but Amelia surprises me, displays resources I hadn't known were there. She makes jokes about the itching, the constant cold foot as the raised leg dumps blood into the hip joint. She's taking it in stride, she says, watching our grimaces, and fills the days reading Dick Francis mysteries and planning her "I can dance again" party for when this is all history.

Today Phil has a four o'clock committee meeting. I leave the office early to spend an hour at the hospital. When I push open the big swinging door I find Amelia in fine fettle. The swelling is almost gone and her traction has been lowered. St. Vincent's is an old hospital; they have windows that actually open and the fresh air is laced with jasmine and lilac. I sit on the bed, relaxed by the enforced inactivity. Amelia looks younger to me here. No make-up, no magazines. Just Amelia. What if she'd been mine from the beginning, I wonder. That's the kind of things step-mothers wonder about. Stupid. Useless.

We play Scrabble. She's a genius at this game, all that reading producing a vocabulary she never uses at the dinner table. Between "jungle for 24" and "mica for 10", we gossip; Jessica's budding track career, Sarah's job on the school paper. Amelia has been making plans for her return to the world of the walking. She wants to dance in the Spring musical next year. It'll take her the whole year to rehabilitate the foot, the leg. I don't even know if she can do it. But today she is happy, voluble, reminiscing. "Remember our big fight?" she says. I drop a "w." "Oh yes," I say, "I remember." "You were so mean," she laughs, "so fierce and holier than thou!" I'm stunned. What do I say here? "I was?" I gasp. "Oh yea, man, you were tough! I thought, this woman is a major heavy. I knew I wouldn't get away with jack if I lived with you." She laughs. She's so casual, relaxed in the afternoon light, and easy with this. The fish in my stomach flops over. "Careful," I say to myself, "careful here. Don't blow this." But she's moving on, not even wanting a response. She wants to know if I'll bring her pizza bread tomorrow, if I can stop at the yarn shop for more wool. I remember she's making a scarf for her Dad, and I'm bundling up my things, moving to the door, when she says the last thing. "Hey Barb. I was thinking, would it be okay if I stayed with you guys a couple of weeks when I get out, maybe til I get rid of the crutches? My mom has to be gone most of the day, and I thought I could hang out with Sarah and Jess in the afternoons." My legs stop, my heart beats quickly. "Oh sure," I say, my response as heavily casual as a high school play audition, "that sounds like a good plan." "I mean if it's a hassle, I don't need to," she offers. But my mind is racing, already rearranging bedroom furniture. "Oh no," I answer, "it's a great idea. And no hassle at all. You know, it's no big deal setting another place at the table."

In the following story, a daughter struggles to find a new and broader perpective on her mother, in order to understand and appreciate their similarities.

Night Visitors and Open Windows

Gretchen Scherer

My backpack slouches in the middle of the kitchen, an icon to transience. It is lightweight with an internal frame and a detachable daypack. Clothes lay scattered all around it: dirty socks, cut-off Levi's and T-shirts…the usual signs that I am home again. My mother, who is my travel accomplice, bought it for me after I graduated from college.

"It's so nice when you come home," she says, filling my wine glass. It makes me happy to know I have been missed, especially because it is my mother I miss most when I'm away.

She glances out the window, looking for deer, but there aren't any. She's at war with them, which means she is also, by extenuation, at war with my dad. He constructed a salt lick at the edge of the yard where the meticulously groomed grass meets an alfalfa field. All winter, the deer visited the salt lick, becoming more and more comfortable with the proximity of humans. They began wandering into the yard, leaving a trail of hoof prints in the snow. One night, as my mother and brother were talking in the kitchen, they suddenly noticed a fawn poised warily just outside the dining room window. It cocked its enormous ears and stared at them through the window.

When spring came, the deer found my mother's crocuses during a trip through the yard and ate the tender shoots before they even had a chance to flower. Now, my mother thinks they'll get her tulips, and later, her strawberries, snapdragons and sweet peas, her zinnias and Russian sage. She sneaks a watchful glance out the kitchen window as she pours my wine, just in case the deer are bold enough to come in the middle of a gray Saturday afternoon.

"I am so annoyed with your father," she half whispers.

I raise my eyebrow, intrigued. I have rarely known this patient, congenial woman to be "annoyed" with anyone. This kind of frankness is new in our relationship. Only in the last couple of years has she decided that I am old enough now not to be frightened by confessions that she and my father don't always see eye to eye. Maybe she has decided it is nice to have a confidante.

"I don't know why he had to put that thing so close to the house," she says, referring to the deer feeder.

"Get another dog," I suggest.

She laughs. "Some help that would be. Guess who had to take care of your father's last dog. We couldn't keep that dog around for anything…he wanted to go places."

No matter what my parents did that dog ran away. He never seemed to have anywhere in particular that he wanted to go. He didn't seem to have any particular reason for going either. Norm just liked to go. Usually, we'd find him, sometimes miles away, loping along in the ditch, his black ears flapping against his head and his pink tongue lolling out the side of his mouth. His journeys became legendary around our area, so much so, that whenever someone spied a dark Labrador-type dog roaming the countryside they called our house.

It never occurred to me until that moment that Norm and I had anything in common. My obsession with traveling has become legendary, and my parents often field the question, "Now where's Gretchen these days?" And, like Norm, my reasons for going often aren't even clear to me. Occasionally, I just get the urge to go somewhere, so I pick a direction or a country and I go.

But the more I think about it, the more I suspect there is a reason and that it is rooted somehow in my mother.

As I grow older, my face, which always resembled hers, bears even more similarity. I know her profile well and sometimes try to study mine, wondering how alike they are. I think she is beautiful and relish our point of likeness, especially because, in many ways, we are so different. This connects me to her and I find myself comparing us in other ways as well, measuring the unfolding stages of my adult life against hers, an exercise that does neither of us justice.

Our faces are mirror images of each other but our lives are not. She was the first daughter after three boys in a third generation Irish family. The farm was the defining force in their lives, although my mother hated it. She tells of a gander who used to chase her across the yard, and she even now despises milk because it reminds her of her childhood. As the oldest daughter, my mother helped feed her five brothers and sisters. When she was younger, she helped prepare the noon feast. In high school, it was dinner. My grandmother kept teaching, partly because she wanted to and partly so they could more easily send all their kids to college; so it was my chatty mother, the homecoming attendant, who often left the malt shop or cheerleading practice early to peel potatoes and cook the roast for eight.

Later, she gave up a fledgling nursing career to become a mother and home-maker at the age of twenty-three, a job she excelled at, in part due to her self-sacrificing nature.

This nature allowed me to live a thoroughly selfish high school existence. Because we lived in a somewhat remote area, my mother spent the majority of her time in the car, driving us to gymnastics practice or piano lessons. I went off to college barely able to boil water and thinking of no one but myself. I have entered my late twenties unmarried and childless and still have only minimal cooking skills. When people ask me what "I do," I sometimes answer, "Travel."

My mother's nursing career really began and ended with a one-year missionary station in the Bahamas. When I was nineteen, we took a family trip there, twenty years after she left. In the baggage claim area, my mother smiled at the wet heat. As we grumbled at the empty and stationary luggage conveyer, she seemed delighted things hadn't changed.

"Things move slower here kids," she said.

When we got in the taxi, it was my mother, not my father as usual, who told the driver where to go. My mother who pointed out the mansion where they filmed a James Bond movie.

Later, we went to the house where she had lived with her friend Bonnie, during the year in Nassau. My mother dragged us through the front door, which was standing open and off one hinge.

"This was our living room," she said, swinging her arm out like a model as she showed us the bare stucco house.

She pointed toward a dark doorway, "Over there is the kitchen and upstairs is where Bonnie and I slept," she said.

It seemed impossible. My mother who wears *Donna Karan* and *Claiborne* and likes leather interiors in her car would never live in a dump like this, I thought. Not happily anyway.

Missionaries had long since been replaced by local nurses, and the house, which was on church property, now stood vacant. My mother walked slowly around the empty living room, running her hand along the whitewashed stone walls, which were stained and chipped in several places. Some of the stucco from the ceiling had fallen onto the floor.

"I know it doesn't look like much," she said, "but we had a cozy blue sofa right over there, and two chairs on either side of the window. We made little curtains out of some old material after we got here. They were violet checks, I think. It wasn't bad, really."

In the kitchen, next to a sagging, grease-stained stove, sat a rusting sink. The cracked linoleum was brown and water stained. She told us about the cockroaches that overran the kitchen at night; the only weapon against them was a frying pan kept on the table just inside the door. Before turning on the light, Bonnie or my mother banged the pan against the table. They would hear faint scuttling noises as the roaches raced for cover.

She held her left hand out expectantly, as though planning to find the frying pan still lying there.

"Once," she said, "I turned on the light without banging first. Cockroaches were everywhere…on the counters, the floors."

She made a fist with her hand and stuck her thumb in my face, "See this?" she asked laughing. "They were this big."

She looked around the room one more time and sighed wistfully, "But we loved it here."

In the midst of this squalor, her face read perfect rapture. She ignored my father, who was busy telling us how he came down here and proposed. In the house she transformed, became twenty-one again, with her whole life ahead of her. She became one of the ghosts, merely smiling a vague smile as she walked slowly up the stairs.

It was fascinating to be there with her, to see her oblivious to us all. As she relived her past, I realized for the first time that she had one. My father served in Vietnam, and was even there when I was born, but to me this journey of my mother's was much more significant. Mothers do not have adventures in foreign lands, that was reserved for warriors or explorers, who, in my past, had always been male.

The Bahamas qualified, in my opinion, as an adventure, especially after hearing the story of my mother's intruder. In the bedroom that she and Bonnie shared, she told me about the night she woke up and saw someone at the dresser rummaging around.

"Weren't you scared?" my sister asked.

"Of course," she replied. "I was terrified the first time. At first I thought I was dreaming or seeing a ghost. I didn't know whether to scream or run or what."

She pointed to the window, "He went right out there and jumped to the tree. As soon as he was gone, I woke Bonnie up. She didn't believe me, but when there was a dollar and ten cents missing from the dresser, she had no choice. He hadn't touched our jewelry or anything else."

They reported him to the priest, but nothing could be done. Twice, he came back, always for loose change, and somehow, she told me, they almost got used to him. It was like they had an unspoken agreement, like they were giving spare change to anyone who might have asked them on the street.

"Did you ever speak to him?" I asked.

"No. I think I almost liked thinking it was a dream. Speaking would have broken that spell."

My mother was the last one to leave the house, after we were already restless and waiting outside by the sprawling banyan tree, the same one the robber used to escape.

She observed her family hanging from or leaning on various parts of the tree and said, "We hung our laundry on that tree to dry."

Now, her greatest love is her garden, an anniversary gift from my father. At least three days a week during the summer she is in one of her two flower beds. She wears thongs, heavy gardening gloves and a baseball cap. She weeds around the perimeter of each plant, waters it, sprays it and purrs over it. The sweat and dirt gathers in a fine line across her lip, her face flushes the color of her fuchsias. The flowers flourish and burst under her tutelage, until each garden is one big explosion of color. Once a week, she cuts two armfuls of flowers and carries them back with her to the house.

I wonder if their heady sweetness remind her of the Bahamas.

Perhaps it is because of the nights she had to prepare meals for her siblings, perhaps she never would have had much of an interest in cooking, but the end result is that she's not crazy about feeding us. And even when I come home after a long time away she may only order pizza. The one exception is her cookies. Those she makes all the time. My childhood is filled with memories of bursting through the door after school to the smell of chocolate chip cookies. My mother would be there too, asking us how our day went. To me, they signified that I was loved, that all was right in the world. Maybe to her this symbolizes perfect motherhood…a house that smells of cookies and flowers.

But she also longs to travel, and although she and my father make occasional trips, I know she waits anxiously for the day when my youngest sister graduates from high school and my father retires so she can go on extended trips. Until then, she satisfies herself through hearing my stories, which I write to her in letters, tell over the telephone, and repeat when I come home.

For now, we sit in fading twilight, drink wine and think about deer. I believe it is as close to perfect happiness as we can come.

She picks up the project of the day, some kind of lumpy red material. She is trying to fashion a rooster's comb for my 12-year old sister to wear in her school play. As my mother sews, she tells me about the time she had the lead in a production in high school. She played a mute.

I can see her leaving for the Bahamas. Only twenty-one, she was thin, a pale and dark-haired Irish beauty with "eyes as blue as Bantry Bay" my grandpa used to say. I imagine her and Bonnie leaving the United States for their first time in 1967 with their new mini-beehives, and see her in her white nursing uniform as she spent her days in the clinic with freshly scrubbed Bahamian children in their Sunday best, with names like Gina Lolabriggida Smith and Elvis Jones. I can see their mothers calling to the children, "Don't shame me" as my mother took the children's hands and walked them back to the examining rooms.

Coming from a small, white farming community, this was very possibly her first close contact with people of another race, and I wonder what reaction she had to their dark skin. If it intrigued her. If at first she touched them gingerly.

Lately, my mind keeps returning to the memory of my mother in the Bahamas. I imagine her as I want to see her so that I can find something of myself in her. Something safe and free. I don't want the mother…the role she plays so perfectly, so silently. I want the woman who sashayed down firm, wet beaches, her sandals dangling from her hands. Who relentlessly punched needles into children's arms to protect them from disease.

Sometimes I resent her silence, her selflessness. I resent even more though, when she asks me to be complicit with her. When I am arguing heatedly with my father and I suddenly feel her eyes bearing down on me, expecting me to be the one to give in. When she says,

"I don't agree with you," to my father and he responds,

"You don't have to agree with me," in that way that also says, "because I'm still right," then I cringe and seethe, determined to stick to my guns and know that later she will tell me what she really thinks.

I believe history repeats itself, and I am afraid of becoming the one who gives in.

I am also afraid that if I remain sedentary too long, I will no longer be able to move.

At night, as I lie in bed, I think again of my mother and Bonnie in their bedroom. I see them sitting up in their beds, the screenless window wide open to the moon, their knees pulled tight to their chests. They are young, curious and unmarried. They tease their hair, adorn themselves with mascara and lipstick, and slide into fitted, sleeveless dresses. Then, they saunter through the native side of town where people recognize them as the young nurses from the mission and greet them with a nod of the head. Their favorite restaurant gives nightly shows…Cajun music and a blues singer. There are limbo tournaments for tourists in the winter. Here, my mother eats jumbo shrimp and drinks piña coladas.

When they come back to the house, they talk about home, wondering what they are missing…harvesting, a street dance, a wedding or two…but they say how glad they are that they aren't there, how much more exotic it is here, and they plan to go to the market the next day. They snuggle down under the sheets and my mother falls asleep with a pang of longing for her boyfriend…the man who would become my father…mixed with her delightful independence.

I think about the man who sneaks into their house. I envision how it happens. She wakes in the middle of the night and sees a shadow by her dresser. Before she feels frightened, she wonders if she is dreaming. She leans up a little on her elbows, trying to get a better look. Her bed is under the window and she sees the black banyan tree in the yard, the leaves rattling in the breeze. She thinks about trying to escape out the window and make a dash for the priest sleeping in the pink stucco rectory next to the church. But she doesn't know if she should leave Bonnie.

The figure turns. She feels her heart pounding in her ears. A dog barks somewhere; she thinks she smells bougainvillea. The figure comes toward her. She tries to keep calm, act casually, as though it is a natural thing to have a complete stranger in one's bedroom in the middle of the night. I imagine him young, lithe and taut like a panther from living on the streets. But suave too. In different circumstances he might have been a prince, a dancer.

He steps on her bed with one foot and puts the other on the window sill. She doesn't breathe. Seeing that she is awake, he pauses. Reaching down to where her foot is protruding from the sheet, he touches it gently. It is like a shot of electricity going through her. For a fleeting second, she glimpses his face in the diffused moonlight before he crouches in the window, leaps, and lands with a soft thud on the ground.

I have fallen in love with this vision of my mother, and because of this I will probably never ask her to describe in precise details her year in the Bahamas. The truth could never hold up to my imagining. And it is, I suspect, this fantasy that keeps me moving. I have convinced myself that by seeking out foreign places I can remain the woman she was, that it is only by standing still I will become the mother. Yet, it is my love for this mother that always brings me home.

I wonder if in moments of solitude, she returns in spirit to the Bahamas, if she stands at the window remembering a brief time so vivid that it momentarily eclipses the sedate suburbia of now. In my mind, she must. In my mind she longs to go to the window and look out, but is afraid of how much farther it is now from the window to the ground.

A daughter comes to understand and respect her mother's point of view.

"It's a Man's World and You'd Better Get Used to It."

Nancy Bunge

That my Aunt Helen was one of two women in the country with a PhD. in nursing education failed to impress my mother. She knew that Aunt Helen would rather have a husband. A six foot three inch Professor at Columbia University, Aunt Helen was the most prominent and the most frequently ridiculed of several old maid schoolteachers in my family. The others were shorter, older, less successful, and regarded affectionately because they weren't as "selfish" as Aunt Helen. At thirteen, when I actually started to develop a figure and an interest in boys, I made calculations, and concluded that most of my female relatives had never married. I decided to beat the odds by acting dumb and slouching. My mother urged me to also pitch my voice higher; my father, Aunt Helen's brother, laughed at these lessons and bought my friends and me a letterhead for the law firm he was sure we would form one day.

As I aged, I did well in school and even enjoyed it. On the other hand, my relationships with men were, to say the least, convoluted, perhaps because I tried to follow my mother's advice. She knew her stuff: just as she predicted, men seemed irrationally vulnerable to flattery and ambiguity. On the other hand, as my brother noted when he urged me to "be dark and mysterious for a change," evasion and lies didn't come naturally to me, so I couldn't play the required role well. When I rested from the labor of trying to work my mother's wiles on boys, I studied. It didn't take long to realize that I spent my most pleasant and peaceful hours at my desk. My books didn't nag me to sleep with them; my books didn't care how my hair looked; my books didn't require that I somehow try to balance bottomless adulation with enough distance to make myself desirable. Reading books and writing papers, I could be myself, not try to follow my mother's or my current boyfriend's admonitions. I began to have the terrifying realization that I preferred books to boys and that, as a result, I could turn into Aunt Helen.

As fate would have it, I earned my PhD. at the University of Wisconsin-Madison while my Aunt Helen was Dean of the Nursing School there. I had fled a boyfriend in Chicago, secretly hoping that like the men in my mother's stories, after I left, he would come to understand that I deserved better treatment and reform. And if he didn't, well, I'd moved on. But that I'd settled in the same city inhabited by my aunt seemed ominous. I found the evenings she invited me over for dinner especially frightening because they seemed portraits of the "empty life" I would endure if I didn't make one of my relationships with men work; I would have nothing to enjoy but great music, good food and laughter. I loved my aunt, but I was glad to escape her and Madison for the glittering city of Washington, D.C. where I wrote my dissertation while teaching full time.

There were more men to date in Washington than in Madison, and I was only 25; I thought I had made the right move just in time. But an admired cousin also lived there who had the irritating habit of putting things into perspective: he warned me against "majoring in adverbs," yawned at my scholarship and marveled at my teaching. He had an eye for and an intolerance of games that he did not hesitate to exercise on me. One Saturday evening after supper, when I began talking of having "plans," he handed me the *Washington Post* and told me to pick a movie. When I said I didn't understand the movie we'd just seen, Jim said, "I'm not biting. That's your favorite game: 'I'm Nancy Bunge from La Crosse, Wisconsin and I don't know anything.'" Then we had a real talk. After I got out of the car, he called my name, then said, "I had a good time." Two days later, three young men approached him as he walked to a friend's to return a book. One of them shot him through the chest with a sawed-off shotgun for no discernible reason. Jim's death made everyone lucky enough to know him desolate. It left me with enough bittersweet memories of an authentic friendship with a male to make men who craved flattery and evasion repulsive. Pretense became impossible.

The following summer, I resolutely returned to the dating scene; the usual disastrous fallout with my current flame took place as my Aunt Helen approached death in Madison and my father had his cancerous larynx removed. Before heading west to spend Christmas with ailing relatives, I worried with a friend about the dissolution of my latest relationship; she invited me to a party where I met someone and began cultivating my usual fantasies of making things work this time. In Chicago, my frantic mother complained about my working on my dissertation while relatives faded. I fled from my mother's charges of selfishness to my dying Aunt in Madison. As I walked into Aunt Helen's hospital room, she used the bar over her bed to pull herself up and said, "Nancy, what do you think of the TA strike?" In that instant, I realized that she had had an enormously difficult life, but that despite and perhaps even because of her troubles, she had made the rest of the world her central concern...even as she was dying. At that moment, she changed from a scary possibility to a role model.

When it came to my aunt's richness, I was a slow learner; others easily understood how terrific she was. When I ridiculed my aunt as a child, my best friend's mother, a nurse who knew how hard my aunt had worked to have the nursing profession taken seriously, corrected me for the first and only time. When she insisted, "Your aunt is a wonderful woman," I pointed out that my aunt was 6'3" and an old maid. Mrs. Esch repeated herself: "Your aunt is a wonderful woman." I thought I knew better, but I obviously never forgot Mrs. Esch's remark.

The nursing graduate students who lived in the same apartment building as I in Madison shouted enthusiastic greetings when my aunt appeared at my door with boxes of elegant food that I couldn't afford to buy. I had mentioned to my dissertation director that I had an aunt at the Nursing School, but it wasn't until he saw her on the dais at graduation that he realized she was Dean. He repeatedly commented that I must be proud of her and I made brief noises of assent before turning to the real issue at hand: getting my degree. While I clung to my reservations about my aunt, she made it clear she had none about me. Once she introduced me to her colleague who said that she knew all about me from my aunt's bragging: I was an excellent student and wonderful in every way.

In retrospect, my other old maid aunts were wonderful, too. My Great Aunt Dorothea earned an MA at the University of Chicago in the 30's, and then put her degree to work teaching at a school in Appalachia for extremely low wages. She and my Great Aunt Hannah had cabins at Reserve, an enclave of family huts near an Ojibwa Reservation in northern Wisconsin. Although they've both been gone for more than 30 years, I have sharp memories of the two of them, stomping through the woods in their jeans and boots, leading us to blueberries, explaining Ojibwa customs, or introducing us to Natives. But until my late twenties, all this vitality went unacknowledged because these bright, lively, kind, happy women had failed at life: they never married and it looked as though, despite my best efforts to transform myself into a femme fatale, I would soon share their fate. One Thanksgiving, Aunt Hannah and Aunt Dorothea jointly approved of my naturalness so loudly that I had to hear; I felt ambivalent about the praise: look where their honesty had taken them.

That my spinster aunts were wonderful does not invalidate my mother's perspective. She had it right: married women enjoy many perks: companionship, acceptability, children, and a second income. When she told me, repeatedly, that I'd better get used to the idea that it was a man's world because I wasn't going to change it, she spoke the truth: it was a man's world and it continues to be a man's world and I used to believe it would change in my lifetime. My mother made it very clear that male superiority was a political and historical accident; it had nothing to do with justice. But the fact that men did not deserve their power would, she knew, make them all the more resistant to sharing it. She believed that for me to build a life on the assumption that I could make a life for myself without a male protector was fool-hardy, and to pursue a PhD. was to follow this path. And having warned me as passionately as she could, and having watched me struggle to transform one relationship after another into something I could live with for the rest of my life, when I walked away from potential mates, persisted in my education, won my PhD., then published, then won tenure, no one was prouder of me than my mother. I knew the score because she had reminded me endlessly; but I had done the right thing anyway. So, it was my mother who urged me to cancel my class and go to my last graduation; my mother who bought me the hood I wear at graduations now; my mother who sent copies of my first book to 20 people and my mother who bought me the gold star paper weight that rests on my desk when I was promoted to full professor. And my mother, who surely would have liked me to produce grandchildren for her, eventually referred to my relationships with men as "close calls."

One could dismiss most of my mother's objections as symptoms of being threatened…if they were not totally reasonable. When I decided to major in Philosophy as a freshman, she raised common sense objections which I thought I soundly defeated with concepts lifted from Plato. Her answer, "That old Plato doesn't know everything, you know" became famous among my friends. But I later discovered she was right: philosophy was a mind game and, like her, I needed to engage in activity I thought would make a concrete difference in people's lives.

One Christmas break I was trying to write a paper on a very difficult Yeats poem that my instructor, who had written his thesis on Yeats, could not analyze. After laboring over the poem until I had a reading, I thought that explaining it to my mother might help me understand whether or not my interpretation truly worked; so we sat down at the kitchen table and stared at Yeats' lines and images. I got almost no distance into my exposition when I stopped and asked my mother what she thought. She said, "You know what I think? I think he's crazy. I'm going to bed." She headed for her bedroom, then stopped to turn and say, "It scares me that you spend so much time thinking about such things." In retrospect, she seems correct. English PhD.s can spend enormous amounts of time thinking about things with no empirical worth and, again, these mental convolutions can become an end. My mother was perfectly pleased to see me get a PhD., but she wanted me to use this knowledge to enrich people's lives, not get caught in competitive, mental exercises that separated me from my common sense…and from others.

Even my mother's charge that I was selfish to work on my dissertation had validity. My father had just begun almost a decade of slow dying of one kind of cancer after another. And I worried about finishing my dissertation. Later, when he was truly dying, my mother said, "Dad's life is over and you're still building yours; if you have to work, leave." But she never wanted me to substitute intellectual excellence for emotional knowledge. As I worried about a colleague's charge that I'd been too lenient with a student, my mother said, "I'm proud that you listened to your heart." And when I finally achieved enough to threaten other people into attacking me, I whined to my mother who replied: "Show them what a nice person is like."

So, my mother's ambiguity in regard to my pursuit of a PhD. didn't derive from jealousy. She simply realized that I was moving into territory that would make me threatening to men who would continue to use their political power to protect their interests. She knew I would pay a high price for refusing to make flattering men my life's work and feared that, in order to survive, I might sacrifice part of my feeling life. Probably because I was raised by my mother, I worry over the same possibilities every day. Thanks to how miserably my relationships went and how tranquil the time I spent out of them, the marriage issue resolved itself long ago; but I still fret about making my teaching and research more useful and humane. My mother's reservations and fears have become my own…I hope, forever.

A daughter has a mammoth re-evaluation of her connection to and relation-ship with her mother, on the occasion of her death.

My Mother's Passing

Christina Gibbons

One of the advantages of bearing down on the age of 60 is the perspective it gives me on my life and relationships. My mother died fifteen years ago and I can think of her now with equanimity. There are a lot of good parts of her that still live in me, just as there are things that belonged to her that sit on my shelves and in my drawers. Over and over I have forgiven her for making my life hard at times and often I feel that I've finally gotten over the difficulties we had together.

My mother left my father when I was six years old and moved us back to live with my grandparents in upstate New York. This was 1948; no one else I knew had divorced parents and I guess my mother thought if she didn't talk about it I would hardly notice.

"We just didn't say much about it back then," she told me once later.

But of course I did notice, and cared a lot. I felt as if I had been cut in half. It took me years to find the words to describe what had happened to me, and even longer to stop feeling hurt. During a year of counseling in my forties, I realized that neither of my parents had meant to hurt me, that they were doing the best they could. I never doubted that they loved me.

As a single parent, my mother leaned on me for companionship and emo-tional support. She didn't get along with her own mother very well, and after her father died, we moved to New York City so that she could find a better job and I could go to better schools. But I was turning twelve and changing. Later she told me how hard it was for her to feel me pulling away emotionally, responding to many of her statements with an irony-tinged complaint: "Oh, Mother, really!" I guess it was at this time that I stopped calling her Mom or Mommy and switched to "Mother," which is the way I referred to her ever after that.

Shortly before I was ready for college, my father, whose alcoholism was seri-ously affecting his ability to make a living, reneged on his alimony payments. My mother responded by trying to sue him. I could see what dire straits it put her in; fortunately I got a big scholarship which assured my education. But I also knew what bad shape my father was in. I did not then have the social skills to bridge the warring worlds of my parents. I suffered and felt angry at my mother and both angry at and sorry for my father. I was estranged from him by this conflict, but also, I think, by his disease.

When I got married at the age of 24, he wrote and said he wanted to come to the wedding. I did not have the strength to deal with such a tense meeting and responded that we would come to see him as soon as we could. But we never got the chance. He died a few months later of an apparent heart attack. When my mother called me to tell me, she was in tears and I realized that she had never let go of him.

Looking back now, I can see how guilty I felt about choosing a mate and a life of my own. But I was stubbornly insistent that I had a right to my own life. We moved all the way across the country so my husband could go to school and then we were sent to Japan for two years so he could finish a tour of duty with the Navy. I hardly heard a word from my mother in those two years…rarely a letter, never a phone call, certainly not a visit. I don't remember thinking about her too much.

The day we arrived back in the states, she called me at our hotel to say that she had lost her job some months before and was down to her last $500. Needless to say, I was angry and upset. Of course we sent her some money. We were on our way to Vermont where my husband was going to do a three year residency. I got an office job working at the State employment agency. My mother moved out of her apartment, put her Cairn terrier in her car, and moved into a motel not too far from us. We gave her money to supplement some temporary jobs she found. I felt stifled, and also ashamed that I did not have the skill to deal with her more directly and more compassionately. One of my colleagues at work was able to help her find a professional job and gradually she got back on her feet. She found a house to rent and spent time fixing it up.

My husband finished his training and we moved to the other end of the state so that he could start a permanent job himself. My relationship with my mother improved dramatically with the birth of our first child. I remember that she drove a couple of hours south to see him on his first day and was the first to point out the dimple in his chin. Within a few months she turned 62, quit her job, and moved to be near us. She loved taking care of this first infant and then the one that was born three years later. I found this a big help. She needed extra money to supplement her retirement benefits, but my husband was earning a good salary and it didn't seem too burdensome to us. When her old car wore out, we gave her ours. I have to say that I was happy to be able to help her out and grateful to my husband for not complaining about it. After all, she was helping me as well.

Over the next ten years, my mother's health gradually declined. Hard as she tried, she could not give up her fifty-year dependence on cigarettes. And though she had always encouraged me to take care of my body and get plenty of exercise, she did not follow her own advice. By her early 70s, she could do less and less. She moved from her rented house into a subsidized apartment. "This is probably the last place I will lay my head," she commented as she moved in. I responded awkwardly as usual. In fact, I think I said, "Oh Mother, really." We had just never been good at finding the words to talk about momentous topics such as loving and dying. Her circulation was bad and it was increasingly painful for her to walk. When her doctor told her she had to give up smoking, she gave up going to see the doctor. I remember her telling me around this time that she had a little savings account with $3000 in it to pay for her funeral. She didn't want to be a burden, she said. She was seventy-three. She told me that she did not expect to live past 74, the age at which her beloved father had died. I was embarrassed by these confidences and again, I didn't know what to say. But I understood on a deep level that she was getting ready to die and that I was not quite ready to let her go. I felt vaguely solemn and depressed all summer.

That year I took my annual vacation swim across the lake with a slight cold that turned into pneumonia. It was the sickest I have ever been before or since. My mother-in-law came to take the children to her house and I lay on my couch sleeping for a week. My mother arrived several times a day bearing flowers and soup, or making tea. She would pad into the room tentatively to ask how I was. I didn't realize it until later, but I had gotten her to take care of me one last time.

Shortly after I recovered, I had a very powerful dream. I had an image that somehow I was taking my mother into my body, the reverse of giving birth. She started as a figure, but then ghostlike, dematerialized and swooped into my midsection, perhaps into my womb. I don't quite remember, but when I woke up I realized that I had to go see her right away. I drove down the hill to her apartment and we sat and visited. I didn't describe my dream or talk about anything at all momentous. Instead we discussed how we should celebrate her 74th birthday which was coming up in two weeks. We decided to go out for lunch and then shopping for a new handbag. I knew that was the most she could comfortably manage. I don't remember if we hugged when we said good-bye.

My mother died of a heart attack early the following morning. When she didn't take in her newspaper, a neighbor called the policeman who found her slumped over her kitchen table on top of her crossword puzzle. The policeman called my husband who called me. At first I was shocked, but I soon realized that I had known more than I thought I knew. She had been telling me for six months that she was getting ready to die. Somehow, without words, I believe that I communicated to her finally that I was ready to let her go. And she had waited for that signal. In addition to the upset and the grief, I felt a rush of gratitude for her tact. And I also felt a tremendous awe as I recognized the psychic bond between us. Here all these years I had been struggling with her, angry and resentful. I had never realized how close we really were. Gradually I came to see that I was lucky in my mother's manner of passing. She would have hated having to be sick, hospitalized, fussed over. She slipped out quietly, without words. She exactly chose the manner of her death. At first I complained that I had not had a chance to say goodbye, but then I understood that we had said goodbye in our own subterranean communication. We profoundly, mystically understood each other at the end. And the $3000 she had saved just exactly paid for her funeral.

Parts of my mother still live in me. She had always lavishly praised creative acts, so that now, whenever I sing a song or make a drawing, my self-satisfaction is full of her approval. I appreciate the values she taught me to live by—honesty, loyalty, even tact. (Although I think we are both often too polite for our own good.) I have worked to be more direct than my mother in the expression of my feelings, but even that comes from the bond between us...a kind of reaction to the person she was. And I also feel her in the arranging of flowers, the knitting of sweaters, the smelling of herbs, and the doing of crossword puzzles. Mostly what I feel now is a lot of peace.

A major shift occurs in this daughter's reaction to her mother.

A New Freedom

Christine Olson

My Mother came to visit me a few years ago. I was then a busy Mother myself, with two kids ages 4 and 7. We were in the kitchen together and Mom was help-ing out by sweeping the floor. True to form, she found an opportunity to make a critical comment. It was small. No big deal really. "Gee, Chris, your floor is so dirty." Did I say no big deal? Each time she made one of those little criticisms every nerve in my body went on alert and the old reaction of feeling like I was bad immediately kicked in, followed by my urge to throttle her. But for some rea-son, that wasn't the reaction I had this time. Instead, I greeted her comment with a sense of playfulness, almost glee. "Isn't that great?" I replied with gusto. "That makes it so much more satisfying to clean up!" And I wasn't being the least bit sarcastic. I really meant it.

The fun thing was that this was completely outside my usual pattern and not only was that really a gas for me, I could see that it took Mom totally by surprise. It was subtle, but you could tell that she had lost her bearings for a moment and had to regroup. New territory for both of us.

It's kind of weird really. The whole encounter was just this brief and seem-ingly insignificant, but the amount of freedom that opened for me in that moment was astounding. To bust out with joy and humor and love…to leave a lifetime of icky interactions behind in an instant and have fun doing it. Who ever heard of such a thing? I guess the fact of wanting to write about it proves to me just how memorable this small interaction was. And maybe it has had a lasting effect.

On her last visit (my kids are now 13 and 17) we were sitting down to dinner and as Mom unfolded her cloth napkin she commented with real concern, "Gee, Chris, your napkins are folded wrong side out."

I didn't say anything but inside I felt a big smile spreading through me. "Silly Mom!" I thought to myself. And instead of feeling criticized, I just felt my love for her.

10

Small Miracles

There are awesome shifts that can occur in a relationship as a by-product of unexpected and unwanted occurrences. These are indeed the "silver linings" of the storm clouds. Some of our most dreaded events...Alzheimers, mental illness, the process of dying...can turn out in ways we would never dream of. May these stories of small miracles offer hope to those who may carry fear of the future somewhere in the back of their minds and hearts.

Demeter Backwards

Judith Beth Cohen

1.

Take precautions against eloping patients read the sign on the Psychiatric Unit door.

Mother looked frail in the powder blue outfit that hung off her small frame. Her cheeks sunken, her mouth a puckered hole without her dentures, she greeted me eagerly, gulping back tears. I couldn't predict if I'd find her depressed and hostile, insisting that I wasn't really her daughter, or manic and chatty, giggling for no reason. No longer on Haldol for hallucinations, she was back to anti-depressants, high blood pressure meds and Tagamet for her stomach. Though I'd called ahead for permission to take her out, there was no pass at the nurse's station. Her doctor would have to sign, but his whereabouts were a mystery.

"I phoned from Boston," I explained, as Mother hovered behind me.

"He said I could go," she added.

For over a month she'd been here, alternating between manic highs and severe depression. Now that my father was dead, she had no home to return to, even if she seemed stable. The nurses and aides were distracted by other demanding patients: a woman in a wheelchair howled like a coyote, a black man in striped pajamas dropped a tin cup onto the floor, retrieved it, then dropped it again, enjoying the sound it made. The nurse agreed to find a resident to sign the pass.

"Don't believe a word they say," Mother whispered. "They're all full of crap. Don't you know…it's a madhouse?"

I felt the familiar rush of despair…it wouldn't be all right. Adam, my new live-in boyfriend had insisted that he could deal with my crazy mother, but I had hoped for a smoother beginning. To protect her from the knowledge that we were "living in sin," I had fabricated a wedding. Though I might be divorced and over forty, I couldn't add one more irrational worry to her long list.

"It was a very small ceremony," I explained over the telephone, "with only two friends as witnesses." I named a date so we'd know when to celebrate, then I purchased a wedding band, and we flew to Detroit so Mother could meet my new "husband." Her brother Si, the partriarch of her family, a tiny, wiry man who still practiced law at eighty-six, had warned me against taking her out on a pass, but I visited so rarely.

"Hello Evelyn." Adam gave Mother a generous hug as if seeing her for the first time on a mental ward was an ordinary event. "It's so good to meet you," he bubbled musically, his greeting nearly a song.

I watched her as if she were my child, wanting to feed her the right lines, wishing I could climb inside her brain and make it work right. My breath suspended, I waited…would our presence have a transforming effect?

"It's nice to have a son-in-law," she said, though she might just as easily have accused him of being an imposter who meant to harm me. Relieved, I worked at breathing again as they carried on a polite conversation in the dayroom. She asked about the flight, and where we were staying. Had we seen her brother yet? The TV blared soap operas while an old woman mumbled and gestured at the air.

"That one's crazy." Mother pointed, making no effort to lower her voice.

The nurse beckoned me…her doctor had appeared. I could speak with him in his office. Alone, I went to meet the expert, an Israeli psychiatrist, head of this research unit where she'd been sent after all the other hospitals had failed. The Institute was supposed to be doing cutting edge experimental work on geriatric mood disorders. He questioned me about her history, as if she'd just arrived. Where were those records that went along as she moved from Ypsilanti to Harper to University Hospital to Kingswood, St. Mary's, Botsford, that long list of clinics that had treated her?

"I don't know why she's not responding," he shrugged and I noticed his muscular arms, and very blue eyes. He could have been one of those mythical Israeli freedom fighters straight out of the movie *Exodus*.

"Can you tell me anything that might help me?"

As I searched for clues, a piece of history he may have missed, my spirits drooped even further; another expert with no answers, one more specialist who wasn't special. How I wanted to believe this place would be different, that after all the moving from hospitals to group homes, that she was lucky to land here. He could try one more drug, he said, but if that didn't work, he was out of ideas. There was electroshock, but they'd have to move her for that; they didn't do shock treatment here. Our brief interview over, I rejoined Mother and Adam with the pass. She'd been freed, at least for the day.

"He's good looking isn't he?" Mother said, as if she read my face.

"Yes," I admitted.

"Did he make love to you?"

"What?" I looked at Adam wondering if I'd heard her correctly.

"Did he make love to you?" she repeated. "He tries it with everyone."

The nurses and aides within earshot exchanged nervous grins. Then Mother was on her feet, rushing toward the door.

"Let's go, let's get out of this place. I can't take it one minute longer."

We drove over the bridge to Belle Isle and wandered through the greenhouse and the gardens. This part of Detroit had been foreign territory when I was growing up...not where Jews had lived. My father would drive out here alone, to think. Looking back at the city skyline put some distance between him and his troubles, but he wouldn't take us here..."too dangerous," he always said.

We bought ice cream cones. Mother's melted before she could finish it. Adam snapped a picture of us: Mother and daughter, cheeks touching, her hair still nearly as dark as mine. Chocolate stained the collar of her white-piped blue jersey, a dress made for a suburban golfing life she'd never lived.

On the ride back to the clinic, I thought of Uncle Si's warning and braced myself, expecting a struggle. From the backseat of the rented Ford, she startled us with an announcement:

"I'm changing my name—from Evelyn to Eve."

"Why?" I wondered.

She giggled like a mischievous child with a plan.

"Because they're using my name," she continued. "You've heard of The Purple Gang, haven't you?"

I remembered allusions to the notorious Jewish gangsters active in the twenties.

"They're calling themselves The Evelyn Berman Gang, so I'm going to be Eve Miller instead."

Adam tried to suppress his spontaneous laugh, then he surrendered. It was infectious; I joined him, giggling helplessly. Soon Mother chimed in, laughing with us, as pleased as if she'd deliberately made a joke.

At the unit door, she thanked us for lunch, and wished us a good trip home to Boston.

"He's a good catch," she whispered, pointing at Adam, smiling her full approval.

2.

Nothing about my fifties childhood would have appeared abnormal or unsafe: two parents, mother home baking cookies, Dad's lawyer's income adequate, lots of family values in our synagogue-attending-holiday-celebrating household. Our brick house sat on a Detroit tree-lined street in a neighborhood that hadn't yet turned "dangerous," but behind the picture window and the tall blue spruce,

Mother's mental illness took center stage and rendered my father, my younger sister and I bit players with no script to follow. One day I had an energetic Mommy redecorating the house, inviting strangers home for supper, filling the car with packages we'd never open. A few days later she would refuse food; unable to rise from her bed, she'd lay curled into a fetal position, nearly catatonic. Then she would be hospitalized and I'd take over, her disease stealing my childhood.

The early signals, I was too young to interpret: at four, I became a big sister, and must have sensed the weight of Mother's new responsibilities. One day I found a shiny, round object, slipped it on my finger and stood cooing at my baby sister, smiling through the bars of her crib, showing off. I held up my ringed finger, proof of my maturity. But the "ring" wouldn't come off. My mother pulled at it and soaped it, but it wouldn't budge. As the sharp metal began to carve into my flesh, I began wailing, then the baby screamed and Mother panicked. She couldn't reach my father so she phoned her brother Si's law office, too upset to speak clearly. Suddenly, fire trucks screamed outside our house. Soon this ring of huge men in black rubber coats and boots were sitting cross-legged on our livingroom floor, passing me from lap to lap, each one trying to remove the metal band, while my mother wept. In the midst of the crisis, a rescuer arrived: superman at the door, Uncle Si accompanied by his dentist friend. With just the right steel shears, he cut the metal bolt and freed my finger. The firemen contributed a band-aid from their first aid kit, and Mother pulled herself back together.

In front of the City County building across Jefferson Avenue from the Ford auditorium, they unveiled a statue called *The Spirit of Detroit*. The giant male figure held a family in one hand and the sun in the other. Underneath him the inscription from Corinthians read: *God through the Spirit of man is manifested in the family, the noblest human relationship.* We'd pass him on the way to Daddy's office high up in the Guardian Building, and though the motto wasn't from our Bible, we could have been the family cupped in his palm. The yellow city buses went from our neighborhood near Seven Mile Road through Palmer Park, down Hamilton past Wayne University, further downtown toward the river. Tall buildings lined Woodward Avenue: the J.L. Hudson Company, a massive brick structure with windows full of posed mannikins in fashionable suits and hats, then Crowley's, the department store where mother had worked as an assistant buyer in the hat department before she married.

I imagined her alone after all the customers had left, trying on hats in front of the mirror…hats made from mink, little felt scallops with tight fitting veils, wide-brimmed straw models decorated with molded fruit and flowers. In my version she would look in the mirror, knowing those hats looked better on her than any of her customers. I pictured her boss as a Lauren Bacall figure in a slinky split skirt, holding a cigarette holder, training my mother to be her protegée, to go to the shows in New York, to fly to Paris and watch models slink down the runway, then pick her favorite hats to sell to Detroit matrons. It gave me such hope for her…if she could have held such a job, then surely she could be different.

"Downtown" was an evocative phrase, a destination, a place I yearned to be, grown-up and frightening. The tunnel to Windsor carried us under the river to an exotic world. For only a toll, we could visit a foreign country where our dollar bought more. At the Elmwood Casino we could watch a floor show with a live band; a roving photographer would snap our picture, just as they did in New York City. Uncle Si would take us to The London Chop House or Joe Muer's. Their fish was packed in ice, rushed onto a plane, and flown in from the Atlantic ocean, so we could eat it the day it was caught. That's how fresh it was, they said, and so many varieties: red snapper and scrod, perch and haddock, flounder and swordfish, difficult to choose. At our table there would be a debate: was swordfish kosher or was it a shellfish and therefore taboo? The rabbis disagreed about it, but Daddy played it safe…rabbis could make mistakes.

Uncle Si would order me Shirley Temples, then he'd correct my manners: "Don't talk with food in your mouth. Don't your parents teach you? Chew with your mouth closed." I would look to my parents for signals…would they defend me?

"She's just seven, just a little girl," I longed to hear, but the critical words hung over me, a polluting vapor, suggesting that these parents of mine were inadequate, failing when it came to etiquette, just as Daddy failed to collect from his clients. "Herb doesn't charge enough. He's a pushover," my mother would repeat; it's what she heard from her brother, Si, the successful lawyer. He wasn't like my father, who would rather sleep late than rush downtown to compete. "Mr. Nice Guy," they mocked him. I knew he took care of his older half-brothers from his father's first family: Uncle Ed, a bartender nicknamed Tillie, who marched with the Veterans and hated the democrats, Uncle Lester, a retired printer, a bachelor union man who lived in a residential hotel. And there were his own brothers. Sammy, the younger one, carried a gun on his beat collecting insurance payments in rough neighborhoods; Irving counted on Dad for a daily ride downtown to Simmons & Clark Jewelers, where he'd worked as a salesman all his life. Daddy was the only one to finish school, the only professional, the one they all leaned on, and for that he was faulted by mother's "mishpoha" (family.)

From them, I learned to measure and judge, rate, rank and compare, and I applied those lessons to myself.

When I was nine, I lingered after school to finish my science project: a "Ming Garden" intended as a birthday gift for Mother. I imagined that my scrawny, pale tree might make her rise from her heap on the couch. The dwarfed twig seemed hunched and graceless as I labored, rearranging the moss, trying to turn my creation into a magical oriental garden. I didn't notice the passing time or the school emptying as my little sister waited obediently. Frustrated, I put my unfnished project back on the shelf...it would have to wait. With my sister's hand in mine, I headed home along Outer Drive. When we crossed the large intersection alone, the afternoon sky was beginning to darken.

Mother stood a vigil at the door, her eyes so wild, her mouth so contorted, I knew something terrible must have happened...someone must be dead. So panicked, she could barely speak, she paced, wrung her hands and wept. I soon discovered that the problem was all me, that my dallying with the garden had created this crisis, that it was my death she had foreseen. That day I learned of my power to hurt her, and from then on protecting her from despair and guarding her fragile sanity became my most important life task, more crucial than making gardens.

3.

A phone call from my Uncle Si interrupted my Sunday birdwatching. I'd been trying to spot the elusive Great Blue Herons who lived on our marsh.

He didn't take time for pleasantries. "You must come and get your mother," he said. "She's been in that Institution a year; it's no more than a warehouse, and I'm too old to deal with her."

As I listened, our serene view became just another illusion. Down the river sat the Quincy shipyard, its large crane at rest, no more aircraft carriers in need of repair. Nearby, the Old Edgar Edison plant was dormant, shut down, so filled with asbestos that even demolition would be too dangerous. Just like my marriage story, our tranquil marshland was not what it seemed.

I summoned my arguments, prepared to go head to head against my uncle, the "prosecutor:" "She's being taken care of. You don't need to deal with her. There's no better place for her here in Boston...I know, I've inquired. It would be harmful to take her away. She was born there, she's spent her whole life there."

Friends had regaled me with horror stories of other women's care-taking burdens, but I couldn't say no. I couldn't let the ward door slam and fly back east as I had on countless visits. Reluctantly, I launched a search. I visited nursing homes and boarding houses for released mental patients. I made phone calls to therapists and social workers. No one was encouraging.

In one bedlam-like Boston institution screaming patients lined the hallways. The young social worker led me into her office. She understood my problem…she knew places for the elderly mentally ill were scarce. She'd do what she could to get my mother in here, but even with private pay at $150 a day, it would be difficult to move her from another state. Was fighting for a bed in that unspeakable hell-hole amongst the glassy stares, the plaintive whimpers, the head banging, the best I could do?

Dispirited after many visits, I sought comfort in the view out my window. Off in the tall grass, I spotted a Great Blue Heron standing motionless, all attention, a sentry on guard. I wondered: was he leaving for winter, on his way to a warmer nesting ground? Did Herons make this their permanent residence? After so much wandering myself, living in Vermont, in Boston, on Cape Cod, I couldn't be sure where Adam and I might settle. What would I do with Mother if we moved again?

4.

For Mother's eightieth birthday, I ordered a cake covered with pink and purple sugar-spun roses. The baker who pushed the color scheme called it "very feminine." She also advised against putting numbers on the frosting. How could she know that I needed to broadcast Mother's milestone, as proud as I would be of a daughter turning thirteen, yet I have neither daughters nor sons; my mother has become my only child. After thirty years spent keeping a safe thousand miles between us, she's come to live five minutes from my house, and it seems as if Hades has returned her from the underworld.

As I watched her baffling change unfold, I kept my guard up, expecting more of the same. In her new studio apartment facing Quincy Bay, I helped her unpack. When she undressed, I averted my eyes, trying not to stare at her protruding belly, her boney arms and legs, her curving spine. I worked to block out my image of her, freshly committed to a state hospital, tearing off her clothes and running naked down the grey corridors until they caught her and put her in restraints. Instead I pictured her modeling for her Hadassah chapter's annual fund-raiser. From the front row, I watched her, more beautiful than the other mothers, so svelte and lovely, her bare shoulders alluring in a swishy cocktail dress.

Once she settled into her new apartment, Mother began wearing her teeth. Putting those dentures back into her head seemed to signify a passage. She would now bite and chew; she would seize hold of life. The crises stopped…no more raging manic episodes; no paranoid outbursts with Mother insisting someone had broken into the kitchen and replaced all the food with jello, no more refusals to speak with me, no more depressed withdrawals.

Her voice on the phone is cheerful: "Have you read the *Globe* today? Did you hear about the man who kept a Haitian woman a slave in his house? She couldn't even speak English, poor thing." She decorates her studio apartment, makes friends, turns out vases and figurines in ceramics, and even writes a humor column for the residents' newsletter. As her life stabilized, we reinvented our mother/daughter relationship, transforming it in the process. I became her driver, her go-between in disagreements with her ceramics teacher, but contrary to my fears, it has been no grim nightmare. Celebrating her eightieth birthday together was something I would have done almost anything short of matricide to avoid, but she's no longer the helpless depressive or the raving paranoid, but simply an eccentric old lady. Through some mysterious process, she has emerged from the intractable psychosis that had all her doctors baffled.

When I surprised her at lunch, she sat in the sun-filled dining room of the Bay View Retirement Community, dressed in a smart blue blazer I'd helped her buy years ago. She'd planned on wearing it to synagogue services, but the jacket hung in her closet forgotten through many breakdowns.

She blew out her candles and the room full of seniors sang "Happy Birthday."

As I watched her unwrap her gift, her face caught the winter light and seemed to glow. She held up the pomegranate jeweled sweater for all to admire.

"It's beautiful…it must have cost you a fortune," she said.

"You know me, I always find bargains," I told her.

"I hope I look as good as you do when I'm eighty," the waitress said as she kissed Mother's cheek.

These days, as friends journey long distances to visit ailing parents, I stay put, enjoying those Herons who return each year to rebuild their old nests on the wetlands behind our house. In her apartment five minutes away, Mother tends the plants that now fill her room: tumbling ferns, delicate violets and flowering azaleas. I'm humbled by the resilience of our bond. In our backwards mother-daughter story, I'm like Demeter, whose daughter Persephone returned from the underworld for half the year. Now together and more whole, we watch the gardens bloom again, if only for a season.

Mother Love

Aloha Maxine Brown

As Loolie maneuvered the little car to the nursing home, my eyes absorbed the changes that had taken place in this Midwestern city where I had spent my turbulent teens. Loolie's voice pierced my reverie.

"You gave her financial support for years. I know that was hard for you."

How different we were! Loolie had been put in bed with me when she was three months old. I had virtually become a mother at ten. With blonde hair and blue-green eyes, I was the spitting image of Mother's first husband. Loolie reflected her father's heritage in her brown hair and very brown eyes.

"Loolie, did you think about motherhood when you had Randy and Nicky?"

"What do you mean?" she asked.

"When I became a mother, I lay with each of my three babies and thought and thought about the kind of mothering we had had and the kind I wanted to give my children. She never praised me after she married your daddy when I was eight. Why, Loolie?"

Loolie frowned. "Okay, she looked at you and saw your father's face."

"That's not fair!" I blurted.

"Your father was the only one she ever really loved. My daddy held her sexual attention." Loolie said as she laughed.

"We didn't talk about the important things."

"I know, Sissie."

Loolie pulled into the parking lot and parked the car. We disconnected our seat belts, adjusted our bras, and emerged from the car.

Loolie explained, "Some things you just can't change, Sissie. You have to learn to accept that. You're a changer. Well, you can't change Alzheimer's."

We headed for the entrance. Air came rushing out to welcome us, pure institutional air. Loolie and I smiled at the residents who were in the corridor as we passed by.

We turned left and passed three open doorways. Finally, she paused by the fourth doorway.

"Oh, good. Mother's awake. Hi, toots!"

The small body in the bed did not move. "Who is this stranger pretending to be our mother?" I thought silently.

Without a moment's hesitation, I swallowed and moved rapidly to the bed. I took Mother's hand and kissed it. Mother had such feminine, soft hands. I saw those perfect eyebrows which never needed plucking and those big, blue eyes. Mother's hair was slightly sprinkled with gray, and the skin on her face was free of the wrinkling of her seventy years. She looked like a commercial for an elixir cream. I had been told she had feeling but did not understand pleasure or pain.

"Are you sure she can't understand anything?" I asked Loolie.

"The doctors say she is almost brain dead except she still has the reflex action for swallowing which keeps her off machines."

"When did she stop being able to talk?"

"Several years ago."

"And she can't move her torso or arms and legs?"

"No, that went years ago, also. They massage her regularly so her muscles don't atrophy. They're very good to her here."

After a few minutes, Loolie asked me, "Shall we order lunch?"

"Do the three of us eat the same kind of lunch?" I wondered aloud.

"We'd order out if they did. No, they have a separate menu for relatives and guests. That is, unless you plan to insist on eating what Mother eats." Loolie's brown eyes twinkled. "Let me order our lunches. Be right back." Loolie left.

I went into the bathroom after checking that Mother's blanket was in place and that she was warm. I washed my face and stared at myself in the mirror. I had buried these feelings for so long. Could I wash them away like my tears?

Loolie bounced into the room. "The trays are on their way. I have to go and complete the forms for the county, state, and federal. Usually, they send the forms to the house. You can start eating. I better feed Mother because she chokes easily, and I know what to do."

I assured, "No, I'll wait for you. We'll eat together...all three of us."

I pulled a chair over to the bed. It was difficult to believe that there was no thought behind those clear, alert eyes. Mother's eyes were still her best feature. Suddenly, I began a low, continuous monologue with Mother.

"Why did you never tell me that I was pretty? All daughters want to hear that, whether it's true or not. Was it fair to point out what was wrong with my nose and say it was like my father's and his family? Sitting there was your child with blue-green eyes and every day you said how beautiful Loolie's brown eyes were because you preferred dark brown eyes. What kind of a mother would say that aloud with her two girls? How could you do that to me? When I was seven and that lady opened a dance studio and was giving tap dancing lessons for fifty cents, Aunt Flossie who was single and didn't have any children offered to pay for my lessons, and you forbade her because you decided the lessons were foolishness so it was a waste of her money. I wanted to learn to tap dance so badly I could taste it. How dare you make those choices for me and her! Well, I learned to tap dance, and people paid to see me dance. Why did I have to practice with Pa-Pa's violin way down by the outhouse so all the neighbors had to hear but not you? Why did we have only two books in the house, an out-dated almanac and a used dictionary which someone gave me? Yet, you subscribed to *Photoplay* and those movie magazines which I read in desperation for something to read besides the five book limit from our small library."

The tears flowed freely. As I droned on, anger from all those years spewed from me, dissipating until it was gone. Mother didn't have to answer for me to feel the catharsis within me, the cleansing catharsis washing away the impurities.

Loolie's voice came from the doorway. "Here are our trays. I timed it just right."

Loolie fed Mother, chattering as she spooned the soft food into her mouth. I thought how much I loved Loolie. She was a wonderful mother herself. I realized that to Mother's generation love took the forms of providing shelter, food, and clothing. There wasn't time for much else. Hadn't she been there through all the childhood diseases…before the days of vaccines? Who taught us what organization was? What about all the homilies that were true…like "It's nothing to be ashamed of to be poor, but it's shameful to be dirty"? I began to remember how Mother loved Christmas, and how there was always a doll. That must have been difficult some years. I realized that love has many facets. It's like a prism, diffusing its light with each different move.

After Loolie fed Mother, she and I ate. There was an unvoiced sense of family as the three of us shared the room.

Loolie told me that enough time had passed that Mother's bodily functions had worked and we must change her and wash her. Willingly, we gently removed the smelly pad from under Mother, trying to keep her from becoming chilled. Mother's body was almost devoid of flesh. Loolie got wet cloths and drying towels from the bathroom. In the process of cleansing Mother, we became the mothers as we tenderly but efficiently without complaints cared for her. Then, Mother fell asleep, and we slipped out quietly to sit on the bench in front.

When we returned and Mother was awake, Loolie checked her watch. "We better leave. Say goodbye to Mother, Sissie."

I caressed Mother's face as tears flowed down mine.

"I love you, little lady. Please remember me…remember!"

I was beginning to shout. Mother had been greatly hearing impaired before the Alzheimer's had taken effect.

"Mother, it's Maxine! *Maxine!*" I shouted. "Calvin's girl! *Calvin!* Calvin's Maxine!!!"

A light came into Mother's eyes.

"See? She knows what I mean!"

"No, she's responding because you're shouting!"

Suddenly, Mother raised her left arm, grabbed my shirtwaist, and pulled me to her. Slowly, painfully, her mouth formed my name.

She stared at my face, focusing her eyes or trying to focus. Loolie and I were sobbing hysterically.

Meanwhile, Mother tried to form words. Finally, she was successful.

"Maaaac...seen! Maaaac...seen!" She dropped her arm and fell back into her pillow, exhausted. Soon, she was asleep from the exertion.

Loolie and I were clinging to each other. Without talking, we tucked Mother into the covers and left.

The next morning, I was on a plane for New York. I had a peace within. Later in time I returned for Mother's memorial service, a loving tribute where I delivered the eulogy. Now, I tell my grandchildren funny stories about their wonderful great-grandmother.

Some Final Words

A Cry From the Heart

From earliest childhood, every daughter needs and wants her mother to be the ideal woman that the daughter rightly deserves: wise, loving, smart, competent, confident, strong, expressive yet capable of restraint and discretion, deeply feeling while at the same time optimistic and upbeat, holding high expectations yet completely accepting (clearly, to be all of this is almost impossible). Daughters need their mothers to demonstrate to them that it is safe to be a fully-dimensional human being.

Once daughters have navigated the adolescent struggle to feel their own independence and uniqueness, some may start to fight with their mothers in a new way. They will notice where aspects of their mothers' wholeness have strayed out of sight, and they will demand that their mothers reclaim the parts of themselves that have been abandoned or forgotten.

This fight comes from deep love and concern and also from deep yearning. It is a much more sophisticated expression of the two year old's urgent cry: "I want my Mommy!!" It can be brutal, or it can be polite; it can be explicit or it can be in code; but the message is the same: "I love you and I demand that you be the woman that I know you really are."

Mothers of the world, when you encounter this fight, no matter how confusing or upsetting it is, murmur, "Thank you for telling me", because only your children will do that for you; then listen, reflect and learn what you can.

Daughters of the world, don't give up unless and until you've tried many different approaches (if you keep trying the same one over and over, and it doesn't work, you're being a bit obstinate). If you see that she really can't engage, then it may be time to accept that she's doing the best she can and your energy would be better employed elsewhere.

The Impact of Mothers on Daughters

We mothers feel so often that we have little influence on our daughters, as they grow to be adolescents and adults. We wish they would heed our advice and our warnings, our alarms, our experience, our intuitions about what is best for them.

We feel helpless to guide them any further. They have become headstrong, impatient for their own experiences, impatient with our intrusions into their quest for adventure, for love, for freedom. They want to swallow the world, and we want to caution them against indigestion.

Our daughters' determination to move in their own direction under their own steam blinds us to a glaring reality...we have had a huge impact on them, just by being their mothers. They absorbed our entire way of being in the world with every breath they took, from the moment they were born. That awesome drive to be on their own way is not a sign of our invisibility...on the contrary, it is a loud declaration that our impact has been so powerful, that to discover who *they* are and what is *their* unique way of being in the world takes fierce energy and single-minded focus.

Daughters seek their distinct place in the universe in many different ways: by fighting with us, by ignoring us, by challenging us, by questioning us, by sneering at us, by cutting us off, by distancing from us, by doing everything opposite from us; at the same time, they may also emulate us, love us, listen to us, ask our advice, become our friends and colleagues, even become dependent on us.

But, Mothers, do not be fooled. Your impact has been monumental. Be compassionate towards your daughter's goal, even if you do not like her means of getting there.

All of us, mothers and daughters alike, have a lifelong task—here are two similar descriptions of it from two disparate sources:

The Gnostic Gospel:
    If you bring forth what is within you
    What you bring forth will save you
    If you do not bring forth what is within you
    What you do not bring forth will destroy you

The poet Rumi:
    There is a light seed grain inside.
    You fill it with yourself, or it dies!

Author Bios

Gina Bacon is a freelance writer based near Portland, Oregon. When she's not writing for fun and/or profit, Gina and her husband stay busy raising their two sons.

Catherine Bamji grew up in South Carolina, worked in the banking industry and finally as a trainer and facilitator for a Maryland consulting company. Now as full-time mother and wife, Cathy lives in Silver Spring, MD and writes at a local cafe in her spare time.

Margaret B. Blackman—Margaret B. Blackman, a cultural anthropologist specializing in the Arctic, has recently completed a collection of essays about the village of Anaktuvuk Pass, Alaska. She teaches Anthropology at SUNY Brockport and is the author of two life histories of Native American women, published by the University of Washington Press.

Deborah Bogen is a Pittsburgh poet and fiction writer whose work has been widely published in poetry journals, anthologies and magazines.

Aloha Brown—Aloha had undergraduate and graduate training in theater at Bowling Green University in Ohio. Professional training was in Manhattan. After a career in theater, she taught English for twenty years and raised three children. Retired, Aloha began to write. In 1989, Bantam Books published her adaptation of *Hedda Gabler* in an anthology, *Six Major Tragedies*. Her writings have been published nationally and abroad.

Nancy Bunge is a Professor in the Department of American Thought and Language at Michigan State University. She has published two books and about forty shorter pieces in books and periodicals, including *The Washington Post, The San Francisco Review of Books, The American Poetry Review* and *Poets & Writers Magazine*.

June Calender, born and educated in Indiana, lives in New York City. She gave up playwrighting to write essays and a vast based-on-fact novel, research for which produced her travelogue, *Phantom Voices in Tibet*. She has two daughters and three grandchildren. She loves traveling, alone or otherwise.

Elayne Clift, a writer in Saxtons River, VT, teaches at several New England colleges and universities. Her latest book is *Love Letters to Vermont: A New England Journal* (*OGN Publications*, 2001). Her second anthology, *Escaping the Yellow Wallpaper: Women's Encounters with the Mental Health Establishment* was published in 2002 by *Haworth Press*.

Ann Clizer lives in the backwoods of Northern Idaho, where she operates a construction business with her husband. Ann enjoys hiking, kayaking and playing in the dirt with her grandchildren. Her essays, articles and stories have appeared in a variety of regional and national publications.

Judith Beth Cohen—Professor at Lesley University, Cambridge, Mass. Author of *Seasons*, a novel, *The Permanent Press*, 1984. Stories in many journals including *The Larcom Review*, *The Best of Rosebud*, *The North American Review*. Currently completing a memoir on mother's mental illness. Book reviews in *The Women's Review of Books*.

Maril Crabtree is a writer, energy healer, and environmental educator who draws constant inspiration from grandchildren Jamie, Jessica, and Penelope. She is author of *Sacred Messengers: The Power of Feathers to Change Your Life* and her poems and essays have been published in a number of journals, magazines, and anthologies.

Susan Crane lives and writes in Boulder, Colorado. Her poetry and essays have been widely published in a variety of literary journals and magazines. She is a former columnist for *The Denver Post* and is currently completing a book-length collection of essays surrounding a theme of domestic violence.

Sally DeFreitas grew up on a farm in Michigan, traveled widely, and then returned to her roots. She worked as a registered nurse until 1998, when she became a correspondent for the *Muskegon Chronicle*. Her poetry has been published in several small magazines. She has one daughter, who is the subject of her story.

Susan DeFreitas

Gelia Dolcimascolo is a Writing Lab Assistant and Facilitator of *The Writers Circle* at Georgia Perimeter College in Atlanta. Her poems have been published in *Poets, Artists & Madmen*; *bluemilk*; *Dancing Shadow Review*; *Mediphors*; *The Forum*; and the *Atlanta Journal-Constitution*, as well as *Adagio* and *Encore!*, two poetry chapbooks she coauthored.

Kathryn Dunn lives in Massachusetts with her husband and children. She is a writer, teacher, and organizational consultant. Her work has been published in literary journals including *Exquisite Corpse*, *the minnesota review*, and *Peregrine*; as well as in *Yankee Magazine* and two anthologies.

Karen Ethelsdatter's poems and liturgies, including interfaith celebrations, particularly affirm women and the feminine presence of God. In addition to a number of poems which have appeared in anthologies and magazines, she has published two full-length volumes of poetry, *Earthwalking & Other Poems* (Xlibris, ©2001) and *Thou Art a Woman & Other Poems* (Xlibris, ©2002), as well as two chapbooks, *The Cat Poems* and *Woman Artists & Woman as Art*.

Elizabeth Feidelson is 11 years old. She plans on becoming a screenwriter, and perhaps an actress. She loves writing stories, plays and poems in her spare time. She also likes to play her drums, dance, and listen to rock and roll. This is her very first publication, and she hopes it will not be her last! Elizabeth lives in Brookline, Massachusetts, with her family, friends, and dog.

Maureen Tolman Flannery, author of *Secret of the Rising Up: Poems of Mexico* and *Remembered Into Life*, is an award-winning poet published in over a hundred journals and anthologies. She edited the acclaimed anthology *Knowing Stones: Poems of Exotic Places*. Maureen lives in Chicago with her actor husband Dan and their four children, all of whom provide much poetic inspiration.

Christina Gibbons is an independent scholar who writes essays and reviews and has co-edited a volume on word and image in comics. She is currently developing a lecture on the female reader in art, which combines the histories of women's literacy and book making through the ages.

Kendeyl Johansen's work has appeared in *Woman's World*, *Baby Years* and *Pregnancy*. She lives in Utah with her Norwegian husband and three sons.

Fran Moreland Johns is a San Francisco-based freelance writer, mother of three and grandmother of four. Author of the nonfiction book *Dying Unafraid* (Synergistic Press, 1999), Johns' articles and short stories have appeared in local and national newspapers, magazines and online sites. *The Conversation* first appeared on Beliefnet.com.

Gwyn Johnson

Kimara Glaser Kirschenbaum—Adopted from S. Korea as an infant. Born and raised in upstate NY. Attended Johns Hopkins University majoring in psychology and anthropology. Studied abroad in Italy and Korea. Currently applying to medical schools with a future goal of working in the field of international and relief healthcare.

Ann Leamon writes by the sea in Connecticut. She has degrees in economics and German and an employment history that ranges from economic analyst to pastry chef with detours through bicycle mechanic and strategic planner. She lives with her dog in a 90-year-old cottage whose roof she and her mother will shingle next summer. She has begun competing in triathlons and may even start training for them.

Marjorie Maddox, professor of Literature and Writing at Lock Haven University, has published one book, *Perpendicular As I*, winner of the 1994 Sandstone Poetry Award, four chapbooks, and over two hundred and fifty poems in literary journals. She is the 2001 Paumanok Poetry Award recipient. She lives in Williamsport, PA, with her husband and two small children.

Jean McGroarty lives in Battle Ground, Indiana, with her husband, Dave, daughters Nora and Haley, and son Charles. She works at the Tippecanoe County Humane Society in Lafayette, Indiana, as Director of Education. She also teaches writing and composition at a local community college.

Meredith Morgenstern, a Miami native, is a member of the International Women's Writing Guild. She now makes her living as a freelance and short story writer in New York City. She has written articles and short stories for *Morbid*

Outlook.com, The Pink Chameleon, Dovetail, and *Careers and the DisABLED* magazine.

Mimi Moriarty is the producer and host of *Write Stuff,* a cable access TV program, and a columnist for the Albany, NY weekly *Evangelist.* She runs with wild women writers, and is a fixture every summer at the *Pyramid Lake Women Writer's Retreat.*

Nomi Kluger-Nash—Ph.D. is a Mother and Daughter who followed three lively careers before fulfilling an early promise made to herself to study at the Jung institute. She is currently a psycho-therapist and writer, dividing her time between the city of Jerusalem and the woods of Massachusetts…looking forward to her next incarnation as Grandma.

Christine Olson grew up in a family of five children. Her mother was an active homemaker and her father was an Air Force officer. Her main passions, music and movement, weave throughout her life in various forms. Currently she lives with her husband and two children in Massachusetts and teaches the Alexander Technique.

Stephanie B. Palladino writes poetry, fiction and non-fiction. Her work has been published in the following anthologies: *Detours II: Fiction of Travel by Land, Air, Sea and Mind, Jewish Mothers Tell Their Stories: Acts of Love and Courage,* and *Ophelia's Mom,* released this month. In 2002, her essay *Using Intuition to Find My Way* will be published in the anthology *Counselors Finding Their Way.* By profession she is a school counselor. She lives in Amherst, MA with two of her three daughters and her husband.

Anita Paltrinieri considers herself very lucky, as she has almost always made the right choices. Since an early age she wanted mostly to travel to and live in different countries. So she studied…and still does…languages and picked up journalism as a profession that took her many places. When not travelling, she lives in a small cottage in Umbria, otherwise known as "the green heart of Italy". Lucky her.

Diane Payne—I live in rural Arkansas with my nine-year-old daughter and our dogs. Even though we've been here one year, we still feel a bit of cultural shock. I teach Writing at the University of Arkansas-Monticello.

Annette Peizer: I write freelance articles, poetry, and most recently, children's literature, and have been published in various local and national publications including: *The Seattle PI, Visions International, Parents, Washington English Journal* and *Seattle's Child.* I currently teach high school Creative Writing courses through the Seattle School District. Formerly a single mother, I live in Seattle, Washington with my 5 year old daughter and newly-wed husband.

Jean Quinn—I am a published poet and photographer and write book reviews and articles for several area newspapers as well as teach a course in memoir writing. I have five children and twelve grandchildren and live in the foothills of the Poconos with my dog, Lady. When I'm not writing I'm boating, reading or gardening.

Elisavietta Ritchie's books include: *In Haste I Write You This Note: Stories; Raking The Snow* (co-winners, Washington Writers' Publishing House awards); *Flying Time: Stories* (4 PEN Syndicated Fiction winners); *The Arc Of The Storm; Elegy For The Other Woman; Tightening the Circle Over Eel Country* (won Great Lakes Colleges Association's "New Writer's Award"); *Awaiting Permission To Land* (won Anamnesis award).

Janine Roberts is a professor in the School Counseling and Social Justice Programs at the University of Massachusetts, Amherst, and President of the American Family Therapy Academy. She is the author of *Tales and Transformations: Stories in Families and Family Therapy*, and coauthor of *Rituals for Our Times: Celebrating, Changing, and Healing our Relationships.* She is an avid cross-country skier, pickle ball player, and storyteller.

Barbara A. Rouillard is a teacher and writer from Springfield, MA. Her work has appeared in over eighty-five publications, including *Yankee, Amelia, Midwest Poetry Review, Writer's Journal* and *Byline.* She is the recipient of a NEH Fellowship, and was first place winner in the 1996 Allen Ginsberg Poetry Awards.

Gretchen Scherer's stories have appeared in *Salon.com, The St. Paul Pioneer Press*, and the anthology *Tanzania on Tuesday* (New Rivers Press), which received a Minnesota Book Award. She teaches at the University of Minnesota and the University of St. Thomas and lives in Minneapolis with her husband and son.

Virginia Schnurr—Interest in the word and art has guided my life. I've spent time as a Vista volunteer teaching Spanish-American children to read and encouraging them to paint. I am a trained children's librarian. I wrote a play on Emily Dickinson for use in the elementary school system and spent the last years writing poetry and a novel on lynching.

Barbara Simon is a creative writing teacher for the University of Maryland, Baltimore County. An artist-in-education for the Maryland State Arts Council, she is also president of Maryland State Poetry & Literary Society. She was a 2002 recipient of an individual artist's grant in fiction from the state. Most importantly, she is the mother of a grown daughter/friend Maggie.

Marianne Preger-Simon—Psychotherapist; leads Mother/Daughter workshops and loves mothers and daughters; enjoys drawing, playing Mozart on the piano, dancing, walking; lives with artist-husband and has 6 adult children and step-children and 9 grandchildren.

Rosie Simon—I'm 11 years old, my favorite color is purple, I love to read, visit bookstores, climb trees, sing, write, I love animals, I love my family and my friends. my favorite food is pasta…I'm in a band called *purple candle*…

Dianne Smaniotto—I was born in 1961 in Chicago. My work has recently been published in *A Kiss Is Still A Kiss* and the *Arts Alive! Literary Review*. I am the mother of two children, Tony and Monica, and live in Tinley Park, Illinois, where I am often inspired to write while running.

Kathleen Anne Smith has been astonishing her family as an artist and writer since childhood. By day a government manager, she lives in a cottage with daughter Jane in Loudonville, New York.

Sybil Smith—Fiction and non-fiction has appeared in *The Northern Review, Ithaca Women's Anthology, Spectrum, The Albany Review, Northeast Corridor, Mediphors, Anna's House, Ellipsis, Gulfstream Magazine, Yankee Magazine, Byline, Dartmouth Medicine Magazine, Life On The Line, Ancestry, The Worcester Review, The Connecticut Review, Between The Heartbeats, U.S. Catholic, The Crescent Review, The Larcom Review,* and *The Sun.* Work is upcoming in *Natural Bridge.*

Patti Tana is Professor of English at Nassau Community College and Associate Editor of *The Long Island Quarterly*. Her most recent book includes selections from her 5 earlier books and a section of new poems: *Make Your Way Across This Bridge: New & Selected Writings (Whittier Publications, 2003).*

Grace Tierney

Davi Walders is a writer and education consultant in Chevy Chase, MD. Her poetry and prose have appeared in more than one hundred fifty publications and she is the winner of numerous prizes including a 2001 Maryland State Arts Council grant in Poetry. She developed and directs the *Vital Signs Poetry Project* at the National Institutes of Health and its Children's Inn in Bethesda, MD.

Phyllis Woolf—Farmer, belly dancer, movement therapist, child care teacher and consultant…all my former occupations have barely prepared me for the enormous fun of grandparenting my daughter's splendid new twin boys. Our society's failure to really value children prompts me to work toward change, in my family and in my consulting.

Cherise Wyneken is retired from teaching and raising four children. She lives with her husband in Ft. Lauderdale, FL and has enjoyed sharing her prose and poetry with readers through a variety of journals, periodicals, and anthologies, plus her book of poetry, *Seeded Puffs*, Dry Bones Press, Inc.

Author Index

Author's name and chapter	Title
Johansen, Kendeyl—4	The Rocker
Johns, Fran Moreland—1	The Conversation
Johnson, Gwyn—7	Flying Lessons
Kirschenbaum, Kimara Glaser—2	Talking Things Out
Kluger-Nash—2	Adventuring
Leamon, Anne—6	Feet of Clay
Maddox, Marjorie—6	Fourth Grade Report
McGroarty, Jean L.—6	Talking
Morgenstern, Meredith—6	Car Seats
Moriarty, Mimi—4	Holding the Reins
Olson, Christine—9	A New Freedom
Palladino, Stephanie B.—3	Accident of Time
Paltrinieri, Anita—8	Her Dream Enacted
Payne, Diane—5	The Keyhole
Peizer, Annette—1, 2	Excerpts; That's The Way We Are
Preger-Simon, Marianne—7	You Must Stay
Quinn, Jeanne—2	My Mother/Myself
Ritchie, Elisavietta—6	Marmalade at Midnight
Roberts, Janine—6	A Reminder
Rouillard, Barbara A.—8	How To Let Go of Your Daughter
Scherer, Gretchen—9	Night Visitors and Open Windows
Schnurr, Virginia—5	Children: A Suspect Endeavor
Simon, Barbara M.—3, 8	To a Young Poet; Magic
Simon, Rosie—6	Special Time
Smaniotto, Dianne—8	French Braid
Smith, Kathleen Anne—2	A Moment with Jane
Smith, Sybil—9	Illumination

0-595-30592-X